CW01454767

Animation in Mexico, 2006 to 2022

SUNY series in Latin American Cinema

Ignacio M. Sánchez Prado and Leslie L. Marsh, editors

Animation in Mexico, 2006 to 2022

Box Office, Web Shorts, and Streaming

Editor

DAVID S. DALTON

Cover Credit: Film poster for *Una película de huevos*, Gabriel and Rodolfo Riva Palacio. Alatriste, dirs., 2006. Used with permission of Huevocartoon.

Published by State University of New York Press, Albany

Printed in the United States of America

EU GPSR Authorised Representative:
Logos Europe, 9 rue Nicolas Poussin, 17000, La Rochelle, France
contact@logoseurope.eu

For information, contact State University of New York Press, Albany, NY
www.sunypress.edu

Library of Congress Cataloging-in-Publication Data

Name: Dalton, David Scott, 1984– editor.
Title: Animation in Mexico, 2006 to 2022 : box office, web shorts, and streaming / edited by David S. Dalton.
Description: Albany : State University of New York Press, [2025]. | Series: SUNY series in Latin American cinema | Includes bibliographical references and index.
Identifiers: LCCN 2024039358 | ISBN 9798855801767 (hardcover : alk. paper) | ISBN 9798855801774 (ebook)
Subjects: LCSH: Animated films—Mexico—History and criticism. | Motion picture industry—Mexico—History. | Animation (Cinematography)—Mexico. | Animators—Mexico.
Classification: LCC NC1766.M6 A77 2025 | DDC 791.43/34097209051—dc23/eng/20241230
LC record available at https://lccn.loc.gov/2024039358

To Ariadna, Davidcito, Dan Armando and Isadora

for popping popcorn and watching so many

Mexican animated films with me over the years.

And to my nephew, Finn Martin, who loved cartoons.

I hope you have a TV in heaven so you can watch these films!

Contents

Acknowledgments ix

Introduction: Animation in Mexico: A Brief History 1
David S. Dalton

SECTION I: The Fifth Period: Commercial Animated Cinema in the Domestic Market

Chapter 1
Huevocartoon: New Masculinities and the Poetics of Failure 31
Rodrigo Figueroa Obregón

Chapter 2
On Colonial and Decolonial Ghosting: *La leyenda de la Nahuala* 55
Elissa J. Rashkin

Chapter 3
La revolución de Juan Escopeta: Toward Nonviolent Masculinity and Citizenship 83
Sofía Paiva de Araujo and David S. Dalton

Chapter 4
Es un pájaro, es un avión: The Twenty-First-Century Animated Mexican Superhero 107
Vinodh Venkatesh

SECTION II: The Sixth Period: On Streaming and the Internationalization of Mexican Animation

Chapter 5
Politicized Web Praxis in Mexican Animated Short Films: *Reality 2.0* (2012) and *Retrato Político* (2013) 127
Katherine Bundy

Chapter 6
The Impact of Anime in Mexico-Centered Adult Animation and Global Mexican Representation 149
Yunuen Ysela Mandujano-Salazar

Chapter 7
The Day of the Dead: Mexican Gothic and Animated Cinema 175
Enrique Ajuria Ibarra

Chapter 8
Border/lands of Belonging in Disney-Pixar's *Coco* 195
Molly F. Todd

List of Contributors 223

Index 227

Acknowledgments

I would like to thank the many colleagues, friends, and contributors who helped to advance this project. The authors of the individual chapters have shown the scope of Mexican animation; without their hard work, this book would not have reached its potential. Rebecca Colesworthy was a pleasure to work with as acquisitions editor, and the blind reviewers provided fantastic comments that have made this book so much stronger.

I also need to extend my gratitude to the University of North Carolina at Charlotte, which provided valuable institutional support. I am especially grateful to the College of Humanities and Earth & Social Sciences for providing funding for an index, which Andrew Ascherl compiled.

Finally, on a personal note, I want to thank my family—Ariadna and my three children—for their support. Indeed, this particular project has been one that has truly transcended the division between family time and research; I began to take an interest in animated cinema after watching dozens of movies with my kiddos when they were younger. In fact, we still watch them together when new films come out!

Introduction

Animation in Mexico: A Brief History

David S. Dalton

On March 12, 2023, Guillermo del Toro's *Pinocchio* (2022) won the Oscar for Best Animated Feature.[1] On the surface, the film's distribution by Netflix, its adaption of an Italian novel, and, crucially, its reimagination of a beloved Disney production suggested that the film had few, if any, ties to a specifically Mexican cinema.[2] Rather, it looked like the latest instance where a world-famous " 'Mexican [filmmaker]' " made a movie that could, nonetheless, not "really be called a Mexican film."[3] Such a take would seem especially understandable in a context where an array of scholars and critics have claimed that the national cinema "has not been able to accommodate" the auteurist dreams of major directors like del Toro.[4] Nevertheless, such an assertion would have ignored the fact that del Toro chose to work with the Guadalajara-based studio El Taller del Chucho, an animation company that had been making major contributions to stop-motion animation in Mexico since the early 2000s.[5] As such, the movie was primarily shot in the director's beloved hometown using local talent. Mexican media clearly claimed the movie as their own, latching onto del Toro's presence in the awards ceremony—which featured fewer Mexican productions than normal—and celebrating his victory as a great honor to the nation.[6] Throughout the country, many people saw the award as a testament to the quality of Mexican animation. Far beyond simply recognizing del Toro's auteurist talent, then, this award also spoke to the maturity of a Mexican animation industry that could compete and win on world cinema's biggest stage.

Casual observers both in Mexico and beyond may not have expected to see a Mexican production win the nod for top animated film, especially against competition like Pixar's *Turning Red*, Netflix's *The Sea Beast*, and DreamWorks's *Puss in Boots: The Last Wish*.[7] That said, those familiar with the country's animation knew that it had developed formidable expertise over the last two decades. Gone were the years where critics derided national animated films, complaining about their amateur look.[8] Ever since the summer of 2006—when Gabriel Riva Palacio and Rodolfo Riva Palacio released *Una película de huevos* to roaring commercial success—the national film industry had produced multiple animated films each year.[9] This expansion in production coincided with significant improvements in the overall quality of these movies. In 2011, the Instituto Mexicano de Cinematografía (IMCINE) stated that "national animation is reviving and is gradually becoming one of the driving forces of the Mexican film industry."[10] As such, the institute identified it as a key genre for investment due to its popularity with Mexican moviegoers.[11] That same year, IMCINE reported that "the genre of animation played a very important role in national cinema in 2011, with four releases drawing 32% of attendance, mostly due to the success of the films *Don Gato y su pandilla* and *La leyenda de la Llorona*, both produced by Ánima Estudios."[12] The year 2011 was especially good for Mexican animation, but it was hardly an aberration. National animated films consistently boasted titles among the most successful pictures during any given year. Of the top ten most commercially successful films from 2000 to 2011, three were animated features, a fact that is especially impressive given that animation accounted for only a fraction of all productions and that it only became a truly lucrative medium in 2006.[13]

The popularity of animated films at the national box office held throughout the 2010s. By 2018, IMCINE noted that animated films were the only genre that could consistently compete with romantic comedies in the domestic arena.[14] This fact takes on greater significance when we consider the corpus of research identifying romantic comedies as the national cinema's single-most profitable genre.[15] Animated cinema has proven lucrative due to institutional factors—particularly its popularity and the relatively inexpensive production costs—that make it easier to net a profit.[16] These films attract large audiences in part because they appeal stylistically and ideologically to middle- and upper-class families. As Ignacio M. Sánchez Prado argues, "In order to survive as an industry, Mexican filmmakers needed to bring the middle class back into theaters."[17] While national cinemas throughout the world depended heavily on box-office earnings to swing a

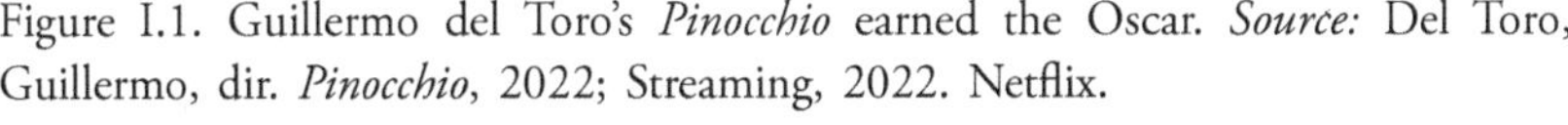
Figure I.1. Guillermo del Toro's *Pinocchio* earned the Oscar. *Source:* Del Toro, Guillermo, dir. *Pinocchio*, 2022; Streaming, 2022. Netflix.

profit in the 2000s and 2010s, the extent of piracy in Mexico made theater screening all the more crucial because DVD sales would bring almost no revenue.[18] In appealing to middle-class families, animated films could better ensure attendance in theaters than could most of their domestic competitors. Producers could sell multiple tickets for a single showing, which meant larger audiences, higher ticket sales, and greater profitability. Animated films were not the first to try to attract parents and children to the same showing; as early as the 1980s, filmmakers had experimented with different types of family cinema as a strategy for remaining solvent.[19] Viewed in this light, contemporary Mexican animation represents, in many ways, the culmination of a model that producers had developed for decades.

Given the strategic importance that the national film industry has afforded to animated cinema, it is especially problematic that it has received such sparse scholarly attention. *Animation in Mexico, 2006 to 2022: Box Office, Web Shorts, and Streaming* seeks to fill this gap. The critical silence surrounding Mexican animation does not reflect any self-evident justification for ignoring this wing of film production. Rather, animated films pose paradigmatic challenges to Mexican film studies because they do not fit particularly well into the narratives that film scholars have constructed about the national cinema. Scholars like Carl Mora and Christian Wehr have, in different ways, argued that Mexican cinema reached something of an apex during the Golden Age (1936–1956) before devolving into crisis in the 1960s and 1970s.[20] As the story goes, the national cinema would later experience a rebirth with the advent of an array of auteurist films in the 1990s and, crucially, the internationally successful, arthouse productions of the post-2000 environment. One of the reasons for the animated cinema's continued relegation to the periphery, then, is that it fits so imperfectly into the master narrative of Mexican cinema. At best, contemporary animation may represent a new era of "return[ing] to commercialism" that serious Mexican cinema supposedly overcame by the dawn of the twenty-first century.[21] Indeed, animated cinema represents an aberration of sorts: a commercially focused cinema that stands in contrast to its independent and critically successful counterparts that have brought significant praise to the nation's cinematic production.

The power of the aforementioned narrative rings clear even in this book's opening vignette. In beginning with Guillermo del Toro's victory at the Oscars, this chapter has justified deeper studies on Mexican animation by explicitly tying it to an auteurist aesthetic that has garnered international recognition. If a Mexican animated picture won an Academy Award, then the country's animation clearly merits greater academic study! Certainly, there are good reasons to begin with del Toro, not the least of which being his consistent work to validate animation as a medium of cinema. In many ways, the director sat at the forefront of the animation renaissance of the 2000s, albeit from a distance. Prior to directing *Pinocchio*, he had both served as producer of Jorge Gutiérrez's *The Book of Life* (2014) and directed the 2013 installment of *The Simpsons Treehouse of Horror*.[22] While he did not carry these projects out from within the national cinema per se, he did develop his skills in that medium. His contributions to *The Book of Life* underscored his penchant for blurring the lines between Mexican and international—particularly US—cinema, a characteristic that Sánchez Prado has signaled as key to his auteurist brand.[23] The film celebrated the Mexican Day of the Dead, but it did so in a way that strove to remain legible to non-Mexican audiences. True to form as a director who "create[s] a symbiotic relationship" between the Mexican and US cinemas, he used his participation in these productions to advocate for including Mexican and Mexican American talent, a fact that rang particularly clearly in the decision to cast Diego Luna, Kate del Castillo, Ana de la Reguera, and several US-Latinx actors in different roles.[24] Beyond his work producing animated films and television, del Toro also supported the animated films that emerged from within Mexico. He heaped significant praise on Carlos

Carrera's *Ana y Bruno* (2017), a gorgeous film that garnered significant critical praise despite struggling at the box office.[25]

Foregrounding del Toro's ties to national animation proves useful in establishing the genre's value as an object of study, but this serves only as a point of departure for the current volume. Indeed, rather than focus on auteurism, the works discussed throughout this book converge more precisely around the concept of commercial cinema. In this way, *Animation in Mexico, 2006 to 2022* answers the call of Sánchez Prado's *Screening Neoliberalism*, which invites scholars of Mexican cinema—particularly those in the US and British academies—to move beyond auteurism and analyze commercial films.[26] Any attempt to understand the national film industry must necessarily grapple with the for-profit nature of the majority of its productions. The commercial nature of the country's animation has led to significant consternation. According to many critics, commercially successful animated films have undermined other, more serious, examples of national cinema. Fernanda Solórzano tapped into this precise feeling in 2007 when she lamented the unprecedented successes of *Una película de huevos* as compared to the more moderate gains of Jorge Estrada's political satire, *Un mundo maravilloso* (2006): "In comparing the four million people that saw *Una película de huevos* to the 711,000 who went to *Un mundo maravilloso*, it becomes clear that, when faced with both visions, Mexico prefers the version that paints eggs over the reality of the country" ["la comparación entre los cuatro millones de personas que acudieron a ver *Una película de huevos* y los 711,000 que fueron a ver *Un mundo maravilloso*, deja claro que, entre retrato y retrato, México elige el que pinta huevos a la realidad del país."][27] Misha MacLaird comes to a similar conclusion, though she does so through a more academic reasoning that centers less judgmentally on the fact that Mexican audiences preferred "narrative simplicity and potty humor" to political satire.[28] Bubbling beneath the surface of these critiques sits an unspoken assumption that a narrowly defined "political cinema" necessarily deserves greater attention—whether popular, critical, or scholarly—than do animated films (which apparently cannot be political) produced for popular audiences. Animated cinema's relegation to critical oblivion thus follows a familiar path when compared to other commercial cinematic traditions that have experienced similar neglect due to "disparaging judgments of taste."[29]

Rather than buy into an elitist narrative about what type of cinema deserves scholarly attention, this book instead follows a trajectory similar to that of Olivia Cosentino and Brian Price in *The Lost Cinema of Mexico:*

From Lucha Libre to Cine Familiar and Other Churros. The contributors to *Animation in Mexico* recognize animated film as yet another "lost cinema" in need of rescuing. Similar to other lost cinemas, this one was never truly "lost." Rather, it was hiding in plain sight as academics overlooked it in favor of other veins of cinema that seemed more worthy of their energy. To date, only a small number of scholars have sought to fit animation into the greater narrative of Mexican cinema. Sánchez Prado, for example, notes "the ability of Mexican cinema to make inroads even in Hollywood's most profitable market: animated cinema."[30] MacLaird acts similarly when she mentions animated film as an especially lucrative market without engaging with the products themselves.[31] Outside of these two scholars, however, the criticism has remained largely silent; *Animation in Mexico* seeks to rectify this oversight in Mexican film studies.

Updating Mexican Animated Film Studies: The Fifth and Sixth Periods

Beyond contributing to Mexican film studies, *Animation in Mexico* also builds on the few studies that exist on animation specifically in the country.[32] The authors of this book stand with Manuel Rodríguez Bermúdez, Rodolfo Peláez, Juan Manuel Aurrecoechea, and a small group of scholars of Mexican animation who express a degree of surprise at the overall dearth of animated film studies given that different types of animation have appeared in the country since at least the 1930s.[33] The term *animation* refers to an array of filmic techniques that create the illusion of movement using different strategies. As such, it is not a genre in the strictest sense. One need look no further than the Claymation of del Toro's *Pinocchio* and the Flash productions of the Riva Palacio Alatriste brothers' Huevocartoon to realize that, in many ways, animated films can differ as much one from another as they do from live-action productions.[34] The different chapters of this book engage with various types of animation while also considering feature films, web shorts, and television shows. In so doing, they show how market forces and a changing technological landscape have created new opportunities and challenges for animation in Mexico.

To date, only a handful of studies exist on Mexican animation. Of these, only two have come out with academic presses, and both were published in Mexico over a generation ago. Aurrecoechea's *El episodio perdido: Historia del cine mexicano de animación* came out in 2004, while Manuel

Rodríguez Bermúdez's *Animación: Una perspectiva desde México* was published posthumously in 2007. Beyond these studies, Luis Gabriel Vázquez Hernández's self-published *Cuentos y recuentos animados. Panorama de la animación mexicana: 2000–2012* came out a decade ago in 2015. A fourth book, Ana Cruz Rodríguez et al.'s *Acervo de animación mexicana* was published in August 2024 following the Festival Internacional de Animación Annecy 2023.[35] This final book provides an "exhaustive" database about previous animated productions in Mexico, but it does not engage in the questions posed in this particular volume.[36] The aforementioned studies provide valuable insights into Mexican animated film studies. That said, with the exception of Vázquez Hernández, they cannot account for what has happened since the mid-2000s, which is when the country's animation underwent its cinematic renaissance. The authors of these books realized that the country's animation industry was shifting beneath their feet. Indeed, Aurrecoechea's book includes a prologue by the director Carlos Carrera, who states, "Let us hope for a complementary text, or a second volume, to come out in the next ten years or so that discusses a new phase of animation that is richer in content and form" ["esperaremos quizá dentro de diez años un complemento, o un segundo volumen con el recuento de una etapa mucho más rica en contendio y forma de la animación mexicana."][37] Carrera's desired volume did not arrive, but the national animated film industry did grow exponentially during those years. *Animation in Mexico* seeks to answer Carrera's call by providing analyses of recent animated films throughout the country.

Key Periods in Mexican Animation: The First through Fourth Periods

In order to chart contemporary trends in Mexican animation, we must first understand the genre's history. To that end, let us turn to the work of Rodríguez Bermúdez, who has put together the most in-depth chronology of Mexican animation of any critic. At the time of his writing in the early 2000s, Rodríguez Bermúdez claimed that Mexican animation had experienced four distinct periods (*etapas*), each characterized by different aesthetic and technical innovations. While a degree of overlap necessarily existed among these periods, the critic also demonstrated an overall evolution of Mexican animation that occurred during these years. As he noted, foreign animated films began to appear in exhibits in Mexico as early as 1907, and audiences loved them.[38] Nevertheless, despite clear demand for animation in the country, the social upheavals of the Revolution and its aftermath meant that Mexican animators lacked the resources to develop a national industry until 1930.[39]

Given this reality, it should come as no surprise that Rodríguez Bermúdez would assert that the first period lasted from 1930 to 1944.[40] By this time, the tradition of animation in countries like the United States was already decades old. Certainly, no full-length animated films existed in 1930—Disney would not release *Snow White* until 1937. That said, Disney had released *Steamboat Willie* in 1928 to international praise, and by 1944 it had already produced six full-length features. As Rodríguez Bermúdez notes, "The quality of [Disney's] animation was incomparable at this time, as were the storylines and the music. Everything came together to make a highly competitive product" ["la calidad de su animación era incomparable en ese momento así como la temática, la música, todo se conjuntaba para hacer una producción de alto nivel competitivo"].[41] Given the level of international competition, domestic animators of the first period attempted to stake out a unique voice in a market where Disney had already established hegemony. The animated productions of this period tended to be very short, and they often lacked the perceived quality of their US counterparts. Nevertheless, filmmakers from the period—many of whom were professionals in other fields who simply had an interest in animation—followed many Disney conventions. Perhaps most important was the emphasis on animated choreographies that integrated visual discourse with music and other types of sound. National films remained short, with the longest one lasting just over eight minutes.[42]

Rodríguez Bermúdez places the second period from 1945 to 1973.[43] Unlike the first period, where most animated films were produced by movie studios with only cursory interests in animation, these years saw the creation of studios that focused specifically on animation. The first of these was Caricaturas Animadas de México, which was founded in 1947. The establishment of a studio with an explicit focus on animation allowed for greater specialization of the genre. Mexican animators could finally access high-quality materials. What is more, this specialized studio began to employ techniques that animators throughout the world had developed to streamline the animation process. Chief among these was shooting on twos, or the use of a single image for multiple frames.[44] These techniques increased the quality of productions while simultaneously cutting costs. Still, animators faced significant challenges. For example, Caricaturas Animados de México's first production, *Noticiero cómico*, was a series meant to parody the news.

However, because it took several months to produce a video, there was always a lag between the release of a video and the event it satirized. As a result, these cartoons were always months behind on current events.[45] In another case, the studio produced *El diablo no es tan diablo*, a full-length feature film that was going to merge live action with animation for the first time in Mexican history. Nevertheless, the tape was lost in a fire as production was wrapping up.[46] Several new studios emerged in the 1960s. Key productions from the decade included *¡Viva la muerte!* (Adolfo Garnica 1965), perhaps the first animated film to celebrate the Day of the Dead, and *Los Súpermachos* (Eduardo Del Río, 1972).[47] In 1968, Cooperativo Producciones Animadas produced *El deporte clásico* (Fernando Ruiz, 1968), a short meant to celebrate the Olympic games.[48] While national audiences continued to consume mostly US productions, Mexican animators were finally establishing a place for themselves within the country. In some cases, they even began working with US producers on well-known television series like *The Flintstones* and *Scooby-Doo*.[49]

Rodríguez Bermúdez places the third period from 1974 to 1993.[50] These years saw the completion of the first feature-length animated film in Mexican history, *Los reyes magos* (Fernando Ruiz and Adolfo Torres Portillo), in 1974.[51] Several more full-length animated films would come out during these years. This period also marked a crescendo in the tension between the domestic and international markets. For example, Fernando Ruiz also produced *Los diez derechos del niño* in 1979 with UNICEF. He showed the film at Cannes as well as at film festivals in the United States, Canada, and the Soviet Union. Despite this international success, however, the film never reached the Mexican box office; instead, it appeared on television a few times before disappearing.[52] Mexico also emerged as the top player in Spanish-language animation more generally during these years. Several animators fled to the country from dictatorships in their home countries and began to work in the Mexican industry. It was under these conditions that Grupo Cono Sur, which consisted of Argentine expat animators, produced *La persecución de Pancho Villa* (1978), a film that followed General Pershing as he attempted to capture the infamous revolutionary leader.[53] The addition of animators from other Latin American countries opened the way for the Puerto Rican animator Francisco López to produce *Crónicas del Caribe* (1982), a thirty-five-minute film that tells of Latin America's long history of colonization.[54]

Rodríguez Bermúdez finishes with the claim that the fourth period lasted from 1994 to 2001 (the year that he finished writing). During this time, Mexican animated films began to achieve international recognition, and animators began to receive greater access to funding.[55] He asserts that the fourth period began with the release of Carlos Carrera's *El héroe* (1994). The film stands out for two reasons: firstly, it won several international awards; secondly, it received financial support from IMCINE, a fact that underscored the incorporation of the country's animation into the national cinema.[56] The period also saw numerous aspiring young animators travel abroad to study animation in foreign universities before returning home.[57] In some cases, Mexican animators received offers to work for studios abroad. Such was the case with Enrique Navarrete, who studied animation at Sheridan College in Canada before accepting an offer to work for DreamWorks.[58] In this capacity, he collaborated on productions like *The Prince of Egypt* (Brenda Chapman, Steve Hickner, and Simon Wells, 1998) and *Antz* (Eric Darnell, Tim Johnson, and Lawrence Guterman, 1998).[59] After working for this US producer, he later opened his own animation company in Mexico called Piánica.[60] At the same time, national universities also began supporting animation as a valid course of study in and of itself.[61] It was also during these years that animation began to take off in Guadalajara; as the vignette at the beginning of this book shows, the development of animation in that city would eventually result in del Toro's *Pinocchio.* Ultimately, the fourth period left a mark on the national film industry because this was the time that animation finally began to truly integrate into the national film industry.

In an afterword to Rodríguez Bermúdez's book, Víctor Ugalde posits that a fifth period emerged in 2002 and lasted until 2007 (the very year the book came out).[62] As he argues, by the end of the fourth period, Mexican animators had demonstrated their expertise, a fact that allowed them to finally find significant commercial success. Vázquez Hernández echoed these sentiments in his own work, though he signaled 2000–2012 as key dates in the national animation.[63] Both Ugalde and Vázquez Hernández recognize how the neoliberalization of the national film industry created the conditions for a radically different animation industry from the previous periods. In no place were these differences clearer than in these new films' focus on the box office and other types of commercialization. This generated unprecedented funding—and thus production opportunities—for domestic animated movies.

Periodization in Contemporary Animation (2006–2024)

In the almost two decades following its publication, Rodríguez Bermúdez's work remains valuable. His demarcations of the first three periods elicit very little pushback. That said, it would appear that some of the proposed dates of the fourth and fifth periods could use some minor adjustments. His choice to signal 2001 as the ending date of the fourth period, for example, appears a bit arbitrary. The problematic end date reflects no error on his part per se; rather, it demonstrates that he had not yet had the opportunity to view the trajectory of the animated cinema of the 2000s with any degree of critical distance. With the help of hindsight, however, scholars in the 2020s can confidently place the fourth period from 1993 to 2005. The fifth period would then start in 2006, the year that *Una película de huevos* showed that domestic animated films could win at the box office.[64] More recently, a sixth period seems to have emerged slowly between 2017 and 2020 that consists of two primary characteristics: the supplantation of box office receipts with streaming and the deconstruction of the divisions between national (Mexican) and international animation.[65] *Animation in Mexico* thus functions as a continuation of Rodríguez Bermúdez's work. The chapters in this book extend his paradigm into the present by interrogating key productions from the fifth and sixth periods, both of which came about after the publication of his book. The essays found herein do not intend to be totalizing; indeed, we recognize that future work will likely help us to refine our understanding of both periods of Mexican animation even more. With greater context and critical distance, for example, future scholars may identify a clear date that divides the fifth period from the sixth.

Regardless of the exact starting date of the sixth period, it is clear that, by the 2020s, Mexican animation—and, indeed, Mexican cinema—had entered a new phase in its history due to the rise of streaming and a decline in box-office attendance. IMCINE had identified streaming as a means to reduce profits lost to piracy during the mid-2010s, with discussions emerging as early as 2013.[66] While the groundwork for streaming began to appear early in the 2010s, it would take several years for it to mature. That said, by 2020, the number of Mexican users with access to Netflix—the largest streaming platform in the country—had risen to 74.3 million.[67] The transition to a more streaming-dominated market intensified in the wake of the COVID-19 pandemic that forced theaters to close, thus leaving filmmakers to distribute their products online. Indeed, the pandemic spurred such significant demand that "the offerings on streaming platforms rose by 35% with respect to 2019. Thus, the gap between theatrical exhibition and that of platforms became significantly smaller."[68] While these conditions have certainly reshaped both world cinema and Hollywood, their effects on Mexican animation specifically cannot be overstated. The rise of streaming allowed filmmakers to make and distribute more films and even series.

Unlike their Hollywood counterparts—which have struggled to navigate an industry disrupted by the sudden dominance of streaming—Mexican films, both animated and not, have, if anything, benefitted from these conditions since streaming has reduced losses through piracy.

This book's focus on commercial cinema challenges the underlying suppositions that have undergirded most studies of world animated cinema. The film scholar Giannalberto Bendazzi—who has uncovered numerous lost animated movies, directors, and producers from every major continent—for example, has argued that film scholars should uncover the "best" works of animated cinema. In so doing, he explicitly argues against interrogating the "transnational market networks" that facilitate animated productions in favor of an aesthetic imperative.[69] We should note that Bendazzi's commitment to world animation necessarily causes him to seek uniting threads that will connect his analyses across time and space. Unfortunately, at least in his brief discussions of Mexican cinema, this preference for aesthetics over markets leads to numerous misreadings. On the one hand, he highlights many major accomplishments of recent animation in the country: the founding of Ánima Estudios; the release of *Una película de huevos* (Riva Palacio and Riva Palacio 2006); the release of *Top Cat* (Alberto Mar 2007); and the successes of *La leyenda de la nahuala* (Ricardo Arnaiz 2007).[70] On the other hand, however, while he provides the information in an almost encyclopedic fashion, he does not contextualize these productions within the neoliberalization of the national cinema that allowed these developments to occur in the first place. He also lacks the familiarity necessary with the local context to explain how changes in production and consumption have influenced national animation in recent years. As *Animation in Mexico* shows, we cannot truly make a contribution to the field of twenty-first-century Mexican animation without first familiarizing ourselves with the cinematic ecosystem from which it operates. A focus on "best" or "great" works simply cannot suffice because it imposes subjective expectations onto the films.

Viewed in this light, beyond its focus on the fifth and sixth periods of Mexican animation, this book also must engage with Bendazzi's disparaging criticism surrounding Mexican animated cinema's "impulse to look 'Mexican' " on the one hand and/or the drive "to imitate Disney" on the other.[71] Once again, his criticisms underscore a lack of familiarity with Mexican cinema in general. These perceived shortcomings represent tensions that have existed in the national cinema, both animated and not, throughout its history. Indeed, many of the most popular actors, directors, and cinematographers of the Golden Age—Dolores del Río, Emilio Fernández, Gabriel

Figueroa, etc.—learned their trade in Hollywood before taking their skills back home.[72] While indebted to Hollywood in some ways, they also strove to differentiate themselves by building new, authentically Mexican aesthetics that would stand in contrast to those found in the United States.[73] A similar process played out in the country's animation, where the "pioneers" of Mexican animation—Salvador Pruneda, Bismarck Mier, Salvador Patiño, Alfredo Ximénez, and Carlos Manríquez—learned their trade in the United States before returning to Mexico.[74] Some of these men, like Manríquez, would stay in Hollywood through the 1950s and build successful careers; Manríquez himself collaborated frequently with both Disney and Warner Brothers.[75] Others, like Pruneda, returned to Mexico by the 1930s and began producing animations back home.[76] As Aurrecoechea notes, Disney's draw centered primarily on the promise of fame and money; that said, Mexican animators often resisted the urge to work in Hollywood because such a partnership would require them to subordinate their creations to the whims of their US employer.[77] In many cases, this would mean the elimination or essentialization of the Mexican elements in a director's or artist's oeuvre. Fairly or not, then, as early as the first and second periods, Mexican animators confronted two options. On the one hand, they could "stay true," as it were, to their cultural roots by producing films directed at national audiences. On the other hand, they could risk selling out by working with more lucrative companies like Disney.

These dynamics have led to no shortage of anecdotes about how different animators navigated their tumultuous relationship with the colossal animation studios of the North. That said, no story surpasses that of Gabilondo Soler, the creator of Cri-Cri el Grillito Cantor, a beloved animated cricket who, to this day, is frequently touted as "the most impactful Mexican children's character" ["el personaje infantile más impactante de México"].[78] Cri-Cri's songs originally appeared on radio, but Gabilondo Soler later created animated choreographies that gave the songs greater personality and popularity. During the 1940s, Disney attempted to woo him to the company in order to use his music and animation to promote the Pan-American ideals of the Good Neighbor Policy.[79] Nevertheless, Gabilondo Soler refused to "cede before the monster of children's cinema" ["ceder ante el monstruo infantil"].[80] He almost certainly chose wisely; Disney released *The Three Caballeros*—a film where Donald Duck scrambles around Latin America to learn the history of its peoples—in 1944. The abysmal reviews from throughout the region dissuaded the studio from producing more films for Latin American audiences.[81] Had he sold his music to Disney, Gabilondo

Soler's work likely would have undergone a similar fate. Instead, Cri-Cri became one of the crowning achievements of the first period that remains cherished into the present.

Gabilondo Soler's refusal to sell the rights to Cri-Cri has made both him and his character into nationalistic legends of sorts. Unlike perhaps any other animated character, Cri-Cri can claim to have Disney's seal of approval without having to actually become the corporation's intellectual property. After all, Gabilondo Soler rejected the Hollywood studio and not the other way around. Every so often, a story will surface in the media reminding people that the animator chose Mexico over millions, and his quote, "Cri-Cri is a legacy for Mexican children" ["Cri-Cri es un legado para la niñez mexicana"] has been immortalized.[82] While Gabilondo Soler refused to sell the rights to Cri-Cri to the US behemoth, he clearly *did* collaborate with the studio on other occasions. More than a few critics have noted major similarities between Gabilondo Soler's Ratón Miguelito and Disney's Mickey Mouse, for example.[83] Moreover, in 1963, Carlos Amador—a Mexican producer who had attempted to facilitate Cri-Cri's assimilation to Disney—filmed *Cri-Cri, el Grillito Cantor*, a movie that included a sequence of Disney's *Three Little Pigs*.[84] Ultimately, then, a collaboration did emerge between Disney and Gabilondo Soler, though it happened on the animator's terms rather than on those of the studio.

Despite the clear (often nationalistic) support that Mexicans have expressed for Cri-Cri, Hollywood—and especially Disney—has infiltrated the Mexican market over the last several decades. The quantity and quality of the productions have meant that national productions have struggled to keep pace. Gabriel Riva Palacio signaled an implicit competition with the studio in 2015 while discussing the impressive success of his film, *Un gallo con muchos huevos* (2015), which had earned $9 million USD domestically and $17 million internationally, a haul that made it the most commercially successful Mexican film not only of 2015, but also in Mexican history up to that point.[85] As he proudly proclaimed, "this is the first movie that begins to compete in the international market" ["esta es la primera película que empieza a competir en el mercado internacional"].[86] That said, he also recognized the predominance of Hollywood in the realm of animated cinema when he added that "to beat DreamWorks and Pixar we still need more money, talent, time, preparation, and schooling" ["pero contra DreamWorks y Pixar todavía nos falta muchísimo dinero, talento, tiempo, preparación y escuela"].[87] This sentiment was especially common during the fifth period, as Mexican animated films sought commercial success through the box office, a fact that generally meant that they would need to entice at least some viewers to attend their movie rather than one by a Hollywood studio.

While this tension still exists, it has largely diminished during the sixth period, which has coincided not only with a rise in streaming, but in greater collaboration between US distributors and Mexico. Certainly, much of this has been because major streaming services in the United States like Netflix have proactively sought out talent from beyond the United States when creating original content. Guillermo del Toro took advantage of this precise tendency from the streaming platform when he produced and directed *Pinocchio*. That said, the sixth period has also seen collaboration with major traditional studios, a fact that became especially clear with the production of Adrián Molina and Lee Unkrich's *Coco* (2017), a Disney/Pixar production that included a great deal of collaboration with Mexican animators. Audiences did not hold *Coco*'s Hollywood roots against it; indeed, the film enjoyed what was, at the time, the greatest attendance in the history of the Mexican box office.[88] National audiences clearly viewed Pixar's production as a validation of Mexican cinema and culture. Ultimately, this book seeks to identify some of the draws that Mexican animated cinema developed in the fifth period while also looking at how this has begun to play out during the sixth period.

Organization

Animation in Mexico consists of eight chapters by scholars trained in the US and Mexican academies. The first four chapters discuss films from the fifth period, a time when Mexican animated films enjoyed significant successes in the domestic box office. The films discussed here often tend to focus on distinctively Mexican cultural forms and, occasionally, even concepts of *mexicanidad*. That said, these productions also frequently eschew *mexicanidad* in favor of more contemporary political, aesthetic, and popular trends that will reverberate with twenty-first-century audiences.[89] The second section deals with different manifestations of sixth-period productions. These films tend to skew a bit more universalist or cosmopolitan because they want to attract streaming audiences from all over the world. When they do deal with *mexicanidad*, they tend to do so in folkloric ways that exploit Mexican Otherness to attract viewers, both domestic and international. At the same time, sixth-period animations often borrow liberally from established, popular transnational film genres like anime, and then they distribute their productions on major, international streaming platforms. Once again, producers strive to reach audiences both within and beyond Mexico. While there is admittedly a degree of slippage across this division—the most successful domestic films almost always try to tap into foreign markets, and the most successful cosmopolitan films tend to win big in the domestic sphere after achieving recognition internationally—such a framework for approaching Mexican animation still proves useful. Ultimately, this division allows us to focus on the strategies that different animations have used to engage the Mexican and international publics respectively.

Section 1: *Animation During the Fifth Period*, consists of four chapters. The first two deal with productions from the country's two most commercially successful animated franchises: Huevocartoon and Las leyendas. In chapter 1, Rodrigo Figueroa Obregón discusses the irreverent Huevocartoon films and their surprisingly progressive approaches to twenty-first-century masculinity. Rather than reflect a paradigm along the lines of Octavio Paz's "Los hijos de la Malinche" in which men must repress their feelings and actively "chingar" or "ser chingado," Figueroa Obregón argues that the films advocate for a paradigm of masculinity that can include men who acknowledge their emotions and even those who do not conform to traditional sexual and gender norms. His observation proves especially interesting given the franchise's association with crude, base, and often sexualized humor. In chapter 2, Elissa Rashkin discusses Anima Estudios's commercially successful, if aesthetically flawed, *La leyenda de la nahuala* (Ricardo Arnaiz, 2007). Rashkin explores colonial and decolonial elements intertwined in the film's ghosting, as well as its comic appropriation of traditional storytelling as a means of "Mexicanizing" the medium of animated film. Through this means, she teases out the movie's approach to such notions as race and nation. In chapter 3, Sofia Paiva de Araujo and David S. Dalton discuss Jorge Estrada's *La revolución de Juan Escopeta*, a film set during the Mexican Revolution. Similar to Figueroa, they identify a strong critique of traditional Mexican masculinity that emerges throughout the animation. While they identify several ties to *mexicanidad* and Golden Age cinema, Paiva de Araujo and Dalton also argue that the film communicates an antibellicist politics that is directly opposed to traditionalist conceptualizations of *mexicanidad*. In aiming this film primarily at younger viewers, it strives to change how people—particularly young men—throughout the country conceive of "proper" masculinity.

While situated in section 1, chapter 4 discusses films that serve as a bridge between the fifth and sixth periods. Here, Vinodh Venkatesh explores how Mexican animators have attempted to capitalize on the current popularity of superhero movies by resurrecting the Mexican superhero genre and transplanting it into the realm of animation. He begins with a discussion of *El Santos vs. La Tetona Mendoza* (2012) in the key of parody, juxtaposing the animated film against a plethora of live-action intertexts from the Golden Age of the *luchador* genre. He then turns to two animated series, *El Chapulín Animado* and *Santo vs. los clones*, both of which circulated through televised and web platforms. Through these analyses, he explores the production possibilities opened up by animation, as well as the circulatory drawbacks that it may pose.

Section 2, "Animation During the Sixth Period" also consists of four chapters. In chapter 5, Katherine Bundy discusses the participatory nature of *Reality 2.0* (Víctor Orozco 2012) and *Retrato politico* (Güicho Nuñez 2013), two animated short films posted online. These films represent a type of "proto-sixth-period" production where people could produce and distribute animated shorts online. While they clearly lacked the emphasis on commercialization that would typify the rise of streaming, the shorts discussed here are important in that they are early examples where animators have shared content online. In Bundy's telling, online comment forums make short, socially driven productions into an ideal vehicle for social critique and even organization. In this way, both animated short films incorporate web usage and tools from the Web 2.0 as an aesthetic lens through which they critique Mexican national politics. In chapter 6, Yunuen Ysela Mandujano-Salazar discusses anime in Mexico. She begins with a discussion of how Japanese cartoons grew in popularity through internet use and lucrative television contracts in the 1990s and 2000s, and she finishes with a discussion of two anime-inspired animation series in Mexico: *Seis manos* (2019) and *Onyx Equinox* (2020). These programs clearly came about as a result of Japanese anime's popularity in the country. Mandujano-Salazar shows how popular animation forms have made their way into Mexico and how Mexican animators have striven to reach out to broad audiences, both domestic and international. In so doing, she demonstrates how both of these programs embody the opportunities that the sixth period has opened for Mexican directors who can now produce programs that will reach beyond the national territory.

The final two chapters deal with a unique form of cosmopolitan animation because they focus on films that foreground the Mexican Day of the Dead for audiences, both domestic and international. In chapter 7, Enrique Ajuria Ibarra considers Jorge Gutierrez's *The Book of Life* (2014) and Carlos

Gutiérrez Medrano's *Día de Muertos* (2019) through the lens of the Gothic. This chapter gauges the appropriateness of the Gothic as an analytical tool for addressing filmic representations of the Day of the Dead, particularly with movies aimed at international audiences. The films may not be Gothic per se, but they do contribute to a revised look at death and remembrance in contemporary global culture. More importantly, the chapter shows how Mexican attitudes can contribute to understanding these issues on a global stage. In chapter 8, Molly Frances Todd discusses Adrián Molina and Lee Unkrich's *Coco*, a film that, while technically a Hollywood production, was filmed using significant Mexican talent both in the area of voice actors and among animation consultants. This chapter gets at the heart of many of the ethical questions that commercial cinema poses in the neoliberal era. As she argues, there are elements both within the film and surrounding its production that mirror hegemonic worldviews and structures of power, ones that in turn produce violence for the very populations represented in *Coco*. Through her analysis, she discusses an ethics of representation—particularly for non-Mexican audiences—when creating a film like *Coco*. As she argues, a colonialist backdrop undergirds much of the film's production.

In the end, *Animation in Mexico, 2006 to 2022: Box Office, Web Shorts, and Streaming* makes important contributions to our understanding of the nation's animated cinema by focusing on previously unstudied animated productions that have, nevertheless, embedded themselves in Mexico's cultural zeitgeist. That said, this volume also signals many areas for greater research. While the book focuses almost exclusively on animated films from the neoliberal era—and, really, since 2006, when Mexican producers realized they could earn significant money by making these movies—very little work exists on animation from the previous periods. Clearly, the field of Mexican animation would benefit from a study focused on twentieth-century productions as well. Another area that has received only scant attention is the production side of Mexican animation. Future research should engage this topic because the conditions of production dictate what types of movies may be produced. What is more, there are other topics that this book touches on that, nevertheless, deserve deeper attention. For example, this volume discusses certain ways through which internet aided in the popularization and distribution of cinema. Nevertheless, as the sixth period continues, it will open opportunities not only to produce popular cinema but also television programs. The country's animation will undergo continued changes as new technologies create innovative distribution strategies. Clearly, this book sheds an important light on the Mexican animated film industry of the first decades of the twenty-first century. In so doing, it has hopefully opened a line of inquiry that remains ripe for future inquiry as well. For now, let us turn to the chapters that comprise this volume.

Notes

1. "The 95th Academy Awards," *A.Frame: The Digital Magazine of the Academy*, 2023, https://www.oscars.org/oscars/ceremonies/2023, accessed May 13, 2023.

2. Del Toro's film after all, adapted both Carlo Collodi's novel, *The Adventures of Pinnochio: Story of a Puppet* (1883), and Disney's *Pinocchio* (1940).

3. Ignacio M. Sánchez Prado, *Screening Neoliberalism: Transforming Mexican Cinema 1988–2012* (Nashville, TN: Vanderbilt University Press, 2014), 156.

4. See Deborah Shaw, *The Three Amigos: The Transnational Filmmaking of Guillermo del Toro, Alejandro González Iñárritu, and Alfonso Cuarón* (Manchester: Manchester University Press, 2013), 1. Dolores Tierney, Deborah Shaw, and Ann Davies, "Introduction," in *The Transnational Fantasies of Guillermo del Toro*, eds. Ann Davies, Deborah Shaw, and Dolores Tierney (New York: Palgrave Macmillan, 2014), 1–2.

5. Carmen Elisa Gómez Gómez and Cecilia Andalón, "Exploraciones estéticas y simbólicas sobre la muerte y la infancia en los cortos *stop motion* de las realizadoras de la escuela Jalisco," *Con A de Animación* 15 (2022): 49. For a discussion of del Toro's deep ties to the company, see Gómez Gómez and Andalón, "Exploraciones estéticas," 50.

6. "¡Guillermo del Toro gana Mejor Película Animada por 'Pinocho' en Premios Oscar 2023!," *Marca*, 13, March 2023, https://www.marca.com/mx/trending/cine/2023/03/13/640e6e0346163f40548b4584.html.

7. Certainly, another nominee, *Marcel the Shell with Shoes On* (Dean Fleischer Camp 2022) was a small-budget film.

8. Following the release of Ricardo Arnaiz's *La leyenda de la nahuala* in 2007, María Celeste Vargas Martínez and Daniel Lara Sánchez wrote: "what we want is for Mexican filmmakers to recognize how they are failing so that national animation can begin to excel and have international quality" ["lo que deseamos en [sic] que los realizadores mexicanos se den cuenta de aquello en lo que están fallando, para que la animación nacional empiece a despuntar y tenga calidad internacional"]. María Celeste Vargas Martínez and Daniel Lara Sánchez, "*La leyenda de la nahauala* . . . ¿Dónde están los guionistas en la animación?" In *Animación Mexicana*, http://animacionenmexico.blogspot.com/2007/. This changed in 2014, with the release of *La leyenda de las momias de Guanajuato*, a film that officially marked *Las leyendas* as the country's first animated film franchise, a fact that the duo celebrated. María Celeste Vargas Martínez and Daniel Lara Sánchez, "De la

nahuala a las momias . . . Leyendas animadas." *Animación Mexicana*, November 17, 2014, http://animacionenmexico.blogspot.com/2014/11/.

9. Following its release, *Una película de huevos* was the second-most commercially successful film in Mexican history. Unlike its competition, *El crimen del Padre Amaro, Una película de huevos* earned almost all of its profits from domestic showings at national movie theaters. See Box Office Mojo, "*The Crime of Padre Amaro*," https://www.boxofficemojo.com/release/rl1666287105/weekend/; Box Office Mojo unfortunately lacks the domestic earnings of *Una película de huevos*, though it does capture the roughly $0.8 million USD that it earned internationally. Box Office Mojo, "*A Movie of Eggs* (2006)," https://www.boxofficemojo.com/title/tt0824696/?ref_=bo_se_r_1. For the overall gross (domestic and international), see Edgar Apanco, "Taquilla MX: Los Huevos le ganaron al oso," *Premiere*, https://www.cinepremiere.com.mx/55406-taquilla-mx.html.

10. Instituto Mexicano de Cinematografía, *Anuario Estadístico de cine mexicano/Statistical Yearbook of Mexican Cinema* (Mexico City: IMCINE, 2011), 209, http://anuariocinemx.imcine.gob.mx/Assets/anuarios/2011.pdf.

11. IMCINE, *Anuario Estadístico* 2011, 103.

12. IMCINE, *Anuario* 2011, 23, 23–30. The commercial reach of animated movies becomes all the clearer when we realize that they represented less than 5% of the overall filmic output that year despite drawing nearly one third of the overall attendance to all domestic motion pictures.

13. See IMCINE, *Anuario* 2011, 33.

14. Instituto Mexicano de Cinematografía, *Anuario Estadístico de cine mexicano/Statistical Yearbook of Mexican Cinema* (Mexico City: IMCINE, 2018), 38. Rather than focus on gross earnings, these data focus on the number of attendees at movie theaters. The advantage is that this provides a baseline for popularity. That said, there are at least two significant disadvantages to this measure. Firstly, attendance and gross earnings are not always perfectly synonymous; a film could earn a higher gross with a lower overall attendance if, on average, ticket prices for one film are higher for one film than the other. Of course, even gross earnings can be misleading because, unlike the net, they fail to compare overall revenue against the price of production. That said, the domestic gross for *Ya veremos* was $9.93 million USD. See Box Office Mojo, "*Ya veremos*," https://www.boxofficemojo.com/title/tt7948540/?ref_=bo_se_r_1. That of *La boda de Valentina* was $8.24 million USD. See Box Office Mojo, "*La boda de Valentina*," https://www.boxofficemojo.com/release/rl1980073473/. That of *La leyenda del Charro Negro* was $5.35 million USD. See Box Office Mojo, "*La leyenda del Charro Negro*," https://www.boxofficemojo.com/title/tt6772418/?ref_=bo_se_r_1.

15. Sánchez Prado, *Screening Neoliberalism*, 62–104; Misha MacLaird, *Aesthetics and Politics in the Mexican Film Industry* (New York: Palgrave Macmillan, 2013), 59–61.

16. IMCINE, *Anuario* 2011, 83–84; 90–91; Víctor Ugalde, "Epílogo: Quinta etapa: 2002–2007," in *Animación: Una perspectiva desde México*, by Manuel Rodríguez Bermúdez (Mexico City: UNAM, 2007), 193–94.

17. Sánchez Prado, *Screening Neoliberalism*, 5.

18. See IMCINE, *Anuario* 2012, 119–37. Certainly, financial models shifted significantly with the rise of streaming in the mid-2010s.

19. Olivia Cosentino, "*Un cine familiar*: Recovering the 1980s Mexican Family Film," in *The Lost Cinema of Mexico*, edited by Olivia Cosentino and Brian Price (Gainesville: University of Florida Press, 2022).

20. Mora, *Mexican Cinema*, 102; Christian Wehr, ed., *Clásicos del cine mexicano: 31 películas emblemáticas desde la Época de Oro hasta el presente* (Madrid: Iberoamericana, 2016), 9.

21. Carl Mora has called the 1960s to the 1980s a return to commercialism; animated cinema would be yet another case of this that coincided with the critical successes of the 1990s and, especially, the 2000s. See Mora, *Mexican Cinema*, chapter 5.

22. Paul Julian Smith, foreword to *The Transnational Fantasies of Guillermo del Toro,* eds. Ann Davies, Deborah Shaw, and Dolores Tierney (New York: Palgrave Macmillan 2014), x. For a discussion of del Toro's *Simpsons* installment, see Glenn Ward, " 'There Is No Such Thing': Del Toro's Metafictional Monster Rally," in *The Transnational Fantasies of Guillermo del Toro.*

23. Sánchez Prado, *Screening Neoliberalism*, 156–62.

24. Shaw, *The Three Amigos*, 2. For a discussion of *The Book of Life* through the lens of Mexican cinema, see Enrique Ajuria Ibarra's chapter in this book.

25. The producers of the film highlighted del Toro's praise of the film in trailers leading up to its release. See *Ana y Bruno*, https://www.youtube.com/watch?v=4M-FURbSQbpw. *Ana y Bruno* won an Ariel in 2019 for Best Full-Length Animated Film; A Premio Quirino in 2018 for Best Ibero-American Animation Feature Film; and 2018 Premio Canacine for Best Animated Film.

26. Sánchez Prado, *Screening Neoliberalism*, 9.

27. "Fernanda Solórzano, "El lugar del espectador. ¿Para quién es el cine mexicano reciente?" *Letras Libres*, April 30, 2007, https://letraslibres.com/cine-tv/el-lugar-del-espectador-para-quien-es-el-cine-mexicano-reciente/. The term "pintar huevos" has a vulgar connotation that essentially means "do nothing."

28. MacLaird, *Aesthetics and Politics*, 71. Aurelio de Reyes González Rojas makes a similar critique when he disparages "double entendre" and other types of low cinema even as he calls on critics to better understand these productions. See Aureliano de los Reyes González Rojas, "Presentación," *Miradas al cine mexicano*, coord. Aureliano de los Reyes González (Mexico City: IMCINE, 2016), 10.

29. Olivia Cosentino and Brian Price, "Introduction: El Santo Versus The Cineteca Nacional de México: Rethinking the Lost Cinema of Mexico," in *The Lost Cinema of Mexico* eds. Cosentino and Price, 7.

30. Sánchez Prado, *Screening Neoliberalism*, 211.

31. MacLaird, *Aesthetics and Politics*, 61–62.

32. In this way, this book follows in the footsteps of Stefanie Van de Peer, who has written extensively on animation from a single region, the Middle East in this case. See Stefanie Van de Peer, *Animation in the Middle East: Practice and Aesthetics from Baghdad to Casablanca* (New York: I.B. Tauris, 2017).

33. Rodríguez Bermúdez, *Animación*, 17; Rodolfo Peláez, "Una perspectiva integral de la animación," in *Animación*, by Rodríguez Bermúdez. Juan Manuel Aurrecoechea identifies apocryphal animations that may have appeared as early as the 1920s. However, we no longer have access to these productions, even if they ever existed. See Juan Manuel Aurrecoechea, *El episodio perdido. Historia del cine mexicano de animación* (Mexico City: Cineteca Nacional, 2004), 15.

34. In recent years, IMCINE has taken to documenting whether an animated film is 2D or 3D in its annual publications. While this does not identify the type of animation (Claymation, paper, computer) of a specific film, it does allow for greater specificity. See Instituto Mexicano de Cinematografía, *Anuario Estadístico de cine mexicano/Statistical Yearbook of Mexican Cinema* (Mexico City: IMCINE, 2022), 51.

35. Compiled by Ana Cruz Rodríguez, Lourdes Villagómez Oviedo, Lucía Cavalchini, Tania de León Yong, and Sofía Carrillo, this book provided a valuable chronology of Mexican animated cinema.

36. Rodríguez et al., *Acervo de animación mexicana*, 65.

37. Carlos Carrera, "Prólogo," in *El episodio perdido*, by Juan Manuel Aurrecoechea, 12.

38. Rodríguez Bermúdez, *Animación*, 123.

39. There is some evidence that there may have been a few animated films produced during these years, though none would have lasted longer than a few seconds. In any event, anything that may have been produced during these years has been lost for nearly a century. As a result, any such productions had minimal, if any, effects on the national film industry. Rodríguez Bermúdez, *Animación*, 124–25.

40. Rodríguez Bermúdez, *Animación*, 124–30.

41. Rodríguez Bermúdez, *Animación*, 124.

42. Rodríguez Bermúdez, *Animación*, 124–26.

43. Rodríguez Bermúdez, *Animación*, 130–36.

44. Rodríguez Bermúdez, *Animación*, 130.

45. Rodríguez Bermúdez, *Animacíon*, 131.

46. Rodríguez Bermúdez, *Animación*, 131.

47. Rodríguez Bermúdez, *Animación*, 134–35.

48. Rodríguez Bermúdez, *Animación*, 135.

49. This was especially the case with César Cantón and Ángel Cantón, two brothers who formed Gamma Productions. They worked with US studios to provide animation services for these and other television programs. See Rodríguez Bermúdez, *Animación*, 135–36.

50. Rodríguez Bermúdez, *Animación*, 136–49.
51. The film was released in 1976.
52. Rodríguez Bermúdez, *Animación*, 136.
53. Rodríguez Bermúdez, *Animación*, 138–39.
54. Rodríguez Bermúdez, *Animación*, 139–40.
55. Rodríguez Bermúdez, *Animación*, 149–90.
56. Rodríguez Bermúdez, *Animación*, 149–50.
57. Rodríguez Bermúdea, *Animación*, 150, 154–57.
58. Rodríguez Bermúdez, *Animación*, 156.
59. Rodríguez Bermúdez, *Animación*, 157.
60. Rodríguez Bermúdez, *Animación*, 156–59.
61. Rodríguez Bermúdez, *Animación*, 150.
62. Ugalde, "Epílogo"; see also Aurrecoechea, *El episodio perdido*, "Adenda (2003–2004)."
63. Vázquez Hernández, *Cuentos y recuentos animados. Panorama de la animación mexicana: 2000–2012* (Puebla: Self Published), chapter 4, 166.
64. Ugalde seems to identify *Una película de huevos* as the crowning achievement of the fifth period in his afterword. Nevertheless, with hindsight it becomes clear that the film was actually the first great achievement of the fifth period. See Ugalde, "Epílogo," 199–202.
65. Even the most successful productions—Las leyendas and Huevocartoon—have given up on theatrical releases in favor of streaming on Vix, which is currently the largest Spanish-language streaming platform in the world. Vix released *Huevos congelados* in 2022, and *La leyenda de los chaneques* in 2023.
66. Instituto Mexicano de Cinematografía, *Anuario Estadístico de cine mexicano/Statistical Yearbook of Mexican Cinema* (Mexico City: IMCINE, 2013), 184–90; Instituto Mexicano de Cinematografía, *Anuario Estadístico de cine mexicano/Statistical Yearbook of Mexican Cinema* (Mexico City: IMCINE, 2014), 204.
67. Cristóbal Fernando Benavaides Almarza and Ligia García-Béjar, "¿Por qué ven Netflix quienes ven Netflix?: experiencias de *engagement* de jóvenes mexicanos frente a quien revolucionó el consumo audiovisual," *Revista de Comunicación* 20, no. 1 (2021): 31.
68. Instituto Mexicano de Cinematografía, *Anuario Estadístico de cine mexicano/Statistical Yearbook of Mexican Cinema* (Mexico City: IMCINE, 2020), 43.
69. Giannalberto Bendazzi, *Animation: A World History: Volume I: Foundations—The Golden Age* (New York: Routledge, 2015), 1.
70. Giannalberto Bendazzi, *Animation: A World History: Volume III: Contemporary Times* (New York: Routledge, 2016), 311–12.
71. Gianalberto Bendazzi, *Animation: A World History: Volume II: The Birth of a Style—The Three Markets* (Boca Raton, FL: CRC Press, 2016), 408.
72. Ana M. López, "From Hollywood and Back: Dolores del Río, a trans(national) star," *Studies in Latin American Popular Culture* 17 (1998); Gloria Tuñón,

"Emilio Fernández: A Look Behind the Bars," trans. Ana M. López, in *Mexican Cinema*, ed. Paulo Antonio Parangará (London: British Film Institute, 1995); Ceridwen Rhiannon Higgins, "Pulling Focus: New Perspectives on the Work of Gabriel Figueroa," (PhD diss., Durham University, 2007), 8–15.

73. Andrea Noble, *Mexican National Cinema* (New York: Routledge, 2005). Charles Ramírez-Berg has explored in depth how Mexican auteurs like Emilio Fernández tried to differentiate themselves from Hollywood—a context with which he was intimately familiar—through nationalistic film techniques. Charles Ramírez-Berg, "The Cinematic Invention of Mexico: The Poetics and Politics of the Fernández-Figueroa Style," in *The Mexican Cinema Project*, eds. Chon A. Noriega and Steven Ricci (Los Angeles: UCLA Film and Television Archive, 1994); see also John Mraz, *Looking for Mexico: Modern Visual Culture and National Identity* (Durham, NC: Duke University Press, 2009), chapter 3. At another level, however, Carl Mora asserts that, at least as far back as the Revolution, "the popularity of Hollywood films was a challenge that the undercapitalized and largely unoriginal national companies were unable to overcome." Mora, *Mexican Cinema*, 22. See also David S. Dalton, *Mestizo Modernity: Race, Technology, and the Body in Postrevolutionary Mexico* (Gainesville: University of Florida Press, 2018), chapter 3.

While filmmakers have generally avoided *mexicanidad* in recent years, their productions still tend toward essentialistic representations of the country through tropes of "exotic violence"—aimed at foreign audiences—and "neoliberal fear," aimed at domestic, middle-class audiences. See Ignacio M. Sánchez Prado, "*Amores perros*: Exotic Violence and Neoliberal Fear," trans. Kara N. Moranski, *Journal of Latin American Cultural Studies* 15, no. 1 (2006).

74. Aurrecoechea, *El episodio perdido*, 15–17.

75. Aurrecoechea, *El episodio perdido*, 16.

76. Aurrecoechea, *El episodio perdido*, 16–17.

77. Aurrecoecchea, *El episodio perdido*, 15–17.

78. "¿Mickey es el 'Ratón vaquero'? Francisco Gabilondo Soler se negó a vender a Walt Disney." *Milenio* May 9, 2023. https://www.milenio.com/cultura/francisco-gabilondo-soler-nego-vender-cri-cri-walt-disney.

79. Gerardo Australia, *Francisco Gabilondo Soler: Su obra y sus pasiones; una herencia para México* (Mexico City: Fundación Francisco Gabilondo Soler, Cri Cri, A.C., 2016), 206.

80. "¿Mickey es el 'Ratón vaquero'?," *Milenio*.

81. For a discussion of the Good Neighbor Policy and its effect on Mexico's access to funding for its cinema, see Maricruz Castro Ricalde and Robert McKee Irwin, *El cine mexicano "se impone": Mercados internacionales y penetración cultural en la época dorada* (Mexico City: Universidad Nacional Autónoma de México), 53–58.

82. "La historia oculta del Ratón Vaquero: Disney intentó comprar las canciones de Cri-Cri." *México Desconocido*, https://www.mexicodesconocido.com.mx/cri-cri-disney-segunda-guerra-mundial.html; "¿Mickey es el 'Ratón vaquero'?," *Milenio*.

83. Aurrecoechea, *El episodio perdido*, 20; Australia, *Francisco Gabilondo Soler*, 206.

84. Australia, *Francisco Gabilondo Soler*, 206–7.

85. Box Office Mojo, "Huevos: *Little Rooster's Egg-cellent Adventure*," https://www.boxofficemojo.com/release/rl2357036545/; Instituto Mexicano de Cinematografía, *Anuario Estadístico de cine mexicano/Statistical Yearbook of Mexican Cinema* (Mexico City: IMCINE, 2015), 70–72.

86. "Los cineastas Riva Palacio estrenarán película animada en EE.UU.," *LaConexiónUSA*, https://laconexionusa.com/noticias/201507141056397_lc105639714.asp.

87. "Los cineastas," *LaConexiónUSA*. Interestingly, by 2020, animation was a driving component of film schools throughout the country. IMCINE, *Anuario* (2020), 68; Instituto Mexicano de Cinematografía, *Anuario Estadístico de cine mexicano/Statistical Yearbook of Mexican Cinema* (Mexico City: IMCINE, 2021), 120.

88. Box Office Mojo, "*Coco*." https://www.boxofficemojo.com/release/rl3650455297/weekend/.

89. For a discussion of how *mexicanidad* has ceased to be a meaningful construct for Mexican audiences, see Sánchez Prado, *Screening Neoliberalism*, 4–5.

Bibliography

Aguilar Pérez, Erika Ivonne. "Matlalcuéyetl y Zeatonaly: Animación stop-motion en la la lengua náhuatl como material visual en la educación primaria de San Miguel Canoa Puebla." Master's thesis, Benemérita Universidad Autónoma de Puebla, 2022.

Aurrecoechea, Juan Manuel. *El episodio perdido. Historia del cine mexicano de animación*. Mexico City: Cineteca Nacional, 2004.

Australia, Gerardo. *Francisco Gabilondo Soler: Suo bra y sus pasiones; una herencia para México*. Mexico City: Fundación Francisco Gabilondo Soler, Cri Cri, A.C., 2016.

Benavides Almarza, Cristóbal Fernando, and Ligia García-Béjar. "¿Por qué ven Netflix quienes ven Netflix?: experiencias de *engagement* de jóvenes mexicanos frente a quien revolucionó el consumo audiovisual." *Revista de Comunicación* 20, no. 1 (2021): 29–47.

Bendazzi, Giannalberto. *Animation: A World History: Volume I: Foundations—The Golden Age*. New York: Routledge, 2015.

———. *Animation: A World History: Volume II: The Birth of a Style—The Three Markets*. Boca Raton, FL: CRC Press, 2016.

———. *Animation: A World History: Volume III: Contemporary Times*. New York: Routledge, 2016.

Carrera, Carlos. "Prólogo." In *El episodio perdido. Historia del cine mexicano de animación*, edited by Juan Manuel Aurrecoechea, 9–12. Mexico City: Cineteca Nacional, 2004.

Castro Ricalde, Maricruz, and Robert McKee Irwin. *El cine mexicano "se impone": Mercados internacionales y penetración cultural en la época dorada.* Mexico City: UNAM, 2011.

Cosentino, Olivia. "*Un cine familiar*: Recovering the 1980s Mexican Family Film." In *The Lost Cinema of Mexico*, eds. Cosentino and Price, 166–91.

Cosentino, Olivia and Brian Price. eds. *The Lost Cinema of Mexico: From Lucha Libre to Cine Familiar and Other Churros.* Gainesville: University of Florida Press, 2021.

———. "Introduction: El Santo versus the Cineteca Nacional de México: Rethinking the Lost Cinema of Mexico." In *The Lost Cinema of Mexico*, eds. Cosentino and Price, 1–33.

Cruz Rodríguez, Ana, Lourdes Villagómez Oviedo, Lucía Cavalchini, Tania de León Yong, and Sofía Carrillo. *Acervo de Animación Mexicana: Base de datos para la investigación y exhibición.* Mexico City: Secretaría de Cultura, 2024.

Dalton, David S. *Mestizo Modernity: Race, Technology, and the Body in Postrevolutionary Mexico.* Gainesville: University of Florida Press, 2018.

Del Toro, Guillermo, dir. *Pinocchio.* 2022; Streaming, 2022. Netflix.

De los Reyes González, Aureliano. "Presentación." In *Miradas al cine mexicano*, coord. Aureliano de los Reyes González, 9–11. Mexico City: IMCINE, 2016.

Gómez Gómez, Carmen Elisa, and Cecilia Andalón. "Exploraciones estéticas y simbólicas sobre la muerte y la infancia en los cortos *stop mostion* de las realizadores de la escuela de Jalisco." *Con A de Animación* 15 (2022): 46–61.

Higgins, Ceridwen Rhiannon. "Pulling Focus: New Perspectives On the Work of Gabriel Figueroa." PhD diss., Durham University, 2007.

Instituto Mexicano de Cinematografía. Anuario Estadístico de cine mexicano/Statistical Yearbook of Mexican Cinema. Mexico City: IMCINE, 2011.

———. Anuario Estadístico de cine mexicano/Statistical Yearbook of Mexican Cinema. Mexico City: IMCINE, 2012.

———. Anuario Estadístico de cine mexicano/Statistical Yearbook of Mexican Cinema. Mexico City: IMCINE, 2013.

———. Anuario Estadístico de cine mexicano/Statistical Yearbook of Mexican Cinema. Mexico City: IMCINE, 2014.

———. 2015. Anuario Estadístico de cine mexicano/Statistical Yearbook of Mexican Cinema. Mexico City: IMCINE.

———. Anuario Estadístico de cine mexicano/Statistical Yearbook of Mexican Cinema. Mexico City: IMCINE, 2018.

———. Anuario Estadístico de cine mexicano/Statistical Yearbook of Mexican Cinema. Mexico City: IMCINE, 2020.

———. Anuario Estadístico de cine mexicano/Statistical Yearbook of Mexican Cinema. Mexico City: IMCINE, 2021.

———. Anuario Estadístico de cine mexicano/Statistical Yearbook of Mexican Cinema. Mexico City: IMCINE, 2022.

López, Ana M. "From Hollywood and Back: Dolores del Río, a Trans(national) Star." *Studies in Latin American Popular Culture* 17 (1998): 5–32.

MacLaird, Misha. *Aesthetics and Politics in the Mexican Film Industry*. New York: Palgrave Macmillan, 2013.

Mariscal Avilés, Judith and Carlos Brambila Paz. "Institutional Connectivity: The Case of Mexico." *Information Technologies and International Development* 8, no. 4 (2012): 1–20.

Mejías, Roberto J., Jonathan W. Palmer, and Michael G. Harvey. "Journal of Global Information Technology Management." *Emerging Technologies, IT Infrastructure, and Economic Development in Mexico* 2, no 1 (1999): 31–54.

Mora, Carl J. *Mexican Cinema: Reflections of a Society 1896–1980*. Berkeley: University of California Press, 1982.

Mraz, John. *Looking for Mexico: Modern Visual Culture and National Identity*. Durham, NC: Duke University Press, 2009.

Noble, Andrea. *Mexican National Cinema*. New York: Routledge, 2005.

Peláez, Rodolfo. "Una perspectiva integral de la animación." In *Animación: Una perspectiva desde México*, by Manuel Rodríguez Bermúdez. Mexico City: UNAM, 2007.

Ramírez-Berg, Charles. "The Cinematic Invention of Mexico: The Poetics and Politics of the Fernández-Figueroa Style." In *The Mexican Cinema Project*, edited by Chon A. Noriega and Steven Ricci, 13–24. Los Angeles: UCLA Film and Television Archive, 1994.

Rodríguez Bermúdez, Manuel. *Animación: Una perspectiva desde México*. Mexico City: UNAM, 2007.

Sánchez Prado, Ignacio M. "*Amores perros*: Exotic Violence and Neoliberal Fear." Translated by Kara N. Moranski. *Journal of Latin American Cultural Studies* 15, no. 1 (2006): 39–57.

———. *Screening Neoliberalism: Transforming Mexican Cinema, 1988–2012*. Nashville, TN: Vanderbilt University Press, 2014.

Shaw, Deborah. *The Three Amigos: The Transnational Filmmaking of Guillermo del Toro, Alejandro González Iñárritu, and Alfonos Cuarón*. Manchester: Manchester University Press, 2013.

Smith, Paul Julian. "Foreword," in *The Transnational Fantasies of Guillermo del* Toro, edited by Ann Davies, Deborah Shaw, and Dolores Tierney. New York: Palgrave Macmillan, 2014.

Solórzano, Fernanda. "El lugar del espectador. ¿Para quién es el cine mexicano reciente?" *Letras Libres*, 30 Apr, 2007. https://letraslibres.com/cine-tv/el-lugar-del-espectador-para-quien-es-el-cine-mexicano-reciente/.

Tierney, Dolores, Deborah Shaw, and Ann Davies. "Introduction." In *The Transnational Fantasies of Guillermo del Toro*, ed. Davies, Shaw, and Tierney, 1–8.

Tierney, Dolores, Deborah Shaw, and Ann Davies, eds. *The Transnational Fantasies of Guillermo del Toro*. New York: Palgrave Macmillan, 2014.

Tuñón, Gloria. "Emilio Fernández: A Look Behind the Bars," translated by Ana M. López. In *Mexican Cinema*, edited by Paulo Antonio Parangará. London: British Film Institute, 1995.

Ugalde, Víctor. "Epílogo: Quinta etapa." In *Animación: Una perspectiva desde México*, by Manuel Rodríguez Bermúdez. Mexico City: UNAM, 2007.

Van de Peer, Stefanie. *Animation in the Middle East: Practice and Aesthetics from Baghdad to Casablanca*. New York: I.B. Tauris, 2017.

Vargas, María Celeste, and Daniel Lara. "Un cuento de hadas fracturado: historia de la 'maquila' animada en México." *Cinémas d'amérique latine* 19 (2011): 53–58.

Vázquez Hernández, Luis Gabriel. *Cuentos y recuentos animados: Panorama de la animación mexicana: 2000–2012*. Puebla, Mexico: Self Published, 2015. https://www.dropbox.com/scl/fi/lffcvly43c7862ymhs7nd/Cuentos_y_REcuentos_animados-Luis_Vazquez.pdf?rlkey=dp7xdtezxgrk4l8g6ahgj92pf&e=1&dl=0.

Ward, Glen. " 'There Is No Such Thing': Del Toro's Metafictional Monster Rally." In *The Transational Fantasies of Guillermo del Toro*, edited by Davies, Shaw, and Tierney, 11–28.

Wehr, Christian Wehr, ed. *Clásicos del cine mexicano: 31 películas emblemáticas desde la Época de Oro hasta el presente*. Madrid: Iberoamericana, 2016.

SECTION I

The Fifth Period

Commercial Animated Cinema in the Domestic Market

Chapter 1

Huevocartoon

New Masculinities and the Poetics of Failure

Rodrigo Figueroa Obregón

Huevocartoon produced its first animated short film in 2001. It was created by the Riva Palacio Alatriste brothers: Gabriel and Rodolfo. They distributed it online and gained instant success. Mexicans had had access to commercial internet for eight years at that point, and the brothers used that medium to distribute the first Huevocartoon short film. With the support of their father and another partner, they launched *huevocartoon.com* in 2002 with the goal of distributing their short animations to broad audiences throughout Mexico. Five years after they produced their first short film, they began creating full-length movies: *Una película de huevos* (2006), *Otra película de huevos y un pollo* (2009), *Un gallo con muchos huevos* (2015), *Un rescate de huevitos* (2021) and, most recently, *Huevos congelados* (2022).[1] According to Mexico's National Chamber of the Cinematographic Industry (CANACINE), this is the most financially successful trilogy in the history of Mexican animated cinema.[2] This animated series' success is an especially extraordinary feat considering that Manuel Rodríguez Bermúdez said in 2007 that, at that time, there were no conditions to develop a market or an audience for animated movies in Mexico.[3]

One of the reasons why Huevocartoon has been so successful is its unrestrained use of *albures* (double entendre). Since the brothers distributed their Huevocartoon clips online, they avoided censorship. Article 25 of the

Federal Cinematography Law (1992, amended in 1999) classified movies as follows:

A. For all audiences.

B. For 12-year-old audiences or older.

C. For audiences of legal age (18 years old).

D. For adults, with explicit sex, obscene language, or a high degree of violence.[4]

This law does not mention what distinguishes one classification or the other. More importantly, it does not state what constitutes "obscene language," nor does it explain why this is sufficient to put a movie that includes it in the same classification as one that depicts explicit sex. By distributing their clips on the internet, the brothers circumvented the possible arbitrariness of the Mexican system of movie classification. It needed to be so because double entendre and explicit language were at the core of the humor used in the Huevocartoon clips. The name of the production company itself is a somewhat dirty pun: *huevo* in Spanish means literally *egg*, but it also may mean *testicle* in Mexican Spanish. In this and other dialects, there is a vast array of expressions that include the word *huevo* and are considered vulgar and offensive. *Una película de huevos*, for instance, may mean *A Movie about Eggs* or *An Awesome Movie*; however, since the expression used for *awesome* is *de huevos*, it is considered vulgar. In the same vein, *Un gallo con muchos huevos* may mean *a rooster with many eggs* or *a very brave rooster*, considering that *con muchos huevos* can mean *with a lot of balls*. Also, *Otra película de huevos y un pollo* may mean *Another Movie about Eggs and a Cock,* since in European Spanish "polla" is vulgar slang for penis. The explicit reference to male genitalia, besides the problems with classification that it could entail, highlights an issue around which Mexican identity has always gravitated: that of masculinity.

Samuel Ramos published in 1934 *El perfil del hombre y la cultura en México*, in which he affirmed about double entendres: "The *pelado*'s terminology abounds in sexual allusions which reveal his phallic obsession; the sexual organ becomes symbolic of masculine force. In verbal combat he attributes to his adversary an imaginary femininity, reserving for himself the masculine role. By this stratagem he pretends to assert his superiority over his opponent."[5] According to Ramos, double entendre aims at feminizing a rival through discourse.[6] Octavio Paz agrees with him: "One word sums up the aggressiveness, insensitivity, invulnerability and other attributes of the *macho*: power. It is force without the discipline of any notion of order: arbitrary power, the will without reins and without a set course."[7] Both authors agree on the idea that Mexican masculinity, through words or otherwise, seeks to impose its will violently on anyone else, especially female or feminized subjects. Male genitalia is perceived as the catalyzer of an unbridled will that must subjugate anything and anyone in its way. However, the logical consequence of such an enterprise is failure. Roger Bartra posits that Mexican masculinity suffers from a terrible atrophy: "When they [women] are sympathetic and virginal, he [the male] rapes them; but when they become lustful, he flees in fear, taking refuge in the skirts of the mother-virgin."[8] These authors emphasize, on the one hand, the brutality of Mexican masculinity; on the other, they also recognize its fragility. The slang word for testicles in Mexican Spanish, *huevos*, condenses the idea very effectively: eggs are big (when compared to the size of actual human testicles), but extremely fragile. Furthermore, *huevo* comes from Latin *ovum*, which shares its etymology with *ovule* and *ovary*. Robert McKee Irwin, speaking of Samuel Ramos, has noted clearly the paradox in the egg metaphor: "Ramos argues that Mexicans need to assert a superficial hypermasculinity to mask their inner feelings of weakness."[9]

Huevocartoon animated movies build their concept on this paradox of Mexican masculinity; in them, egg characters are extremely aware of their flimsiness, and their peripeteia is directly linked to the threats that the outside world poses for them. In the third installment of the series, we see Toto involved in a professional fight, the Mexican way par excellence of attaining manhood. The importance of professional boxing and cockfighting in Mexican culture derives from the conflation of masculinity and violence in it. Samuel Ramos and Octavio Paz stress the importance of violence in the national character. However, as mentioned before, Huevocartoon movies are extremely aware of the fragility of masculinity and put forward a new masculinity, different from the one that Ramos and Paz analyzed. Therefore, Toto does fight and defeat a stronger gamecock, but his main tactic to do so is evasion.

As the previous example shows, the Huevocartoon movies question the types of traditional Mexican masculinity about which authors like Ramos, Paz, and Bartra wrote. In so doing, they dialogue with current scholarship on masculinity in Mexico in interesting ways. On the one hand, the movies embody Héctor Domínguez-Ruvalcaba's assertion that, in the early twentieth century, "the hegemony of masculinity is put into question."[10] That said, where Domínguez-Ruvalcaba seeks to situate crises in masculinity along a spectrum of masculine sensuality and violence, these films ultimately seek to imagine articulations of masculinity that eschew violence. Indeed, each of the movies questions the validity of constructs of masculinity that require men (and male eggs) to turn to violence in the first place.[11] The movies thus come to fit within a current of neoliberal cinema where, according to Samanta Ordóñez, idealistic representations of masculinity "tend to be structured in the cosmopolitan values of Western modernity rather than any type of recognizable Mexicanness."[12] Viewed in this light, many of the patterns for masculinity that we see in the film reflect those of foreign—particularly US—cinema.

Indeed, the Riva Palacio Alatriste brothers seem to draw their inspiration from films like Pixar's *Finding Nemo*, which details the travels of a family of fish who strive to reunite after fishermen capture a baby clownfish and turn him into a pet. Throughout that film, the male (and female) characters confront danger without resorting to violence. A similar dynamic emerges in the Huevocartoon movies, where Toto becomes a chicken without direct confrontation with his enemies, which consist of an array of antagonists that consist of humans, zombie eggs, reptile eggs, scorpion eggs, opossums, cats, and many other predators of chicken eggs. Similar to what we see in *Finding Nemo* and other Pixar films, these antagonists "are less villains than they are distractions, ultimately uninvolved with, or completely ignorant of, their respective films' main narrative journeys toward the protagonists' wisdom and/or idealized 'home.'"[13] Clearly, the Huevocartoon movies reject many midcentury suppositions about masculinity by tapping into the gendered tropes of international animated cinema. That said, the movies frequently have to reference outdated modes of Mexican masculinity as they build new paradigms if only to invalidate them. Viewed in this light, one cannot fully disentangle the films' representations of gender from the thought of Ramos, Paz, and Bartra.

Conflicting Masculinities in *Una película de huevos*

In *Una película de huevos,* it is very clear at the very beginning of the movie that humans are the enemy insofar as they have eggs for breakfast. That said, Toto's main antagonists in this movie are a group of reptilian eggs, who are apparently poultry's sworn enemies. However, the audience quickly notices that reptilian eggs are also learning how to be reptiles, how to behave as such, emphasizing the idea of species (and gender) as a performance. As a matter of fact, Coco—a crocodile egg who hates violence and loves acting—is going through his very own transformational process and is asked to attack Toto and his friends so that he can become a crocodile. It is also very clear to the audience that Coco is not a hitman or a rogue; on the contrary, he wants to be a Shakespearean actor and behaves like someone who is acting, not like a reptilian egg who wants to kill avian eggs. In the end, Coco finds himself one of the most likable characters insofar as his lack of natural violence allows Toto to succeed, and he confronts his father as well as the stereotypes of violent masculinity. Coco demonstrates, by being a strong and yet sensitive character, that "masculinity, then, is not internal; it is determined more by the judgments of others by than an intrinsic quality."[14] The movie seems to advance the idea that there is no such thing as a natural violence between men/testicles/male eggs, but a social construction of it. Rather than follow in the footsteps of his carnivorous parents, Coco ultimately performs a type of queer subjectivity by pushing back against the demands that he impose himself on others. In rejecting the violent nature of his family, Coco comes to challenge Paz's paradigm where, according to Ben. Sifuentes-Jáuregui, "masculinity is most present or persistent when most challenged."[15] The film ultimately validates Coco's queer masculinity over more violent articulations of masculinity when another reptile egg—a rattlesnake egg—accidentally kills himself in his attempts to destroy the

Figure 1.1. A character prepares to eat eggs for breakfast. *Source:* Riva Palacio Alatriste, Gabriel, and Rodolfo Riva Palacio Alatriste, dirs. *Una pelicula de huevos*, 2006; Mexico City, 2007. DVD.

chicken eggs. Clearly, the film posits a more peaceful masculinity with an emphasis on the arts as preferable to one of violence.

The coming-of-age stories of both Toto and Coco entail a very different relationship with their nature. As a chicken egg, Toto does not face the same pressures to be outwardly violent. Nevertheless, this seems to be the central message of the movie: there is no nature, only individuals who are, as Rousseau supposed, inherently good. In the first installment of the Huevocartoon saga, Toto has a fragile shell until he returns home, where he becomes a chick after hatching in his mother's perch. Toto emerges from there with the song "El Son de la Negra," an unmistakable staple of mariachi music, and some eggs wearing mariachi and other traditional outfits, thus reinforcing the idea of a new Mexican masculinity: "As conceptions of masculinity change over time, so change notions of *lo mexicano*."[16] Double entendre, especially that which highlights homosexual desires, is a fundamental feature of this and the rest of Huevocartoon movies. That said, not all puns are meant to express sexual innuendo. When Toto exits the perch as a chick, Willy asks him: "¿Quién lo quiere?" He then answers his own question by saying, "¡Po' yo!" This double entendre is, unlike traditional ones, harmless; Willy asks Toto "Who loves you?" and answers "Why, I do!" "Po' " is a very common contraction in oral Mexican Spanish of "pues," and if one adds "yo" it produces the aforementioned translation, but it also sounds exactly like *pollo* (chick). Toto's transformation into a chick has been possible because of his friends' love toward him and his ability to dodge situational threats.

By the time the film ends, the clash between two individuals over who is more masculine seems to be over. Toto and Coco can coexist and attain their dreams of being a chick and an actor respectively without killing or harming each other. Their assumed rivalry, which they inherited from previous generations, is canceled as soon as they start following their own dreams and ignore tradition. Toto is impelled to let himself go, for everything will be alright; however, Coco needs to deny his nature as a predator, a fact that aligns him with an array of 2000s animated films, where characters must "behave in a way that is entirely unnatural both for him as an individual and for clownfish as a species . . . becom[ing] something other than what he is naturally meant to be."[17] Far from negative, this fact allows the characters to grow as they challenge societal pressure on them to act in ways that do not align with their values or personalities.

The extent of Toto's effects on constructs of masculinity in Mexico rings particularly clearly in light of Brian L. Price's observation that, ever since the

Figure 1.2. Coco befriends and joins the chicken eggs. *Source*: Riva Palacio Alatriste, Gabriel, and Rodolfo Riva Palacio Alatriste, dirs. *Una pelicula de huevos*, 2006; Mexico City, 2007. DVD.

publication of Paz's *The Labyrinth of Solitude*, there has been a cult of defeat in Mexican popular imagination.[18] One of his main tenets "is that authors connect with the tragic moments of their history by employing a series of discursive strategies that highlight, reinterpret, and even poeticize perceived cultural, political, and social shortcomings."[19] He adds that "these [failure] narratives are fiercely nationalistic and intimately tied up with the nation's guiding fictions."[20] The idea of basing one's national identity on failure and defeat may seem odd to some readers; however, Price propounds that such is the case due to Mexico's long history of domestic and international lack of success, from the nineteenth century onward. Given the numerous defeats Mexico has suffered during the last two centuries, the only way to feel some historical pride resides in extolling Mexicans' stoical endurance instead of its rare military feats: "The emotional appeal of failure in the construction of national identity finds its most important expression in the ability to invest the present with the transcendental value of martyrdom."[21] No matter what the history of a country might be like, since Greek tragedy a narrative requires an order and someone or something who breaks it: "It has often been suggested that heroic fictions presuppose some sort of failure of social arrangements—or their violent disruption by a figuratively or literally alien force—in a way that makes redemptive intervention from without necessary."[22]

What is the social arrangement that Toto disrupts in a nation that praises endurance toward failure as the pinnacle of masculinity? Foremost, the very notion of failure as the core of masculinity formation. Toto succeeds: by the end of *Una película de huevos*, he has become a chick. He is the only character in the first movie who hatches and becomes what he is supposed to become. He also fractures the food chain: humans are supposed to have eggs for breakfast. Toto is a farm egg, a fact that entails the idea that, according to the owners of Granjas El Pollón, the purpose of his existence is to be food for humans. However, the opening scene of the movie shows the audience the act of consuming eggs from the eggs' perspective by placing the viewers' gaze at the ground level when eggs are running from people, making them terrifying. The audience assumes Toto's outlook and sees the otherwise quotidian act of having breakfast as a horrifying practice, highlighted by the use of red tones in the scene. Toto must go against and overcome this cycle of creating life for consumption. He is a hero whose fate is not marked by failure. Sergio de la Mora argues that "if there are two stereotypical ideas associated with *mexicanidad*, they are surely machismo and a taste for suffering," since they usually go hand in hand.[23]

Otra película de huevos y un pollo: The Quest for Ethical Consumption in a Neoliberal Era

After escaping the food chain and becoming inedible for humans as a chick, Toto's new phase brings a new challenge: he may have not been eaten, but now he needs to eat. Thus the franchise's second installment, *Otra película de huevos y un pollo*, poses a new hurdle in Toto's path toward masculinity and adulthood. Now that he is no longer an egg, the new challenge for him is to obtain his own food: earthworms. When his mother tries to teach him how to look for worms for food, he refuses to eat them, and his mother says "así tiene que ser" [it has to be that way], to which he adds that if that is the case, he does not want to be a chick anymore. When his egg friends Willy and Bibi say goodbye to him, Toto hugs him without realizing that now he is stronger and can break his friend's shell (and therefore kill him). He confides to Tocino that sometimes he would like to be an egg again, an idea that is completely alien to Tocino because if he went to his previous state, he would be a pig about to be butchered. Toto now faces a world in which he is no longer someone's breakfast, but one in which he needs to consume other beings to continue his way toward manhood. This fundamentally ethical question does not exclude the fact that he may be someone else's victim. Toto is no longer edible for humans as an egg, but his heart can be used for *brujería* [traditional Latin American witchcraft]. There is a very common expression in Mexican Spanish for when someone cannot do something because of mercy: "tener corazón de pollo" [to have the heart of a chicken]; it means that someone is as peaceful and harmless as a chicken. Therefore, this organ in them is also a symbol of compassion and naïveté. This movie's villain, who is actually a villain and not someone entangled in social constructions or hierarchies (as Coco), is a talisman who wants Toto's heart for a potion.

The talisman looks like a gray egg, but we learn at the end of the movie that he is a stone. This character catalyzes Toto's realization of a deeper truth about his own nature. In this way, the film follows in the footsteps of Hollywood animated cinema where, according to Amy Davis, "The presence of a villain—and the chance for the character(s) to be heroic—means that the narrative has the opportunity to present a victory which has been snatched from the jaws of defeat, a form of storytelling which is a necessity."[24] To avoid defeat, Toto must confront his fear of eating earthworms and the threat to his own life. Interestingly enough, the witch stone has an emblem right on his chest that resembles Spanish's question marks: "¿?"; Toto later learns that they are the source of the stone's power. As such, we can infer that interrogation and introspection are the origin of Toto's weakness. The young chick faces a very serious moral issue: Is it acceptable to eat sentient beings in order to survive oneself? The other option is starvation. At the beginning of the movie, it seems like the problem cannot be solved. Toto's tender heart might bring about his own demise. Nevertheless, the film begins to suggest an ethics of killing and consumption when the talisman conjures an army of zombie eggs to capture and destroy Toto.

David S. Dalton has explored the power dynamics of killing in *Otra película de huevos y un pollo,* in which he finds an issue of utmost interest for the ethical problems that Toto confronts: "Justifiably or not, the zombie eggs' undead performance signals them as the only ones whom Toto and his friends can deliberately kill without first negotiating," since he eventually learns that he can eat worms without killing them.[25] The witch stone's army of zombies includes all sorts of avian eggs. Technically, they are closer to Toto and his friends as species than earthworms, and yet they are the ones whom the hero kills indiscriminately. The fact that this is the only instance in which the heroes kill in this film—or in the others—proves especially interesting. Dalton's understanding of it supports the idea that I posited

Figure 1.3. Toto and his friends prepare to battle the zombie eggs. *Source*: Riva Palacio Alatriste, Gabriel, and Rodolfo Riva Palacio Alatriste, dirs. *Otra película de huevos y un pollo*, 2009; Mexico City, 2010. DVD.

about *Una película de huevos*: individuality is what makes life worthy. He understands the hero's disregard for zombie existence as a rejection of the masses as valuable subjects. Toto's quest is ultimately a singularity, for no other character is going through it. He does get help from other eggs and characters, but his path toward manhood is unique. He feels lonely when he is stuck between different life phases, but in the end, he is the only character that progresses from one stage of life to the next. Thus, Toto rejects tradition, or he simply ignores it. As an individual, there is no source of evil or good but himself, a trend in post-NAFTA Mexican cinema that De la Mora links with "individualist, middle-class, gender-based issues."[26] The masses are inherently evil or unpredictable, as the scorpion eggs, who can kill on command. However, scorpion eggs do follow a moral compass that tells them that it is wrong to kill Toto after he saved them from freezing to death. Zombie masses, on the other hand, are absolutely expendable.

Throughout *Otra película de huevos y un pollo* we see references to William Shakespeare and Kentucky Fried Chicken. On a smaller scale, Toto goes through Hamlet's own questioning: "Whether 'tis nobler in the mind to suffer / the slings and arrows of outrageous fortune, / or to take arms against a sea of troubles / and by opposing end them."[27] Contrary to Hamlet, Toto chooses a more joyous path that leads him to manhood instead of death. In Mexican folk culture, death is a stoic and commendable outcome to any enterprise taken by a man; in "Caminos de Guanajuato," José Alfredo Jiménez, one of the most beloved mariachi singers and lyricists, says: "la vida no vale nada" [life is worthless]. However, Toto goes against this folk sentiment and decides that life is worth living and that he will not suffer stoically. José Alfredo Jiménez in that very song insists: "[la vida] comienza siempre llorando / y así llorando se acaba" [life always begins weeping / and so it ends]. Toto decides that, even though he has gone through his share of tragedy, he will not endure life's slings and arrows passively. Life is meaningful for Toto as long as he finds his own destiny, as he does not succumb to the burden of questioning, symbolized by the talisman's emblem on his chest. However, the road to meaning is paved with death and the need to kill to survive.

Dalton emphasizes the importance of Toto's refusal to consume other animals, but kills zombie eggs: "Toto's refusal to consume the worms represents his rejection of the agricultural system that has commodified his body. Toto's entire life leads to the moment when his charred flesh will end up on someone's plate. The worms play a key role in this process because they will make him fat (and strong) enough to fight. This shared identity as consumed beings connects both predator and prey as cogs in the machine of industrial agriculture."[28] Thus, zombie eggs are not meant for consumption by humans and are therefore expendable. Toto cannot

Figure 1.4. The talisman egg prepares to kill Toto. *Source*: Riva Palacio Alatriste, Gabriel, and Rodolfo Riva Palacio Alatriste, dirs. *Otra película de huevos y un pollo*, 2009; Mexico City, 2010. DVD.

relate to them insofar as they do not share the same destiny, apparently at least, since he and they are just cogs serving higher authorities. As Dalton points out, Toto eventually learns that he can eat part of the earthworms, and they will regenerate, which means that they do not need to die for him to continue living. Hence, Toto can eat them and not clash with his inner self as Hamlet did. Since he does not need to kill or harm earthworms to survive, Toto does not confront a major ethical problem. Toto can kill zombie eggs insofar as he does not identify himself with them. They seem to be rotten and therefore unusable. It is important to note that "one of the key components of officialist literary and cultural production was the assertion that the state could modernize the indigenous masses by fusing their bodies with technology."[29] That said, the masses in this movie cannot be modernized; they are simply useless.

In the neoliberal era, the male individual is much more important than the masses, as Samanta Ordoñez propounds regarding one of the most important post-NAFTA movies, *Y Tu Mamá También* (2001): "Cuarón attempts to dramatize the separation of individual subjectivity from specious nationalist fictions of collectivity by focusing on the gradual breakdown of the friendship between Julio and Tenoch, whose affective attachments are represented in terms of retrograde/immature Mexican masculinity."[30] In *Otra película de huevos y un pollo*, Toto comes to good terms with his nature as consumer insofar as he does not need to kill other beings and worms can regenerate their bodies and continue the cycle of consumption. Dalton emphasizes the idea that this movie, unlike the first one in the trilogy, is about the individual against his "nature." However, when the individual fights against it, he does not change the system; on the contrary, the system he is involved in continues unaltered. The farm keeps producing eggs and poultry for human consumption.

There are two other characters involved in consumption: Tlacua and Cuache. These opossums participate in each film of the trilogy, in which they are looking for food. Obviously, an egg or a chick would be an ideal meal for them. However, they play a satirical role in the movies, for they do not seem to be able to secure the food they need, mostly because of their own incapacity to do so. Furthermore, they do not participate in the main narrative line, but their appearances are limited to side narratives for the most part. Nonetheless, they are characterized as rural Mexicans (which can be noticed by means of their stereotypical accent) who want to go to the United States because they cannot find the food they need in Mexico. Regional accents seem to indicate foreignness; those who have an accent are from other countries, want to leave Mexico, or live in border towns (most actors who dub the main characters of the series are from Mexico City or central Mexico, and only three among all the voices are from northern and eastern states, even if their regional accent is unnoticeable). Despite their comicality, Tlacua and Cuache point at a major issue in Mexico: its expelling of working-class citizens to the United States, looking for opportunities to find a market in which their labor is needed and better compensated. According to the US Census of 2010, 11,580,000 of Mexican-born individuals lived in the United States.[31] According to Mexico's National Institute of Geography and Statistics (INEGI), during that same year the country's population was 112,336,538.[32] This means that approximately 10 percent of Mexican citizens lived in the United States. From 1850 to 1970 the Mexican population in the United States remained relatively the same in terms of its size, but in the 1970s there was an immigration boom that did not recede until the 2010s.[33] NAFTA's economic policies did not alleviate the harsh living conditions of rural Mexicans. Just like Tlacua and Cuache, this population was left at the margins of Mexican society to deal with their problems by themselves. The open-market economy that benefitted some Mexicans and some Americans did not yield any fruits in rural Mexico and was thus unable to stop the economic exodus toward the north. Toto champions individualism and an ethical chain of consumption, but the mass of zombie eggs and the starving opossums face only death or starvation. Toto's road to masculinity is paved by those who are not fit to participate in an open-market economy; Olivia Cosentino propounds that, in the movie *Por la libre* (2000) by Juan Carlos de Llaca, we can see that a globalized Mexico does not guarantee the fulfillment of all its citizens' desires.[34]

NAFTA played a major role in how Mexican cinema changed and created new models of masculinity. For several decades after the revolution, the rural farmworker was the archetype of the Mexican citizen.[35] Many films of the Mexican Golden Age depict a main character who is a poor male who suffers stoically the slings of fortune. All of these movies were produced before NAFTA. This trade agreement "dictated a smaller role for government in film production, a reduction of screen quotas for Mexican films, the sale of its national chain of theaters, and the deregulation of ticket prices, which immediately doubled."[36] One of the direct effects of these policies was that producing films in Mexico became more difficult financially.[37] Mexican films were no longer to be wholly funded by the state but by private entrepreneurs or companies first, and only then by the state. Also, the Mexican government no longer has power over the industry, which now resides in the hands of distribution companies.[38] Furthermore, ticket price deregulation made it impossible for many Mexicans to go to the theaters: "The deregulation of ticket prices, as a new implementation of neoliberal policy in preparation for NAFTA, raised ticket prices, on average, to the equivalent of Mexico's daily minimum wage."[39]

These changes meant that going to the theater to watch a domestic feature film was no longer affordable for blue-collar and working-class Mexicans. However, the middle class was still able to watch movies at the theaters, but it also wanted to see their sensibility and ideology on the screen. Therefore, the myth of the self-made man was welcomed placidly. The struggles of rural farmers no longer made sense for middle-class Mexicans: "Post-1992 films [were] unashamedly catering to the interests of the new, more affluent audience."[40] Middle-class Mexicans liked to think of themselves as individuals who owed their success to no one but themselves. Also, they wanted to believe that social ascent was possible. In Mexican soap operas, the main character, a poor but morally incorruptible individual (usually a beautiful woman), can climb social hierarchies by means of marriage. But soap operas usually aim at working-class women, whereas post-NAFTA cinema tends to cater to middle-class males. Therefore, this new cinema, produced under different economic dynamics, championed a new form of masculinity, one devoid of struggle, failure, and defeat.[41] In order to participate in this new market, Huevocartoon movies had to put aside the anonymous masses and those who have not enjoyed neoliberalism's fruits, such as Tlacua and Cuache, whose dullness in the movie is to blame for their lack of success. Furthermore, neoliberal sensitivity—that is, petit-bourgeois—required a new kind of character, one that did not remind it of Samuel Ramos's *pelado* or Paz's *pachuco.* The middle-class hero needed to be a male adult in the making insofar as, according to neoliberal ideology, one can become a billionaire by means of a free market. Toto will become a rooster eventually, the archetype of masculinity: the expression "ése es mi gallo" [that's my rooster] in Mexican Spanish means that one man authenticates another one as being the best at a difficult enterprise.

Finding a Voice: *Un gallo con muchos huevos*

In *Un gallo con muchos huevos* [literally "A Rooster with Many Eggs," but more accurately "A Cock with Big Balls"], the audience witnesses Toto's transformation from being a cockerel to a rooster. There are two main conflicts in this movie: as I mentioned before, the professional fight in which Toto partakes and finds his rooster voice—crowing. In Mexican Spanish, having *muchos huevos* does not only imply the idea of being fierce or brave but also that one imposes his will over others', usually by violent or offensive means. In general, the audience does not see Toto being violent or rude, but in this movie, he needs to come to terms with one idea: he is the main rooster on the farm, and now he must lead the flock. This is the summit of his individual journey. He will no longer be a chick who needs to take care of himself because of his frailty; he must become a rooster that takes care of the whole flock and determines the times of production at the farm. Toto needs to overcome his own fears and become some sort of Nietzschean *Überhahn*. Unlike the German philosopher's gay science, Toto does not create his own moral code but follows his innate goodness. Once again, he does not need to question himself or the system; he just follows what his heart (the one that the talisman wanted to extract from him) dictates.

In *Un gallo con muchos huevos*, Toto is not violent and does not want to fight. However, it is the world around him that forces him to do so. The owner of the farm is in economic distress and one way to help her to keep the farm is through betting in professional fighting. That is his future father-in-law's choice, and Toto is drawn into it reluctantly. Nonetheless, he wants to impress a pullet, which is the axis of the encounter between his masculinity, adulthood, and role as a leader. For the first time in the trilogy, Toto wants to impress a female character, and his passage to the next stage in life is directly linked to her. The main character's voice becomes of utmost importance in this movie insofar as he needs to learn how to crow but also how to talk to women. Toto seems terrified about telling Di that he likes her, but also about everything of becoming a rooster. The film, as previous installments of the Huevocartoon franchise, emphasizes that Toto's rooster voice is found in his inner self. Therefore, his quest for "appropriate" masculinity and adulthood is an individual enterprise, and the masses are yet again put aside.

Bankivoide, the gamecock Toto must fight in order to save Granjas El Pollón, displays Mexico's national colors all over his body. His hackle is red, the midsection of his body is white, and his tail is green. Bankivoide can certainly be a symbol of traditional postrevolutionary Mexican masculinity: he must fight to reach the top of the social hierarchy, he is cocky (pun intended), and he is attractive to Chiquis, the most beautiful bird. Later in the film Bankivoide learns that most of his life had been an illusion insofar as the people around him wanted him to win his fights and made shady arrangements for it to happen. Cockfighting in his case seemed more like the spectacle of "Suffering, Defeat, and Justice" that Roland Barthes sees in professional wrestling.[42] On the contrary, Toto's win is authentic and even Bankivoide's boss bets on Toto. It is also important to notice that Bankivoide's girlfriend is a peacock (*pavo real* in Spanish [literally "royal turkey"]), whereas Toto's is a pullet. Bankivoide's interspecies relation does not seem to be working very well, while Toto's, one among the same species, does work (although he needs to find his rooster voice first). Both Irwin and Emily Hind have highlighted the importance of the penis (and its conflation with masculinity) as a kind of incontrollable god in Mexican literature.[43] However, we see in the Huevocartoon trilogy that Toto does not need to control his penis/voice, but to find it. Domínguez-Ruvalcaba states that "aggressive machismo is explosive and uncontrollable. [. . .] These depictions [Ramos's on machos] explain the intersection of macho fatalism with the misfortune of the nation. Presentation of the macho's simulative actions as forms of defense, compensation, and relief, interpret social behavior as a syndrome of irrationality."[44] Thus, Toto's journey is mostly calm and comical and devoid of the "challenging delirium of the deadly passions" that are characteristic of the Golden Age movies' masculinity.[45]

Toto's individual quest for masculinity is looked up to by younger eggs, who see in him the *súper vengador,* the *super avenger*, emphasizing the idea of an *Überhahn.* His main issue is to face the difficult crossroads at which he is without quailing or quitting, as Don Poncho did. This is important insofar as he is allowed to dodge threats or attacks, but he will need to eventually face them. Nonetheless, he will have to fight, crow, and tell Di that he loves her at some point. He should not let down the eggs that admire him. Their admiration is a mix of respect, awe, and love: one of them tells him several times throughout the movie "lo quiero mucho" [I love you very much], using the formal way of addressing someone in Spanish. As a matter of fact, the way in which Toto finds his voice is when Bankivoide calls him "gallina" [hen] and he remembers his mother, Di, and one of the kids. Therefore, his masculinity depends on being called a female (and therefore, according to Bankivoide's view, a coward) and the people he loves, two of them women. Sergio de la Mora "contend[s] that machismo needs the *joto* to define and affirm itself as much as it needs a clingy woman."[46] This is the most stereotypical masculine that Toto gets: the maternal figure has played an essential role throughout Mexican history: from Malinche to Virgin of Guadalupe to Golden Age cinema.[47] That said, Toto diverges from notions like Paz's "la Chingada" in that he does not expect his mother and romantic interest to be suffering mythical figures. As someone who has undergone an individual transformation and owes nothing to the masses or to history, he trusts his inner self to give him an ethical way to relate to women. Ironically, Di and Toto's mother remain on the sidelines of the story; they passively watch how a man-to-be tries to maintain their way of life. It is important to note that "for women to be recentered in narrative fiction–literature or film—it stands to reason that a degree of subversion was and still is required and that this subversion must take place over time, and repeatedly, to push back against the weight of 'universal' (sexist) culture."[48] It is very clear that Toto's journey to "proper" masculinity does not include women as independent beings or as individuals who can have a meaningful impact in their societies. His path to masculinity is individual and, excuse the pleonasm, masculine.

Toto's path to masculinity throughout the Huevocartoon trilogy is not one of defeat. His passage into it is not defined by how bravely he can withstand failure. On the contrary, he becomes a respectable, grown-up rooster by means of success. However, its terms need to be analyzed meticulously, for they entail a convoluted and problematic relation with traditional postrevolutionary masculinity. Karl Marx and Friedrich Engels asserted that "the bourgeoisie, historically, has played a most revolutionary part. The bourgeoisie, wherever it has got the upper hand, has put an end to all feudal, patriarchal, idyllic relations."[49] However, we see that a neoliberal champion who opposes the masses keeps excluding female characters from the narrative of his success. Toto does overcome the idea that men become so by enduring failure and/or violently imposing their will on other people. Nonetheless, Di and his mother only play the role of the male's supporters, of his emotional inspiration. Bibi could be seen as a female character that is independent, but her feats are not the center of the trilogy, and Toto constantly sees her as Willy's girlfriend (even though she claims that she needs her own space and a differentiated identity from his). Toto's masculinity is unique in the postrevolutionary cultural landscape in Mexico insofar as he finds it within himself, not by homosocial relations (unlike De la Mora's analysis of Pedro Infante's movies) or destruction (of individuals, for he can kill zombie masses).[50] However, at the end of the trilogy, Toto does not alter patriarchal or capitalist systems. For instance, the movie's soundtrack does not contain any traditional or folk music from Mexico; it is mostly billboard hits in English or in Puerto Rican Spanish, the one exception being Javier Calderón's pop rock songs, appealing to middle- and upper-class musical taste. Toto becomes the farm's alpha male, which entails the idea that he will be in charge of impregnating multiple hens (it is important to notice that Toto's father is never shown in the movie, for his role is that of a stud), and eggs are still being sold for human consumption. Toto saves himself and those around him, but by keeping the farm functioning he assures that other eggs will be consumed and that Di will need to share him with other hens, as opposed to what Marx and Engels state about the bourgeoisie's vision of women, who believe communists want women to be shared.[51] Don Poncho kept his wattle (even though it is removed from gamecocks so that it will not interfere when they fight) as a symbol of his testicles. Which means that other roosters are capons. They will also become food for humans and be below Toto in the farm's social hierarchy.

Although the Huevocartoon trilogy promotes a more individualistic and less violent path to masculinity, it keeps several remnants of postrevolutionary ideology of manhood. NAFTA changed the way in which animated cinema represented the middle class's conflicts but also reproduced some of its most troublesome approaches to gender ideology. The fact that homosexuality is still seen as something of which it is acceptable to make fun by means of *albures* is a clear manifestation of it. Nonetheless, it is remarkable that the whole idea of failure as a national characteristic was discarded for a more triumphant approach to identity formation. Since this chapter focused primarily on an individualistic form of masculinity, I would

Figure 1.5. Toto wins the boxing match. *Source*: Riva Palacio Alatriste, Gabriel, and Rodolfo Riva Palacio Alatriste, dirs. *Un gallo con muchos huevos*, 2015. Mexico City, 2016. DVD.

dare to suggest that a possible path for further investigation could include the ways in which homosocial bonding among males has changed how boys and men are portrayed in animated cinema and how this has also affected how girls and women are depicted.

Notes

1. This chapter focuses on the first three films of the series, since the last two take place after Toto, the main character, becomes a father. Therefore, given that the main argument of this chapter deals with the formation of Toto's masculinity, whose fatherhood implies his coming of age, the last two movies of the series are beyond the chapter's scope.

2. "Películas Animadas 2000–2018," CANACINE, accessed May 23, 2020, https://canacine.org.mx/peliculas-animadas-2000-2018/.

3. Manuel Rodríguez Bermúdez, *Animación. Una perspectiva desde México* (Mexico City: UNAM), 190.

4. Mexico. Cámara de Diputados del H. Congreso de la Unión. "Ley Federal de Cinematografía." (Mexico, 2015), 11–12.

5. Samuel Ramos, *Profile of Man and Culture in Mexico* (Austin, TX: University of Texas Press, 1962), 59–60.

6. Robert McKee Irwin, *Mexican Masculinities* (Minneapolis: University of Minnesota Press, 2003), 190.

7. Octavio Paz, *The Labyrinth of Solitude. Life and Thought in Mexico* (New York: Grove, 1961), 81.

8. Roger Bartra, *The Cage of Melancholy. Identity and Metamorphosis in the Mexican Character* (New Brunswick, NJ: Rutgers University Press, 1992), 162.

9. Irwin, *Mexican Masculinities*, 188.

10. Héctor Domínguez-Ruvalcaba, *Modernity and the Nation in Mexican Representations of Masculinity* (New York: Palgrave Macmillan, 2007), 2.

11. Domínguez-Ruvalcaba, *Modernity and the Nation*, 2.

12. Samanta Ordóñez, *Mexico Unmanned: The Cultural Politics of Masculinity in Mexican Cinema* (Albany: State University of New York, 2021), xix.

13. Stella Bruzzi, *Men's Cinema: Masculinity and Mise-en-scène in Hollywood* (Edinburgh: Edinburgh University Press, 2013), 83.

14. Irwin, *Mexican Masculinities*, xviii.

15. Ben. Sifuentes-Jáuregui, *The Avowal of Difference: Queer Latino American Narratives* (Albany: State University of New York Press, 2014), 9.

16. Irwin, *Mexican Masculinities*, xiii

17. Keith Booker makes such an observation with regard to Pixar's *Finding Nemo*. See Keith Booker, *Disney, Pixar, and the Hidden Messages of Children's Films* (Westport, CT: Greenwood, 2010), 90.

18. Brian Price, *Cult of Defeat in Mexico's Historical Fiction: Failure, Trauma, and Loss* (New York: Palgrave Macmillan, 2012).

19. Price, *Cult of Defeat*, 3–4.

20. Price, *Cult of Defeat*, 4.

21. Price, *Cult of Defeat*, 9.

22. Richard Sparks, "Masculinity and Heroism in the Hollywood Blockbuster," *British Journal of Criminology* 36, no. 3 (1996): 357.

23. Sergio de la Mora, *Cinemachismo. Masculinities and Sexuality in Mexican Film* (Austin: University of Texas Press, 2006), 104.

24. Amy Davis, *Handsome Heroes and Vile Villains: Masculinity in Disney's Feature Films* (Bloomington: Indiana University Press, 2015), 188.

25. David S. Dalton, "Worms, Scorpions, and Zombies: Egg-splaining the Zombie Aesthetic in Gabriel and Rodolfo Palacio Alatriste's *Otra película de huevos y un pollo*," Children's Literature Association Conference, Tampa, Florida, June 22–24, 2017.

26. de la Mora, *Cinemachismo*, 151.

27. Coco explicitly poses this question in a performance of the play early in the film.

28. Dalton, "Worms, Scorpions, and Zombies."

29. David S. Dalton, *Mestizo Modernity: Race, Technology, and the Body in Postrevolutionary Mexico* (Gainesville: University of Florida Press, 2018), 177.

30. Ordóñez, *Mexico Unmanned*, 40.

31. "Foreign Born: 2010 Current Population Survey Detailed Tables," United States Census Bureau, accessed May 23, 2020, https://www.census.gov/data/tables/2010/demo/foreign-born/cps-2010.html.

32. "Censo de Población y Vivienda 2010," INEGI, accessed May 23, 2020, https://www.inegi.org.mx/programas/ccpv/2010/.

33. Ana Gonzalez-Barrera, "More Mexicans Leaving Than Coming to the U.S.," *Pew Research Center*, November 19, 2015, https://www.pewresearch.org/hispanic/2015/11/19/more-mexicans-leaving-than-coming-to-the-u-s/.

34. Olivia Cosentino, "Configuring Desire and Social Order in the Contemporary Mexican Youth Road Film." In *The Latin American Road Movie*, eds. Verónica Garibotto and Jorge Pérez (New York: Palgrave Macmillan, 2016), 204.

35. Víctor M. Macías-González and Anne Rubenstein. *Masculinity and Sexuality in Modern Mexico* (Albuquerque: University of New Mexico Press, 2012), 11.

36. Jacobo Asse Dayán, "*Güeros*: Social Fragmentation, Political Agency, and the Mexican Film Industry under Neoliberalism," *Norteamérica* 12, no. 1 (2017): 138.

37. Misha MacLaird, *Aesthetics and Politics in the Mexican Film Industry* (New York: Palgrave Macmillan, 2013), 23.

38. Frederick L. Aldama, *Mex-Ciné: Mexican Filmmaking, Production, and Consumption in the Twenty-first Century* (Ann Arbor: University of Michigan Press, 2013), 83.

39. MacLaird, *Aesthetics and Politics*, 45.

40. Asse Dayán, "*Güeros*," 149.

41. Ignacio M. Sánchez Prado, *Screening Neoliberalism: Transforming Mexican Cinema, 1988–2012.* (Nashville, TN: Vanderbilt University Press, 2014), 112.

42. Roland Barthes, *Mythologies* (New York: Hill and Wang, 1972), 19.

43. Irwin, *Mexican Masculinities*, 112; Emily Hind, *Dude Lit. Men Writing and Performing Competence, 1955–2012* (Tucson: University of Arizona Press, 2019), 112.

44. Domínguez Ruvalcaba, *Modernity and the Nation*, 105.

45. Domínguez Ruvalcaba, *Modernity and the Nation*, 80.

46. de la Mora, *Cinemachismo*, 5.

47. Octavio Paz in *The Labyrinth of Solitude* posits that the search for a mythical mother is at the very core of Mexican identity: "Who is the *Chingada*? Above all, she is the Mother. Not a Mother of flesh and blood but a mythical figure. The *Chingada* is one of the Mexican representations of Maternity, like *La Llorona* or the 'long-suffering Mexican mother' we celebrate on the tenth of May. The *Chingada* is the mother who has suffered—metaphorically or actually—the corrosive and defaming action implicit in the verb that gives her her name." See Paz, *The Labyrinth of Solitude*, 75; see also Bartra, *The Cage of Melancholy*, 147–62.

48. Ilana Dann Luna, *Adapting Gender: Mexican Feminisms from Literature to Film* (Albany: State University of New York Press, 2018), 3.

49. Karl Marx and Friedrich Engels, *Selected Works* (Moscow: Progress, 1969), 113.

50. See de la Mora, *Cinemachismo*, 71.

51. Marx and Engels, *Selected Works*, 123.

Bibliography

Aldama, Frederick L. *Mex-Ciné: Mexican Filmmaking, Production, and Consumption in the Twenty-first Century.* Ann Arbor: University of Michigan Press, 2013.

Asse Dayán, Jacobo. "*Güeros*: Social Fragmentation, Political Agency, and the Mexican Film Industry under Neoliberalism," *Norteamérica* 12, no. 1 (2017): 137–68.

Barthes, Roland. *Mythologies.* New York: Hill and Wang, 1972.

Bartra, Roger. *The Cage of Melancholy. Identity and Metamorphosis in the Mexican Character.* New Brunswick: Rutgers University Press, 1992.

Booker, Keith. *Disney, Pixar, and the Hidden Messages of Children's Films.* Westport, CT: Greenwood, 2010.

Bruzzi, Stella. *Men's Cinema: Masculinity and Mise-en-scène in Hollywood.* Edinburgh: Edinburgh University Press, 2013.

"Censo de Población y Vivienda 2010," INEGI, accessed May 23, 2020, https://www.inegi.org.mx/programas/ccpv/2010/.

Cosentino, Olivia. "Configuring Desire and Social Order in the Contemporary Mexican Youth Road Film." In *The Latin American Road Movie*, edited by

Verónica Garibotto and Jorge Pérez, 195–214. New York: Palgrave Macmillan, 2016.

Dalton, David S. "Worms, Scorpions, and Zombies: Egg-splaining the Zombie Aesthetic in Gabriel and Rodolfo Palacio Alatriste's *Otra película de huevos y un pollo.*" Children's Literature Association Conference, Tampa, Florida, June 22–24, 2017.

———. *Mestizo Modernity: Race, Technology, and the Body in Postrevolutionary Mexico.* Gainesville: University of Florida Press, 2018.

Davis, Amy. *Handsome Heroes and Vile Villains: Masculinity in Disney's Feature Films.* Bloomington: Indiana University Press, 2015.

De la Mora, Sergio. *Cinemachismo. Masculinities and Sexuality in Mexican Film.* Austin: University of Texas Press, 2006.

Domínguez-Ruvalcaba, Héctor. *Modernity and the Nation in Mexican Representations of Masculinity. From Sensuality to Bloodshed.* New York: Palgrave Macmillan, 2007.

"Foreign Born: 2010 Current Population Survey Detailed Tables," United States Census Bureau, accessed May 23, 2020, https://www.census.gov/data/tables/2010/demo/foreign-born/cps-2010.html.

Gonzalez-Barrera, Ana. "More Mexicans Leaving Than Coming to the U.S.," *Pew Research Center,* November 19, 2015, https://www.pewresearch.org/hispanic/2015/11/19/more-mexicans-leaving-than-coming-to-the-u-s/.

Hind, Emily. *Dude Lit. Men Writing and Performing Competence, 1955–2012.* Tucson: University of Arizona Press, 2019.

Irwin, Robert McKee. *Mexican Masculinities.* Minneapolis: University of Minnesota Press, 2003.

Luna, Ilana Dann. *Adapting Gender: Mexican Feminisms from Literature to Film.* Albany: State University of New York Press, 2018.

Macías-González, Víctor M., and Anne Rubenstein. *Masculinity and Sexuality in Modern Mexico.* Albuquerque: University of New Mexico Press, 2012.

MacLaird, Misha. *Aesthetics and Politics in the Mexican Film Industry.* New York: Palgrave Macmillan, 2013.

Marx, Karl, and Friedrich Engels. *Selected Works.* Moscow: Progress Publisher, 1969.

Mexico. Cámara de Diputados del H. Congreso de la Unión. "Ley Federal de Cinematografía." (Mexico, 2015), 11–12.

Ordóñez Robles, Samanta. *Mexico Unmanned: The Cultural Politics of Masculinity in Mexican Cinema.* Albany: State University of New York Press, 2021.

Paz, Octavio. 1950. *The Labyrinth of Solitude. Life and Thought in Mexico.* New York: Grove, 1962.

"Películas Animadas 2000–2018," CANACINE, https://canacine.org.mx/peliculas-animadas-2000–2018/.

Price, Brian. *Cult of Defeat in Mexico's Historical Fiction: Failure, Trauma, and Loss.* New York: Palgrave Macmillan, 2012.

Ramos, Samuel. 1934. *Profile of Man and Culture in Mexico.* Austin: University of Texas Press, 1962.

Rodríguez Bermúdez, Manuel. *Animación. Una Pespectiva desde México.* Mexico City: Universidad Nacional Autónoma de México, 2007.

Sánchez Prado, Ignacio M. *Screening Neoliberalism: Transforming Mexican Cinema, 1988–2012.* Nashville, TN: Vanderbilt University Press, 2014.

Sifuentes-Jáuregui, Ben. *The Avowal of Difference: Queer Latino American Narratives.* Albany: State University of New York Press, 2014.

Sparks, Richard. "Masculinity and Heroism in the Hollywood Blockbuster," *The British Journal of Criminology* 36, no. 3 (1996): 348–60.

Chapter 2

On Colonial and Decolonial Ghosting

La leyenda de la Nahuala

Elissa J. Rashkin

La leyenda de la Nahuala, directed by Ricardo Arnaiz for his own Animex Producciones in 2007, takes up a favorite Mexican storytelling form—tales of the supernatural set in the colonial period—and translates it to the format of an all-ages animated feature film. The story of a boy facing and conquering his fears through a series of encounters with the phantasmal inhabitants of an abandoned mansion in the city of Puebla brings into play familiar representations of cultural identity, such as the Afro-descendent nanny Dionisia; the Nahuatl-speaking ghost Xochitl, servant to the also ghostly Teodora; Fray Godofredo, erudite and tolerant Franciscan; the Nahuala herself, dimly outlined yet easily identifiable as a common figure in popular legend; and other figures broadly associated with the social order of New Spain.

These representations are to a great extent stereotyped, as Julian Woodside has noted.[1] What interests me in this film, however, is how the commotion set off by Leo and his brother Nando's presence in the mansion on the doubly significant date of Day of the Dead and Fuego Nuevo, the transition from one cycle to the next in the ancient Mesoamerican calendar, creates an atmosphere of rupture that correlates with the film's setting in 1807, just prior to the beginning of the struggle for national independence. This scenario reconfigures the national narrative as ghost story and allows for the intertwining of what I will provisionally call colonial and decolonial elements in the film's ghosting; moreover, these elements emerge precisely through the creators' comic appropriation of traditional storytelling as a means of "Mexicanizing" the film animation medium.

My (perhaps cavalier) adaptation of the term "decolonial" to describe the film's conjuring of ingredients favorable to the cause of Mexico's independence from Spain via the armed struggle inaugurated by Miguel Hidalgo in 1810 is intentionally anachronistic, as I hope will become clear later in this chapter. Presumptive heir to earlier radical projects such as those of Frantz Fanon, Paolo Freire, or Che Guevara as channeled through cultural movements like the New Latin American Cinema of the 1960s and 1970s, *decolonialidad* in contemporary Mexico has become an academic buzzword associated with theoretically dense maneuvers that, at times, inadvertently recall Black feminist theorist Audre Lourde's warning that "the master's tools will never dismantle the master's house."[2] Her proclamation resonates especially well in the film's Villavicencio-Nahuala mansion.[3] However, before setting out on the prickly conceptual paths of analysis, an introduction to *La leyenda* is in order.

On Nahuala Street

La leyenda de la Nahuala is set in the city of Puebla, a quintessential site of the Mexican picturesque. Puebla is associated with a religiosity expressed in an abundance of baroque churches, gastronomic creations like *mole de guajolote* or the more prosaic *camote* and, to a certain extent, national identity, due to the city's status as site of the 1852 battle against the invading French army commemorated in the Cinco de Mayo holiday and the less well-known contribution of the Serdán family to the early moments of the Mexican Revolution.[4] In the commentaries that accompany the DVD edition of the film, director Arnaiz and screenwriter Omar Mustre mention finding, on a map consulted in the early stages of production, the Calle de la Nahuala—a haphazard trace, perhaps, that would become the center of the narrative.[5] Apocryphal naming is itself a part of Mexican storytelling: while formal names refer to political figures or dates in official history, small streets and alleys frequently receive nicknames that pay homage to the supernatural and/or to tragic crimes situated in the colonial era.[6] That these crime tales often invoke gender or sexual transgression is a striking aspect that also makes its way into *La leyenda*; although the street's extratextual identity is unclear, as we will see, the Nahuala's Indigenous female monstrosity is nothing if not intersectional.

Leo San Juan, the film's protagonist, lives with his brother Nando, their grandmother Toñita, and Nana Dionisia. The Nana's relationship to the others is essentially that of "Mammy," that is, a domestic worker whose apparent member-of-the-family status conceals the economic basis of her role in the household, as I will discuss shortly. The pairing of Dionisia and the grandmother as keepers of tradition for the orphaned boys emerges as the family prepares for Day of the Dead, preparing the altar that will honor the deceased parents and other relatives.

Leo, coded as traditionalist by his role as church acolyte and virtuosity with the Mexican wooden cup-and-ball *balero* toy, is harassed by Nando due to an apprehensiveness that makes him an easy target of practical jokes. When a spooky retelling of the Nahuala legend causes Leo to wet his pants, Nando gives him the unkind nickname of "Chisguete."[7] Leo's narrative trajectory will allow him to overcome his fears and emerge as hero, squelching Nando's hubris in the process. The Day of the Dead preparations underline the differences between the brothers: while Leo becomes melancholy thinking of his lost parents, Nando sneaks the treats from the altar that are meant to be enjoyed by the visiting spirits. The holiday, a gateway celebration in which the worlds of the living and the dead mingle, provides the opening through which ghosts will return to Puebla, their visit welcomed via the numerous festive practices depicted in early sequences of the film. To incorporate the Nahuala into this scenario, however, another temporal window must be opened: the lighting of the Fuego Nuevo, inauguration of the Mesoamerican fifty-two-year "century."

This association is made after Leo is sent to deliver bread to an address on the Calle de la Nahuala and is given a mysterious medallion by Santos, the candy seller who also introduces the latest novelty: Chinese fireworks. Nando follows Leo and succeeds in scaring him to the point of wetting himself; he then seizes the medallion and, intending to take the joke even further, steps into the Casa de la Nahuala and calls to his brother, asking for help. When Leo steps inside, Nando laughs and opens the medallion, from which a supernatural light escapes and illuminates the house, accompanied by dramatic music. Leo, sensing another joke, refuses to be taken in. Just as he wishes aloud that his brother would disappear forever, ghostly forces suck Nando into the mansion's dark interior.

After a restless interval at home, Leo sneaks out to visit Fray Godofredo. The priest takes Leo to the Biblioteca Palafoxiana, a famous library coded as center of historical knowledge, where he directs the boy to a large, dusty book of legends. He then recounts a tale that adds information to what we have already heard from Nando and is now reenacted in flashback, beginning with the Fuego Nuevo ceremony, in which a young Godofredo takes part along with Indigenous participants (fig. 2.1). The portentous event—the liminal moment between the death of one cycle and the birth of another—empowers the Nahuala to carry out her malevolent mischief.

At the Villavicencio mansion, the Nahuala takes possession of the household's Indigenous cook: mother of the candy vendor Santos. She also attempts to enslave the spirits of three girls: Teodora, her servant Xochitl, and Teodora's friend Toñita—Leo and Nando's grandmother. Toñita is saved by the group of Fuego Nuevo celebrants, but the witch succeeds in taking over the mansion. "Tonight," concludes the priest, "the medallion must be destroyed, or the Nahuala will return." The Miquistli image from the medallion, as replicated in the book, reinforces the double authority of his words, as a priest and as a man of science, conversant with the spirit world and the native cosmovision with which the legend is purportedly connected.

The scene-setting described to this point occupies the first thirty minutes of *La leyenda de la Nahuala*.[8] Besides introducing characters and invoking, with admirable detail, local color connected with Día de Muertos, it also establishes various interlocking time frames: the story's present, in 1807,

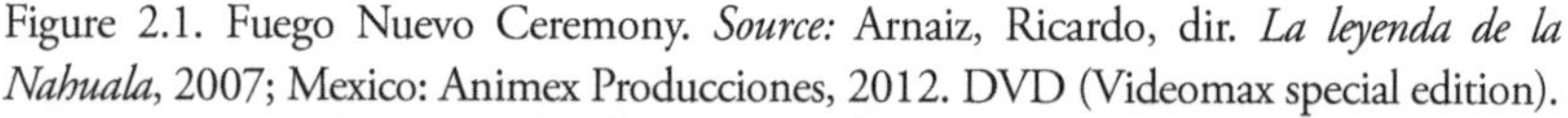
Figure 2.1. Fuego Nuevo Ceremony. *Source:* Arnaiz, Ricardo, dir. *La leyenda de la Nahuala*, 2007; Mexico: Animex Producciones, 2012. DVD (Videomax special edition).

on the eve of the Independence struggle and also Day of the Dead and a key date in the local—active although suppressed—Indigenous calendar; the moment fifty-two years earlier in which the Nahuala's power was released, and the Villavicencio mansion became haunted; and, implicitly, the creators' and spectators' present, in which elements such as spooky legends, wooden toys, mystical aboriginal rites, Day of the Dead altars, and fireworks form part of a cultural imaginary associated with national identity. This comes about most notably through the discourse of tourism that juxtaposes folklore and the picturesque with "modern" aspects of Mexican and specifically Pueblan life, such as industrial growth and the technological advancement necessary to promote activities such as animated filmmaking.[9]

The returning Nahuala, in this scenario, emerges as a vehicle through which to reexamine Mexican temporalities, not in terms of the static tableaux shown, for instance, in the promotional clip included in the *leyenda* DVD, but rather via the uncomfortable implications of the spectral, as we will see in the next section. First, however, a brief note about origins.

Legend(s) behind the Legend . . .

La leyenda de la nahuala was a box office and critical success. Perhaps as a result of its speedy incorporation into Mexican pop culture,[10] the "witch known as La Nahuala" was assumed to be a figure of folk legend adapted to the screen. However, attempts to locate an "original" or specifically Pueblan Nahuala legend have been, to date, fruitless. Rather, all searches lead back to the film: a cultural product whose convincing presentation of "authenticity" allows it to "invent tradition" in the small discursive sphere devoted to the subject.[11] Interestingly, shortly after its debut at the Morelia Film Festival, director Ricardo Arnaiz responded to an interviewer's question about the film's inspiration: "We looked for core elements of Mexican films, we were inspired by movies like *Dos fantasmas y una muchacha*" ["Buscamos elementos pilares de las películas mexicanas, nos inspiramos con cintas como *Dos fantasmas y una muchacha*"]—a haunted house comedy directed by Rogelio A. González in 1958.[12]

Dos fantasmas y una muchacha features Germán Valdés "Tin Tan" as well as his brother Manuel "El Loco" Valdés, the voice of Lorenzo Villavicencio in *La leyenda de la Nahuala*. Among the *Leyenda*'s many references to the earlier movie are the characters named López and Pérez, and Lorenzo Villavicencio's "Witch Doctor" dance that replicates the one performed by

"El Loco" Valdés (fig. 2). The comic sensibility of Arnaiz and his team thus pays homage to Mexican film history while offering, in the director's words, "a universal theme with Mexican identity" ["una temática universal con identidad mexicana"].[13] It is also, as repeated viewings reveal, a thoroughly researched, lovingly rendered depiction of early nineteenth-century Puebla. But, what of the Nahuala?

Nahualismo and Hegemony

As readers who have sat around a table late at night sharing tall tales will surely recognize, *nahualismo* is a paradigmatic source of the Mexican ghost story. However, what constitutes *nahualismo* is not always clear. In contemporary oral tradition, it generally involves malevolent shapeshifting: a woman or man who clandestinely assumes nonhuman form to carry out evil deeds, such as bloodsucking or stealing the hearts of infants as rejuvenating nourishment. Stories of encounters with mysterious animals, animal shapes or sounds also fall into this category, as the *nahual* is the animal double of the witch or sorcerer and may sometimes act on the latter's behalf without the direct physical transformation. The association of black magic with

Figure 2.2. Lorenzo Villavicencio treats his guests to a "Witch Doctor" dance, in homage to "El Loco" Valdés. *Source:* Arnaiz, Ricardo, dir. *La leyenda de la Nahuala.* 2007; Mexico: Animex Producciones, 2012. DVD (Videomax special edition).

ancient indigenous beliefs is taken for granted—as in the aforementioned articles referring to the film's villain as "a witch known as La Nahuala." Yet, as cultural representation, its history is far more complicated.

The literature on *nahualismo*, particularly in regard to the colonial period that concerns us here, includes such important works as Gonzalo Aguirre Beltrán's *Medicina y magia. El proceso de aculturación en la estructura colonial* (1992) and Roberto Martínez González's monumental study *El nahualismo* (2011).[14] For our purposes, it is helpful to note the diversity of meanings of the phenomenon among past and present native cultures, and also the slippage, noted by Aguirre Beltrán, between *nahualismo* and related ideas such as *tonalismo*, both based on the idea of a human's nonhuman animal double. Tracing these phenomena historically in part through a critical reading of Sahagún, Aguirre Beltrán argues that in cultures where the two coexist, "every individual has their *tona*, but not every individual is a *nahual*" ["todo individuo tiene su *tona*, pero no todo individuo es *nagual*"].[15] The *tona* is the particular animal spiritually linked to each person at birth, whereas the *nagual* is a class of specialists whose ability to transform themselves into nonhuman animals is only one of their extraordinary powers or skills. Yet both are part of a worldview that emphasizes relationships between human beings and the surrounding environment: relationships that, in response to colonial domination, would come to represent cultural survival and resistance.[16]

Martínez González, building on Aguirre Beltrán's pioneer understanding of cultural practices related to medicine and magic as dynamic and fundamentally reconstituted as a result of the Conquest, evangelism, and Spanish rule, devotes a full chapter to the evolution of *nahualismo*: specifically, to the transformation of the *nahual* into the witches and sorcerers created, via persecution, by the Inquisition, prior to their more recent discovery and appropriation by the global New Age movement.[17] He begins by looking at the processes by which the figure of the witch emerged in Europe in the fourteenth and fifteenth centuries as a means of combating deviation from Catholic dogma: in response first to Arab expansionism—non-Christian practices as Satanic—and later to unorthodox beliefs persistent among nominally Christian, but subaltern, communities.[18] Women in particular were liable to accusations of acquiring strange powers through pacts with the devil; many of the acts condemned by the church were associated with midwives and other female healers in an effort to reassert authority over the spiritual terrain occupied by these women whose existence outside of patriarchal norms was justified by the usefulness of their skills.[19]

Although the idea of the witch/sorcerer suffered modifications over the years and also inspired different degrees of persecution in response to varying social circumstances, it is clear that the Spaniards viewed the native inhabitants of what would become New Spain through well-developed filters that transformed Indigenous practices and beliefs into sorcery, native deities into demons, and ritual specialists—such as the shape-shifting *nahualli*—into *brujos*, *hechiceros*, *nigrománticos* (witches, sorcerers, necromancers).[20] In the early years of colonization, native transgressors of the Catholic norm often were ignored by the Inquisition, given their assumed unfamiliarity with Christian doctrine; as time went by, however, the seeming failure of evangelization, in spite of the conciliatory introduction of the Guadalupan apparition in 1531, led to increased persecution.

At the same time, parts of the dominant European imaginary regarding witchcraft came to influence Indigenous thought and practices as well, to the point that, centuries later, phenomena like *nahualismo* were/are not simply resistant remnants of earlier, repressed cultural complexes, but rather sites in which Mesoamerican, African, European and other elements intermingle, sometimes becoming, as in the representation under discussion, part of a cultural formation seen as mestizo and/or Mexican.[21]

Nearly five centuries after the arrival of Catholicism and its demonic imaginaries, *La leyenda de la Nahuala* draws on this history of conquest and transculturation and also makes some bold moves of its own. First, in order to consummate the association between the Indigenous *nahual* and the European witch, the malignant spirit in question receives the hybrid name *Nahuala*, adding the Spanish feminine gender to the gender-neutral Nahuatl term. Her persona is that of the emblematic *nahualli*-witch identified by Sahagún: s/he who frightens men and sucks the life force of children by night.[22] However, unlike other such beings, in the film she seeks not only to terrorize individual denizens of Puebla, but also to dominate the entire population. Her powers emerge, as we have seen, during the cosmic renovation of the universe symbolized in the lighting of the Fuego Nuevo. Visually, in her human form she is a dark-skinned and dark-robed menacing version of the cook whose body she possesses, but outside of this body, she is a sinuous, spectral version of the plumed serpent heads at the well-known archeological site Teotihuacan, representations associated with the deity Quetzalcoatl.

What does this spirit want and why? The use of the Quetzalcoatl imagery from an oft-visited historical site close to Mexico City, along with the medallion of Miquistli (death) and the Tezcatlipoca mask that—together with the Franciscan's cross—is crucial to her defeat, embodies the tradition of utilizing ancient relics in Indiana Jones–style adventure movies and television shows; the association between objects of "lost" civilizations, often made of precious metals and stones, and supernatural energies can be seen as a continuing apologia for colonialist plundering, although recent versions like *Dora and the Lost City of Gold* (James Bobin, 2019) not only thwart and punish would-be looters but also appear to vindicate the cultures decimated by colonialism and their present-day descendants.[23]

In *La leyenda*, however, the Nahuala and her objects are not part of an archeological past to be discovered, defended or expunged per se. Her power, unleashed only fifty-two years earlier—that is, during the lifetimes of the older adult characters and those who, as ghosts, remain youthful—is operative in 1807 and poses a threat to the colonial city, dominated by the Catholic church and, presumably, viceregal political authorities (who play no overt role in the film). Acting through Santos, who believes her to be his mother rather than a spirit occupying his mother's body, she attempts to entrap Nando in order to have sufficient children's souls in her possession to carry out this rebellious plan.

The figure of Santos is striking in that his complicity with the Nahuala derives from his mestizo status: son of an absent/unknown father and a violated—demonically possessed if not actually raped—Indigenous mother, he resembles the melancholic "hijo de la chingada" that Octavio Paz famously posited as national archetype in *The Labyrinth of Solitude* (1950).[24] This may (or may not) be why, the night on which he is set to consummate the Nahuala's vengeance, the animation team dresses Santos in the colors of the Mexican flag (fig. 3). Meanwhile. the learned Franciscan, the only character with knowledge of the Nahuala's abilities and intentions, repeats the historical role of priests like Sahagún whose detailed accounts of Mesoamerican worldviews, distorted by their own cultural filters that impelled them to see the devil in all non-Christian belief systems, were motivated less by science than by the evangelical imperative.

This curious configuration of tropes exceeds the scope of local legend—the initial witch's house on the corner as a spooky site to be avoided—and brings us into the realm of the spectral. In the twelve chapters of *Espectros: Ghostly Hauntings in Contemporary Transhispanic Narratives*, scholars draw on theorists such as Jacques Derrida and Avery F. Gordon in order to analyze ghosts and their meanings in a variety of Latin American and Spanish texts.[25] While none of the literary or filmic works discussed bear any particular resemblance to an animated comedy like *La leyenda de*

Figure 2.3. Dressed in the red, white, and green of the Mexican flag, Santos plots his revenge. *Source:* Arnaiz, Ricardo, dir. *La leyenda de la Nahuala*, 2007; Mexico: Animex Producciones, 2012. DVD (Videomax special edition).

la Nahuala, the volume offers insight into the relationship between ghosting and the long history of violence in colonized societies. In their introduction to the second part of *Espectros*, Ribas-Casasayas and Petersen note that "the concept of foundational trauma is important to Transhispanic studies, which examines five centuries of biological and cultural genocide in the Americas, the enslavement and exclusion of populations of African descent, religious persecutions" as well as dictatorships, civil wars, political oppression, and ecological devastation.[26] Ghosts populate narratives as a reminder of unfinished business, unhealed wounds, justice not rendered. In doing so they disrupt conventional chronologies and force the present to confront the past. The Inquisition, as I have already suggested, forms part of this traumatic past, not only in terms of its suppression of heretical practices but also its remodeling of imaginaries.[27] The *nahual-brujo* complex is a result of this process; moreover, given the elements that deviate from typical tall tales of witchcraft and associate her clearly with a pre-Hispanic ritual calendar and aesthetic, it is possible to see the film's Nahuala as the reemergence of Puebla's autochthonous spirit, poised to take vengeance on a caste-based society in which white Spaniards and Creoles maintain their political and economic hegemony through religion and myriad forms of the social construction of difference.[28]

This potentially subversive decolonial project, though enticing, is not actually pursued by the film; the Nahuala's fury is not limited to the villa's elites, but acts equally against the upper-class Villavicencio family and that of Toñita, Leo, and Nando San Juan, as well as the humble Santos and his mother and the clearly Indigenous figure of Xochitl. These and other characters, moreover, are distinguished by tropes of identity that draw on easily recognizable stereotypes, leading Julián Woodside to critique what he sees as the film's illusory multicultural discourse.[29] Woodside's analysis compares *La leyenda* with *Héroes verdaderos. Episodio: Independencia* (Carlos Kuri, 2010), using a typology of characters to argue that both films reproduce harmful stereotypes and, as products directed at a young audience, serve to perpetuate racism in Mexico. This reading, like my attempt to position the Nahuala as a subversive figure, is undoubtedly incomplete; yet the living and dead characters in *La leyenda*, as bearers of stereotyped traits and also in their relationships to one another in a stratified social order whose segregation is somewhat interrupted by the appearance of the spectral as a common threat, warrant further examination.

The Living and the Dead: Social Hierarchies and Otherness

As Woodside notes, *La leyenda de la Nahuala* re-creates traditions, customs and daily life of the late colonial period by means of characters who coexist "de manera armónica, pero claramente segregada" [harmoniously, but clearly segregated]:

> However, said characters are represented via a present-day perspective on what it means to come from these strata; that is, the script shows aspects of Mexican cultural memory with respect to each of the identities represented from that time period, but with a contemporary air based on stereotypes and conventions.

> [Sin embargo, dichos personajes son representados a partir de una perspectiva actual de lo que significa provenir de dichos estratos, es decir, el guión muestra aspectos de la memoria cultural mexicana que se tiene con respecto a cada una de las identidades representadas de aquella época, pero con un aire contemporáneo basado en estereotipos y convenciones].[30]

Most evident in this regard is Teodora, frozen in time as a ghost. Spoiled only child of the well-to-do Villavicencios, she treats those she sees as below her with exaggerated contempt; for instance, she orders Xochitl to serve her water only to spit it out, complaining of its wetness (fig. 4). Her snobby manner of speaking, however, is that of the contemporary upper class, known colloquially as "fresa" at the time of the film's release, or more recently, "whitexican." Her attachment to the fluffy dog Chichí evokes contemporary pop figures like Paris Hilton, and her vocabulary includes English phrases, culminating in her farewell toward the film's end: "Dicen que en el más allá, todos somos iguales. O sea, eso es cero *cool*, ¿estás de acuerdo? [They say that that in the afterlife everyone is equal. Like, that is so uncool, right?] *Byecito*."

This stylization allows for young audiences of today to place her socially, creating a link with the colonial past whose hierarchies have not,

Figure 2.4. Ghosts Teodora and Xochitl bring colonial social relations into the twenty-first century. *Source:* Arnaiz, Ricardo, dir. *La leyenda de la Nahuala*. 2007; Mexico: Animex Producciones, 2012. DVD (Videomax special edition).

in fact, been undone but rather, two hundred years on, are recognizable in the extreme class stratification of contemporary Mexico. At the same time, Teodora's bullying presentation reinforces sympathy with the more neutrally depicted mestizo Leo and also with Xochitl, who quickly becomes his guide and protector. Although her own farewell to Leo is spoken in Nahuatl, what distinguishes Xochitl from the elites that she serves is her modest, astute, and slightly flirtatious good nature: a likable "good Indian"—in contrast to the malevolent Nahuala—without clear ethnic markers, and with scant objectives of her own.[31]

Probably the film's most striking racial characterization is that of the Nana Dionisia. Though never explicitly identified as Black or *mulata*, she is recognizable as such due to her physical features and her origins in the Afro-descendent community of Alvarado, Veracruz, a coastal community known for the colorful vocabulary of its inhabitants; indeed, her very name is suggestive of the profane, "Dionysian" folkways associated with her hometown.[32] Given that slavery was widespread and not abolished in Mexico until after Independence,[33] Dionisia is certainly a descendent of enslaved Africans, though probably not enslaved herself, since, as Pablo Miguel Sierra Silva argues, the repugnant institution that was a key part of seventeenth-century life, met a "slow and unremarkable death over the course of the eighteenth century" due to gradual socioeconomic transformations on micro and macro levels.[34]

Although her political-economic condition as a Black woman remains vague, the Nana's Afro-Veracruz cultural identification, diametrically opposed to the Catholic conservatism associated with Puebla, is showcased throughout the film.[35] Large-framed, good-humored, constantly laughing and joking, Dionisia's stereotyped configuration is almost shocking, although it can also be seen as part of the film's homage to Mexican cinema and pop culture—in which caricatures such as the comic Memín Pingüín or songs like "El negrito Sandía" by Cri-Cri have only recently come under scrutiny as potentially offensive. Moreover, a similar cartoonish Blackness can be found in representations such as rag dolls sold in the port of Veracruz as a touristic souvenir of local identity, in which racial heritage is performed through music, dance, and fiesta as a means of distinguishing the region from other parts of Mexico.

The international fame of son jarocho—the festive musical tradition of the Sotavento region, which includes Alvarado along with much of southern Veracruz and parts of neighboring states—has contributed in recent years to a reexamination of Afro-Mexican histories and identities. *La leyenda* participates, however superficially, in this process: Dionisia always appears in the film accompanied by lively harp and jarana music, and climbs seemingly endless sets of stairs singing the "arriba y arriba" chorus of *La bamba*, the best-known piece in the jarocho repertoire. A jovial spirit seemingly free from the social restrictions of staid Pueblan society, the nature of Dionisia's subordinate relationship to the San Juan family is never specified. Her subaltern racialized/sexualized status, however, comes into play in a sinister sequence that unfolds, as it must, in the house of the Nahuala.

After both Leo and Nando are noted to be missing, Toñita and Dionisia follow their trail to the haunted mansion. Climbing stairs to Dionisia's tune of "arriba y arriba," they reach a closed door. The nanny pushes the door open, allowing the grandmother to enter while her own large body gets stuck in the doorframe. Taking the situation with aplomb, she takes out her knitting, but suddenly lets out a shriek and drops the yarn and needles. The camera's point of view shifts from the front to the back of the door, where a skeleton in aristocratic masculine dress is poking her buttocks. "Ñam ñam ñam, se ve suculento" [yum yum yum, looks tasty], he remarks. Other skeletons gather around, emitting similar comments. Slapping the trapped rear end, the host hungrily suggests inviting its bearer to dinner. The film cuts to Dionisia's frightened face (fig. 5), and the scene ends. The imagery is grotesque, particularly—as Woodside would surely agree—in a children's film: the sexualization of the Black female body as object of consumption for white male appetites, doubly carnal as food and—as the skeletons' lewd laughter and double entendres suggest—as erotic plaything. The *mulata*'s status as supporting character and domestic servant explains why her predicament attracts no attention from the others, and is, rather, a comic aside, a minor sacrifice to the urgent mission of rescuing the grandchildren and breaking the mansion's nefarious spell. After all, malignant spirits are at work, and little time remains to restore order and prevent destruction.

Dionisia is not seen again until after the Nahuala's defeat, when, hilarious as ever, she reports her experience with the ghosts: "¿Qué creen? En lo que esperaba, ¡me enseñaron una receta *buenísima*!" [Guess what? While I was waiting, they showed me a *delicious* recipe!]. In contrast to the epic struggle between the anticolonial Nahuala and the church (via the acolyte Leo and Fray Godofredo), the potential drama involving the subaltern brown woman and predatory white elites whose skeletal condition requires parasitic sustenance is defused, leaving the stereotype of *jarocha* carnality intact.[36] The Villavicencios and their guests are dead, as are Teodora and Xochitl, while the other characters mentioned here are alive,[37] yet colonial social divisions have been, if anything, reinforced.

Figure 2.5. Dionisia, stuck in the doorway, is a target for ghostly sexual aggression. *Source:* Arnaiz, Ricardo, dir. *La leyenda de la Nahuala*, 2007; Mexico: Animex Producciones, 2012. DVD (Videomax special edition).

Mayhem in the Master's House

The film's loose play with ethnic and regional stereotypes and national imaginaries regarding the pre-Hispanic spirit world are permitted by its setting: the haunted house, perhaps the heterotopia par excellence of juvenile fiction.[38] Through visual and sound effects, and through the inclusion of whimsical characters such as the pair of sugar skulls Finado and Moribunda whose bouncing is accompanied by lively marimba music, or the Quixotic don Andrés and his giant alibrije companion, the mansion is constructed as an *other* space, superimposed by magical means on the conventional household it contained half a century earlier, prior to its seeming abandonment.

The *casona*, however, bears an interesting relationship to the dynamics of domination and subalternity discussed above in terms of *La leyenda*'s ethnic characterizations. Large houses in town and city centers were long the residence of choice for the wealthy in Mexico and elsewhere, until changes in transportation and communication systems led to the emergence of exclusive zones far from the noise and commotion of the *plebe* or common people. Today *casonas* like that of the Nahuala are rarely inhabited by single families; decaying and abandoned in cases where the owners lack the will or the resources to renovate according to historical building standards regulated by the Instituto Nacional de Antropología e Historia, they have also been made into museums or rehabilitated as restaurants, department stores like Sanborn's, and other commercial uses. In all three cases, they symbolize the past, whether as financial burden,[39] as cultural legacy, or as commercial opportunity. In Puebla as in other sites of historical tourism, they are also frequently associated with spooky legends that are exploited for touristic ends.[40]

In this touristic discourse, the *casonas* represent an ambiguous, spectral relationship between present-day Puebla and the city's colonial origins. As Sierra Silva writes, Puebla is not generally imagined as a site of cultural diversity: "Projected onto the colonial past, the city of Puebla emerges as a site of mestizoness and whiteness. Research on colonial indigeneity in the city has begun to challenge these ideas, but blackness remains a foreign concept," in spite of the prevalence of African and Asian slavery during the sixteenth and seventeenth centuries.[41] Sierra Silva shows that the refusal to acknowledge the pervasiveness of slavery in important urban centers such as Puebla distorts our understanding of Mexican history and that of transatlantic human trafficking, a central aspect of social, economic, religious, and cultural life during his period of study.

A spectral reading, of course, would indicate that a structuring absence of this magnitude cannot but haunt the present. Isabel Cuñado writes: "The ghost is a crossroads where subjective experience and history overlap and feed each other. The ghost speaks of and for the innumerable victims who are expelled from history, when their deaths stop counting or their stories are forgotten. Along with speaking of a lingering past, ghosts expose those gaps and suppressions in our recording of the past that produces *exiles* from history."[42] This role of the ghost complements the notion of the haunted house as heterotopia.[43] For Michel Foucault, one of heterotopia's defining principles is that it "is capable of juxtaposing in a single real place several spaces, several sites that are in themselves incompatible"; another is that "heterotopias are most often linked to slices in time—which is to say that they open onto what might be termed, for the sake of symmetry, heterochronies."[44] They also "always presuppose a system of opening and closing that both isolates them and makes them penetrable," as illustrated in the Nahuala's use of the medallion to ensnare Nando.[45]

Finally, the "last trait of heterotopias is that they have a function in relation to all the space that remains."[46] That is, the strange goings on in the old mansion are only partially contained by its oldness and abandonedness. The Nahuala's occupation of this space has everything to do with the colonial stratification it represents: not supernatural but rather everyday performances of unequal social difference.[47] The *casona de la Nahuala* can be seen as haunted not only by a malevolent spirit in particular but also by the many experiences of social injustice retained in its territorial memory, of which the white elite's cannibal lust for Indigenous and Afro-descendent domestics is an elusive but also allusive gesture.[48]

Ghosts of Independence

The spectral aspect referenced here would seem to be a great deal weightier than what a children's film might support, and indeed, the abovementioned allusions to unequal colonial social relations are matter-of-fact compared with US productions like *The Book of Life* and *Coco*, set largely in fantastic worlds of the dead in order to maximize spectacle while upholding conventional messages along the lines of "follow your heart." Leo San Juan, on the other hand, inherits Fray Godofredo's (post-Inquisitorial?) cross; a year later, when the priest's spirit visits the family during Todos Santos, he gives Leo his next mission, sending him to Xochimilco to look into sightings of La Llorona. This, of course, sets the stage for various sequels,[49] one of which, *La leyenda del Chupacabras* (2016), takes place during the Independence struggle, with Nando in the royalist army and Leo on the side of the insurgents. Yet as I suggested at the beginning of this chapter, Mexico's impending War of Independence is a factor in the first film as well.

The year 1807 is announced at the beginning of the film with good reason. By 2007, plans for the nation's bicentennial celebrations were well underway. The federal government, presided over by Felipe Calderón of the conservative Partido de Acción Nacional, would undertake road repair and construction to encourage tourism to historical sites, revamp primary school textbooks, and issue to all households a history primer containing a text by Luis González y González accompanied by a "great man" style of visual narration that was as notable for its exclusions as for its content.

In the festivities themselves, as Lidia Girola Medina (2012) observes, "The bet was on the confirmation of Mexico's touristic image abroad as a country of colors, tastes, 'fiesta,' a solid and emerging economy" ["la apuesta fue por la confirmación de la imagen turística que se tiene de México en el extranjero, como un país de colores, de sabores, de 'fiesta,' de economía sólida y emergente"].[50] However, due to the already-intense climate of insecurity and violence, it was recommended that audiences stay home and watch the show on television. A lavishly choreographed carnival parade on September 15, followed by the largest-ever military parade the next day, were among the spectacles that national viewers were supposed to passively imbibe.[51] The ghosts of the ongoing Drug War, like those of the 1810 insurgency and the 1910 revolutionary uprising, were displaced by ostentatious pageants proclaiming national identity and unity.

The foregrounding of national independence in *La leyenda de la Nahuala* is important because, in an independent nation that has abolished slavery and established equality between men (and much later, women) as citizens, the intense social stratification of the colonial era seemingly no longer requires resistance. The romanticization of colonial streets and buildings not only as physical sites but as the settings of hair-raising legends is safe because the revolution against colonial occupation, as founding national narrative, ensures that evils such as slavery and religious persecution are frozen in the past, even though they actually persist in racist, classist and sexist constructions of the subaltern majority.[52] This is why Teodora's dismissal of social equality as "zero cool" hits home: in spite of the nominal democracy guaranteed by the constitutions of 1857 and 1917, the scenario in which everyone is equal remains a rumor of the "más allá," the beyond.

In the film's epilogue, set during Day of the Dead one year later, Toñita presides over the visit from last year's spirits, including the Villavicencios and their guests as well as Fray Godofredo, who witnesses his hot-air balloon dream materialize as Leo and his ghostly friends set out for Xochimilco. Given that these ghosts take the place of the ancestors who would normally visit the home altar, it is clear that, with independence on the horizon, the nascent notion of the "national family" implies the erasure of social conflict, or perhaps its magical resolution.

All of this suggests, in an oddly ludic way, the scenarios studied by Solimar Otero in *Archives of Conjure: Stories of the Dead in Afrolatinx Cultures*: ritual spaces in which diverse spirits, both familiar and archetypal, visit and interact with the living, involving these in work whose political nature may not be transparent, but is certainly urgent.[53] Similar to the Foucauldian heterotopia or the performance spaces described by Ngũgĩ wa Thiong'o, the interactions between the living and the dead in *La leyenda de la Nahuala* are traversed by power relations and by conflicts as yet unsettled.[54] The embedding of the haunted house in an audiovisual production that is comic, child-friendly, and touristic does not quite abolish the tensions latent in a situation in which some characters are masters while others are servants or slaves, and in which this colonial inequality, along with sly suggestions of possible decolonial revenge or transcendence, are the substance of humor.

After all, who doesn't love a good ghost story?

Notes

1. Julián Woodside, "Cine y memoria cultural: la ilusión del multiculturalismo a partir de dos películas mexicanas de animación." *Estudios sobre las Culturas Contemporáneas* 18, no. 2 (2012): 65–84.

2. Audre Lourde, "The Master's Tools Will Never Dismantle the Master's House," in *Sister Outsider: Essays and Speeches by Audre Lourde* (Freedom, CA: Crossing Press, 1984), 110–13.

3. For a sample of articles reviewing the "decolonial turn" in Latin America, see Pedro Garzón López, "Pueblos indígenas y decolonialidad. Sobre la colonización epistemológica occidental," *Andamios* 10, no. 22 (2013); Oriana Rincón, Keila Millán, and Omar Rincón, "El asunto decolonial: conceptos y debates," *Perspectivas. Revista de Historia, Geografía, Arte y Cultura* 3, no. 5 (2015); Elías David Morales Martínez and Jéssica Girão Florêncio, "El debate sobre decolonialidad, aspectos indígenas y medio ambiente en América Latina. Un análisis sobre el estado del arte," *Foro Internacional* 58, no. 1 (2018); Claudia Zavala Silva, "El giro decolonial. Consideraciones críticas desde América Latina," *Pléyade* 21 (2018). Recurrent in the bibliographies are the names Ramón Grosfoguel, Santiago Castro Gómez, Enrique Dussel, Boaventura de Sousa Santos, Walter Mignolo and Aníbal Quijano, among others. While this pantheon of decolonial thought would seem to be mostly male, decolonial feminists have long recognized the gendered implications of occidental modernity and have developed a rich critique of "racialized, colonial, capitalist, heterosexualist gender oppression." See María Lugones, "Hacia un feminismo descolonial," trans. Gabriela Castellanos, *La manzana de la discordia* 6, no. 2 (2011): 105. This latter perspective informs the present chapter.

4. In much of Mexico, Cinco de Mayo passes almost unnoticed among other May holidays like International Workers Day and Mother's Day, whereas, in the United States, it has been appropriated as a feast day for consumption of stereotypical elements such as tequila, beer, tacos, and mariachi music. This phenomenon is pertinent to the touristic discourse that *La leyenda de la Nahuala* draws on, although

without the heavy hand wielded in later animated pictures like *The Book of Life* (Jorge R. Gutierrez, 2014), *Día de Muertos* (Carlos Gutiérrez Medrano, 2019) or, most notoriously, Disney-Pixar's *Coco* (Lee Unkrich and Adrian Molina, 2017). As to the siblings Aquiles, Máximo, Carmen and Natalia Serdán, their revolutionary activism and the brothers' martyrdom during a raid on their home two days before the official start of the 1910 uprising has been narrated in a children's book by Silvia Molina (2015) and has put them on the map of historical tourism; their house is now a museum of the Revolution. *Mole de guajolote* is a complex spicy turkey dish and *camote* is a sweet potato candy so common that *camote* is used as a humorous or derogatory reference to Pueblans.

5. Solimar Otero's notion of "residual transcripts" is pertinent here, although her book concerns religions such as Espiritismo and Candomblé, as well as female anthropologists whose study of and participation in these practices converts them into ancestors for Otero's own praxis. Although a comic representation of *nahualismo* involving racial stereotypes is perhaps worlds apart from her focus on Afrolatinx spirituality, Otero's fascinating exploration of conjure and the influence of the dead on living cultural practices has guided me in the writing of this chapter. See Solimar Otero, *Archives of Conjure: Stories of the Dead in Afrolatinx Cultures* (New York: Columbia University Press, 2020).

6. Like most cities in Mexico with pronounced colonial pasts, the site from which I write—Xalapa, in the neighboring state of Veracruz—boasts at least four alleys whose names allude to spectacular murders embedded in urban legend. Two of these are based in marital jealousy while a third takes place during a lovers' tryst. Similar alleys, such as the Callejón del Muerto, exist in Puebla and are featured in the city's tourist literature.

7. *Chis* is a children's word for urine, like *pee*.

8. The film's total running time is eighty-two minutes.

9. The film was financed by the government of Puebla, and a promotional video for the state as touristic and business destination accompanies the 2012 special edition DVD consulted here.

10. Products released alongside the film included a book, soundtrack album, games, and action figures.

11. The invention of tradition, masterfully dissected in the 1983 book *The Invention of Tradition* edited by Eric Hobsbawm and Terence Ranger (Cambridge: Cambridge University Press, 1983), remains a powerful phenomenon in the internet age. For instance, several websites published articles long after the *Leyenda*'s release that purported to reveal the "true story" that inspired the film, yet in fact they simply recount the plot without reference to external sources. See Más México, "¿Quién fue la Nahuala? Conoce esta leyenda del Estado de Puebla," November 13, 2017, https://mas-mexico.com.mx/quien-fue-la-nahuala-conoce-esta-leyenda-del-estado-de-puebla; Mitos y Leyendas de México tradicionales, "La leyenda de la

Nahuala, la historia real que inspiró la película," 2020, https://leyendasdemexico.info/nahuala-historia-real/.

12. Erik Mariñelarena, "Ricardo Arnaiz," *Inkubo MAG* (*Inkuadro* film section), October 20, (2007), http://inkuadro.blogspot.com/2007/11/ricardo-arnaiz.html.

13. Mariñelarena, "Ricardo Arnaiz."

14. Gonzalo Aguirre Beltrán, *Medicina y magia: El proceso de aculturación en la estrucutra colonial* (Xalapa, Mexico: Universidad Veracruzana, 1992). This title was originally published by the Instituto Nacional Indigenista in 1963.

15. Aguirre Beltrán, *Medicina y magia*, 104. *Nahual, nahualli, nagual, tonal, tonalli, tona* are variants of the same two words. Although Nahuatl vocabulary has dominated Mexican studies since Sahagún's time, similar concepts exist in non-Nahuatl-speaking Indigenous groups. See Roberto Martínez González, *El nahualismo* (Mexico: Universidad Nacional Autónoma de México, 2016), https://historicas.unam.mx/publicaciones/publicadigital/libros/el/nahualismo.html.

16. Aguirre Beltrán, *Medicina y magia*, 100–2. See also Federico Navarrete Linares, "Nahualismo y poder: un viejo binario mesoamericano," in *El héroe entre el mito y la historia*, edited by Federico Navarrete Linares and Guilhem Olivier (Mexico City: Centro de Estudios Mexicanos y Centroamericanos, 2000), paragraph 10, paragraph 21.

17. Martínez González's analysis of the spread of the *nahual* idea as a motivational model via Miguel Ruiz's "Toltec" self-help book *The Four Agreements: A Practical Guide to Personal Freedom* (1997) is fascinating, though beyond the scope of this chapter. My reference to the creation of evildoers by religious-political persecution invokes Michel Foucault's "repressive hypothesis." See Foucault, *The History of Sexuality, Volume I: An Introduction*, trans. Robert Hurley (New York: Vintage Books, 1980).

18. Martínez González, *El nahualismo*, 461–63.

19. See Barbara Ehrenreich and Deidre English, 1973, *Witches, Midwives, and Nurses: A History of Women Healers* (New York: The Feminist Press, 2010). Issued in a second edition by its original publisher, it remains an authoritative work on this subject.

20. Martínez González, *El nahualismo*, 464.

21. In Catemaco, Veracruz, in 2010, Alberto Ortiz Brito interviewed two curanderos and a curandera in order to obtain data on the local idea of the *nahual*, such as who can become one and under what conditions. The responses differed, though all three associated the *nahual* with witchcraft and emphasized shapeshifting as their key trait. While the two men emphasized the role of mentoring and discipline in the acquisition of this skill, the woman cited the need for a pact with the devil—reflecting, according to the author, the legacy of colonial interpretations of Mesoamerican cosmovisions. See Alberto Ortiz Brito, "La concepción del nahualismo a través de tres curanderos de Catemaco, Veracruz," in *Memorias y vínculos:*

Un aporte de antropología e historia para la región de Los Tuxtlas, ed. Álvaro Brizuela Absalón and Rubén Montiel Ral (Xalapa, Mexico: Programa de Apoyo a las Culturas Municipales y Comunitarias (PACMyC), Alquimia Branding, 2019), 58. Ortiz's mention of the incorporation of elements such as zodiac signs and tarot cards in contemporary *curandurismo* suggests the importance of distinguishing the eclectic pragmatism of existing popular spiritual practices from the Mexicanist representation of nahualismo/witchcraft in texts such as *La leyenda de la Nahuala.*

22. Martínez González, *El nahualismo*, 466.

23. Dora, face-to-face with the ancient Inca guardians toward the end of the film, addresses them in Quechua and convinces them that she and her group are interested in knowledge, not material plunder. The colonial figure of the "explorer" is refigured as benign ally of the spectral beings of "other" spaces and temporalities.

24. Octavio Paz, *The Labyrinth of Solitude. The Other Mexico. Return to the Labyrinth of Solitude. Mexico and the United States. The Philanthropic Ogre*, trans. Lysander Kemp, Yara Milos, and Rachel Phillips Belash (New York: Grove, 1985). For a related observation involving Paz in light of 1960s–1970s science fiction and *lucha libre* cinema, see David S. Dalton, *Mestizo Modernity: Race, Technology, and the Body in Postrevolutionary Mexico* (Gainesville: University of Florida Press, 2018), 142.

25. Alberto Ribas-Casasayas and Amanda Petersen, eds. *Espectros: Ghostly Hauntings in Contemporary Transhispanic Narratives* (Lewisburg, PA: Bucknell University Press, 2016). See also Ribas-Casasayas's helpful "Editorial. El espectro, en teoría" in the 2019 volume of *iMex. Mexico Interdisciplinario / Interdisciplinary Mexico* entitled *México espectral.*

26. Ribas-Casasayas and Petersen, *Espectros*, 64.

27. Serge Gruzinski, *La colonización de lo imaginario: Sociedades indígenas y occidentalización en el México español, siglos XVI–XVIII* (Mexico City: Fondo de Cultura Económica, 1991).

28. The casting of Ofelia Medina as the voice of the Nahuala supports this reading, as Medina is known for leftist and pro-indigenous social activism as well as film and theatrical performance.

29. Woodside, "Cine y memoria cultural."

30. Woodside, "Cine y memoria cultural," 73.

31. Woodside, "Cine y memoria cultural," 77.

32. It is interesting to note that, in the mid-seventeenth century, Alvarado was assigned to the Diocese of Puebla, coming under Veracruz jurisdiction during the War of Independence. The complex cultural imaginaries summoned by this relationship are intriguing, although quelled by the director's simpler idea of Dionisia as "morenita, la idea original mía era que era mulatona, pero quedó más bien morenita" [brown, my original idea was that she was *mulata* (i.e., Black) but she turned out more like brown], a vague but sharply Veracruz ethnic admixture. Ricardo Arnaiz, commentary track on the *Nahuala* DVD, 2007.

33. In 1829, during the presidency of Afro-descendent insurgent Vicente Guerrero, although insurgent leaders Miguel Hidalgo y Costilla and José María Morelos y Pavón had included abolition in their platforms.

34. Pablo Miguel Sierra Silva, *Urban Slavery in Colonial Mexico: Puebla de los Ángeles, 1531–1706* (Cambridge: Cambridge University Press, 2018), 8.

35. Slave rebellions in Veracruz led to the establishment of the first free Black settlement in the Americas, San Lorenzo de los Negros, today called Yanga after the rebel leader instrumental in its founding. African and Afro-descendent women were often enslaved as domestics in Puebla's Spanish and creole households; yet the emphasis on Dionisia's Veracruzness, along with the fact that slavery had steeply declined by the period in question, permits a less troubling reading of her character as a free woman: indeed, a carefree spiritual daughter of Yanga, although her blackness is never actually mentioned.

36. An against-the-grain reading, though, might see Dionisia in the light of the subversive role that Africans and their descendants, especially women, played in the transgression of Catholic morality during the colonial era. Accusations of witchcraft, heresy, and immoral sexual conduct brought many before the Inquisition. See Yolanda Juárez Hernández, *Persistencias culturales afrocaribeñas en Veracruz: Su proceso de conformación desde la Colonia hasta fines del siglo XIX.* (Miradores, Mexico: Editora de Gobierno del Estado de Veracruz, 2006), 173. Dionisia's out-of-frame activity with the white skeletons, culminating in the transmission of the "recipe," may be proactive rather than submissive, especially given earlier uses of food against the Villavicencios by both the Nahuala and Xochitl.

37. Until the end when Fray Godofredo, having defeated the Nahuala, hands his large wooden cross over to Leo and, as it were, gives up the ghost.

38. Foucault's notion of heterotopias as "other spaces" is developed further on in this chapter.

39. Unmaintained structures, uninhabited or clandestinely occupied, also figure as a safety hazard. See Alba Espejel, "Peligro latente, detectan 14 casonas en ruinas en Puebla capital." *El Sol de Puebla*, June 10, 2020, https://www.elsoldepuebla.com.mx/local/peligro-latente-detectan-14-casonas-en-ruinas-en-puebla-capital-proteccion-civil-5346015.html.

40. *Puebla Legendaria* offers walking tours enhanced with the participation of live actors; tour themes include the Inquisition, legends from beyond the grave, angels and devils, and legendary Puebla, among others (pueblalegendaria.com). Many other easily found websites provide examples of legends associated with sites in the city's historic center.

41. Silva, *Urban Slavery in Colonial Mexico*, 5.

42. Isabel Cuñado, "The Bright Future of the Ghost: Memory in the Work of Javier Marías," in *Espectros: Ghostly Hauntings in Contemporary Transhispanic Narratives*, ed. Alberto Ribas-Casasayas and Amanda Petersen (Lewisburg, PA: Bucknell University Press, 2016), 42, emphasis in original.

43. Particularly the filmic haunted house, itself a projected specter, animated by myriad visual and sound effects that encompass multiple styles and cultural references, leaving aesthetic realism behind.

44. Michel Foucault, 1986, “Of Other Spaces,” trans. Jay Miskowiec, *Diacritics* 16, no. 1 (1986): 26.

45. Foucault, “Of Other Spaces,” 26.

46. Foucault, “Of Other Spaces,” 27.

47. Writing about the politics of the African performance space, Ngũgĩ wa Thiong'o argues that this space is “constituted by the totality of its external relations” with other spaces such as farms, factories, residences, and schools. See Ngũgĩ wa Thiong'o, *Penpoints, Gunpoints, and Dreams: Towards a Critical Theory of the Arts and the State in Africa* (Oxford: Oxford University Press, 1998), 40. Like Foucault's heterotopias, it must also be seen in terms of time, both past and future: “What memories does the space carry, and what longings might it generate?” Ngũgĩ wa Thiong'o, *Penpoints*, 41.

48. In a flashback to the dinner scene of 1755, a Villavicencio guest is portrayed making lewd remarks about the household's new cook, just before the latter is possessed by the Nahuala, who poisons them all using serpents that rise out of the soup, thus exacting a potent decolonial vengeance.

49. *La leyenda de la Llorona* (2011), *La leyenda de las momias de Guanajuato* (2014), *La leyenda del Chupacabras* (2016), and *La leyenda del Charro Negro* (2018), all directed by Alberto Rodríguez for Ánima Estudios, which acquired the *Leyenda* franchise in 2010 and also produced two television series (2017 and 2019). *Las leyendas: el origen*, in which Arnaiz returns as director to explore the world of the calaveras Finado and Moribunda, was scheduled for release in 2020, although ultimately delayed by the Covid-19 pandemic.

50. Lidia Girola Molina, “Representaciones sociales, cambios en los imaginarios y conmemoración. Una propuesta de análisis comparativo entre los Festejos de 1910 y 2010,” in *Conmemoraciones: Ritualizaciones, lugares mnemónicos y representaciones sociales*, eds. Laura Angélica Moya López y Margarita Olvera Serrano (Mexico City: Universidad Autónoma Metropolitana Azcapotzalco, 2012), 223.

51. Girola Molina, “Representaciones sociales,” 220–21.

52. In June 2020, during the pandemic and in the wake of international outcry following George Floyd's murder by police in the United States, a scandal occurred involving the Consejo Nacional para Prevenir la Discriminación (Conapred), an office founded in 2003 during the presidential administration of Vicente Fox. A forum convoked by Conapred to discuss racism and classism in Mexico included as one of its panelists the YouTuber Chumel Torres, known for his violently racist, classist, and sexist “comedy.” Public reaction was such that not only was the forum canceled, but the head of the office and several board members resigned. While commentators decried censorship, President Andrés Manuel López Obrador criticized

the office's dubious commitment to ending discrimination and pledged to reform the Consejo with an Indigenous woman in the directorship. At the time of writing the outcome is unclear.

53. Otero, *Archives of Conjure.*

54. Ngũgĩ wa Thiong'o, *Penpoints.*

Bibliography

Aguirre Beltrán, Gonzalo. *Medicina y magia: el proceso de aculturación en la estructura colonial.* Xalapa, Mexico: Universidad Veracruzana, 1992.

Arnaiz, Ricardo, dir. *La leyenda de la Nahuala,* 2007; Mexico: Animex Producciones, 2012. DVD (Videomax special edition).

Bobin, James, dir. *Dora and the Lost City of Gold.* 2019; USA: Paramount Players, Walden Media, Screen Queensland, Burr! Productions, Media Rights Capital, Nickelodeon Movies.

Cuñado, Isabel. "The Bright Future of the Ghost: Memory in the Work of Javier Marías." In *Espectros: Ghostly Hauntings in Contemporary Transhispanic Narratives,* edited by Alberto Ribas-Casasayas and Amanda Petersen, 33–46. Lewisburg: Bucknell University Press, 2016.

Dalton, David S. *Mestizo Modernity: Race, Technology, and the Body in Postrevolutionary Mexico.* Gainesville: University of Florida Press, 2018.

Ehrenreich, Barbara, and Deidre English. 1973. *Witches, Midwives, and Nurses: A History of Women Healers.* Second edition. New York: The Feminist Press at CUNY, 2010.

Espejel, Alba. "Peligro latente, detectan 14 casonas en ruinas en Puebla capital." *El Sol de Puebla,* June 10, 2020. https://www.elsoldepuebla.com.mx/local/peligro-latente-detectan-14-casonas-en-ruinas-en-puebla-capital-proteccion-civil-5346015.html.

Foucault, Michel. *The History of Sexuality, Volume I: An Introduction.* Translated by Robert Hurley. New York: Vintage Books, 1980.

Foucault, Michel. 1967. "Of Other Spaces." Translated by Jay Miskowiec. *Diacritics* 16, no. 1 (1986): 22–27. http://doi.org/10.2307/464648.

Garzón López, Pedro. "Pueblos indígenas y decolonialidad. Sobre la colonización epistemológica occidental." *Andamios* 10, no. 22 (2013): 305–31.

Girola Molina, Lidia. "Representaciones sociales, cambios en los imaginarios y conmemoración. Una propuesta de análisis comparativo entre los Festejos de 1910 y 2010." In *Conmemoraciones. Ritualizaciones, lugares mnemónicos y representaciones sociales,* coordinated by Laura Angélica Moya López and Margarita Olvera Serrano, 197–238. Mexico City: Universidad Autónoma Metropolitana Azcapotzalco, 2012.

González y González, Luis. *Viaje por la historia de México.* Mexico: Secretaría de Educación Pública, Comisión Nacional de Libros de Texto Gratuitos, 2010.

Gruzinski, Serge. *La colonización de lo imaginario: Sociedades indígenas y occidentalización en el México español, siglos XVI–XVIII.* Mexico City: Fondo de Cultura Económica, 1991.

Gutiérrez Medrano, Carlos, dir. *Dia de Muertos.* Mexico City: Metacube, Symbosys Technologies, 2019.

Gutierrez, Jorge R., dir. 2014. *The Book of Life.* Los Angeles: Reel FX Animation Studios, Chatrone, Mexopolis, Twentieth Century Fox Animation.

Hobsbawm, Eric, and Terence Ranger. *The Invention of Tradition.* Cambridge, UK: Cambridge University Press, 1983.

Juárez Hernández, Yolanda. *Persistencias culturales afrocaribeñas en Veracruz. Su proceso de conformación desde la Colonia hasta fines del siglo XIX.* Miradores, MX: Editora de Gobierno del Estado de Veracruz, 2006.

Lourde, Audre. "The Master's Tools Will Never Dismantle the Master's House." In *Sister Outsider: Essays and Speeches by Audre Lourde*, 110–13. Freedom, CA: The Crossing Press, 1984.

Lugones, María. 2010. "Hacia un feminismo descolonial." Translated by Gabriela Castellanos. *La manzana de la discordia* 6, no. 2 (2011): 105–19.

Mariñelarena, Erik. "Ricardo Arnaiz," *Inkubo MAG* (*Inkuadro* film section), October 20, 2007. http://inkuadro.blogspot.com/2007/11/ricardo-arnaiz.html.

Martínez González, Roberto. *El nahualismo.* Mexico: Universidad Nacional Autónoma de México, 2011. https://historicas.unam.mx/publicaciones/publicadigital/libros/el/nahualismo.html.

Más México. "¿Quién fue la Nahuala? Conoce esta leyenda del Estado de Puebla." *Más México.* November 13, 2017. https://mas-mexico.com.mx/quien-fue-la-nahuala-conoce-esta-leyenda-del-estado-de-puebla/. Accessed 26 Nov. 2022.

Mitos y Leyendas de México tradicionales. "La leyenda de la Nahuala, la historia real que inspiró la película." *Mitos y leyendas de México tradicionales.* https://leyendasdemexico.info/nahuala-historia-real/. Accessed November 26, 2022.

Molina, Silvia. *Los hermanos Serdán.* Mexico City: Secretaría de Educación Pública/Instituto Nacional de Estudios Históricos de las Revoluciones en México, 2015.

Morales Martínez, Elías David, and Jéssica Girão Florêncio. "El debate sobre decolonialidad, aspectos indígenas y medio ambiente en América Latina. Un análisis sobre el estado del arte." *Foro Internacional* 58, no. 1 (2018): 131–60.

Navarrete Linares, Federico. "Nahualismo y poder: un viejo binario mesoamericano." In *El héroe entre el mito y la historia*, edited by Federico Navarrete Linares and Guilhem Olivier, 155–79. Mexico City: Centro de Estudios Mexicanos y Centroamericanos, 2000.

Ngũgĩ wa Thiong'o. *Penpoints, Gunpoints, and Dreams: Towards a Critical Theory of the Arts and the State in Africa.* Oxford: Oxford University Press, 1998.

Ortiz Brito, Alberto. "La concepción del nahualismo a través de tres curanderos de Catemaco, Veracruz." In *Memorias y vínculos: Un aporte de antropología e historia para la región de Los Tuxtlas*, edited by Álvaro Brizuela Absalón and Rubén Montiel Ral, 51–59. Xalapa: Programa de Apoyo a las Culturas Municipales y Comunitarias (PACMyC), Alquimia Branding, 2019.

Otero, Solimar. *Archives of Conjure: Stories of the Dead in Afrolatinx Cultures*. New York: Columbia University Press, 2020. Kindle.

Paz, Octavio. *The Labyrinth of Solitude. The Other Mexico. Return to the Labyrinth of Solitude. Mexico and the United States. The Philanthropic Ogre*. Translated by Lysander Kemp, Yara Milos, and Rachel Phillips Belash. New York: Grove, 1985.

Ribas-Casasayas, Alberto. "Editorial. El espectro, en teoría." In *México espectral*, edited by Ribas-Casasayas, 8–20. *iMex. Mexico Interdisciplinario / Interdisciplinary Mexico* 8, no. 16 (2019). https://www.imex-revista.com/ediciones/xvi-mexico-espectral/.

Ribas-Casasayas, Alberto, and Amanda Petersen, eds. *Espectros: Ghostly Hauntings in Contemporary Transhispanic Narratives*. Lewisburg, PA: Bucknell University Press, 2016.

Rincón, Oriana, Keila Millán, and Omar Rincón. "El asunto decolonial: conceptos y debates." *Perspectivas. Revista de Historia, Geografía, Arte y Cultura* 3, no. 5 (2015): 75–95.

Ruiz, Miguel. *The Four Agreements: A Practical Guide to Personal Freedom*. San Rafael, CA: Amber-Allen, 1997.

Sierra Silva, Pablo Miguel. *Urban Slavery in Colonial Mexico: Puebla de los Ángeles, 1531–1706*. Cambridge: Cambridge University Press, 2018.

Unkrich, Lee, and Adrian Molina, dirs. *Coco*. Burbank, CA: Walt Disney Pictures, Pixar Animation Studios, 2017.

Woodside, Julián. "Cine y memoria cultural: la ilusión del multiculturalismo a partir de dos películas mexicanas de animación." *Estudios sobre las Culturas Contemporáneas* 18, no. 2 (2012): 65–84. Redalyc, https://www.redalyc.org/articulo.oa?id=31624694005.

Zapata Silva, Claudia. "El giro decolonial. Consideraciones críticas desde América Latina." *Pléyade* 21 (2018): 49–71.

Chapter 3

La revolución de Juan Escopeta

Toward Nonviolent Masculinity and Citizenship

Sofia Paiva de Araujo and David S. Dalton

Jorge Estrada's *La revolución de Juan Escopeta* (2011) tells the coming-of-age story of Gapo, a child who confronts orphanhood and violence during the Mexican Revolution. One of the most memorable moments of the movie occurs when Gapo learns that Juan Escopeta, his mentor and traveling companion, is on a mission to kill his brother, Damián. Feeling deceived and enraged, Gapo points a gun at Juan Escopeta. The hitman encourages Gapo to shoot, suggesting it would be a rite of passage: "It's about time you became a man" ["ya es hora que te hagas un hombrecito"].[1] Despite his motive for revenge, Gapo, who had previously shown an affinity for firearms, chooses *not to* shoot. Instead, he replies, "I'm already a man" ["yo ya soy un hombre"] and lowers his pistol. This scene encapsulates the film's nonviolent and antibellicist message. By refusing to give in to a violent rage, Gapo comes to embody a type of nonviolent masculinity that differs radically from the stereotype of the Mexican *machismo* that appears in many films—particularly those of the Golden Age—of the Mexican Revolution.[2] By focusing on Gapo's psychological and moral development, the movie promotes nonviolent articulations of masculinity and citizenship to Mexican audiences.

Released about a year after Mexico's centenary and bicentenary celebrations, which were marked by "fanfare and gunfire," *La revolución de Juan*

Escopeta reflects on societal constructs of gender and violence.[3] Produced from a context where firearms function as a "prosthesis for citizenship" for the oppressed, it is especially interesting to note the film's skepticism of those discourses that would celebrate gun violence.[4] The production draws from a long tradition of cinema of the Revolution that began with films of Pancho Villa and became popular during the Golden Age.[5] Indeed, it embodies many of the tendencies toward cultural nationalism that typified films that came out in the decades following the Revolution. The storyline is especially indebted to Fernando de Fuentes's *Vámonos con Pancho Villa* (1935). On their surface, both films reproduce an array of nationalist symbols—both visual and ideational—that would seem to celebrate the violent Revolution.[6] For example, both films follow young protagonists who begin their quests with a reverence for the Revolution. However, after seeing the senseless violence and corruption that permeates the conflict, they lose faith in the cause and question the validity of a war that has cost so many lives.[7] In this way, *La revolución de Juan Escopeta* continues in the footsteps of its precursor. Even as it re-creates many of the most cinematographically iconic elements of Golden Age cinema, it ultimately undermines simplistic, pro-revolutionary propaganda, thus causing audiences to reflect on the attitudes that have led to the normalization of violence both in the national cinema and in Mexican thought for decades. That said, in using specifically animated cinema, Estrada seeks to reach an especially important demographic—young, Mexican males—and undermine those cultural forces that celebrate violent masculinity.

Certainly, *La revolución de Juan Escopeta* is not the only animated movie to depict the Revolution. Indeed, the movie fits within a body of animated films that came out in and around 2010 to celebrate the centenary and bicentenary of the Revolution and Independence respectively. For example, the full-length film *Tierra de revolucionarios* (Antonio Ramos Sr. and Antonio Ramos Jr.) was released by the Instituto Chihuahense de la Cultura at the Festival Cervantino in Guanajuato in October, 2010, approximately a year prior to the release of Estrada's film. That said, *Tierra de revolucionarios* reads more like a work of propaganda that celebrates the role of the people and state of Chihuahua in the early years of the Revolution than a commercial film aimed at popular audiences. In that same year, the company Batallón released a series of short films, *Suertes, humores y pequeñas historias de la Independencia y Revolución*. These shorts appeared at the Morelia Film Festival, often preceding full-length pictures, and they received a fair amount of attention.[8] More recently, Arturo "Vonno" Ambriz released *Revoltoso* (2020), a stop-motion short that decries corrupt leaders and elites who favored "progress" over people.[9] Each of the aforementioned animated films merits study on its own terms; that said, *La revolución de Juan Escopeta* stands out for several reasons. Perhaps most obviously, as a commercial production, it reached larger audiences than did its counterparts. Certainly, one could argue that the commercial nature of *La revolución de Juan Escopeta* likely forced Estrada to cater to the political attitudes of middle-class viewers in his quest to recoup the production costs.[10] That said, in reaching a greater number of viewers, the film enjoyed a larger platform to promote its antibellicist message.

A brief plot summary will facilitate our discussion. Set during the presidency of Victoriano Huerta (1913–1914), the film revolves around the shared journey of the ten-year-old Gapo and the gunman Juan Escopeta. The story begins in 1914 as federal soldiers (*federales*) raid Gapo's small town, Mineral de la Luz, in search of rebels. They forcibly recruit Gapo and kill his mother, but Juan Escopeta rescues him from the federales' encampment. When Gapo learns that Juan Escopeta is going north, he decides to join the gunman and search for his brother, Damián: a legendary revolutionary hero who left his hometown to fight alongside Pancho Villa. During their journey, they participate in the battle of Zacatecas, and they encounter numerous revolutionary figures: *federales*, *soldaderas*, *villistas*, *colorados*, and a mediocre opportunist, El Gordo, whose connections to powerful people lead him to privileged positions in the government. The setting during the presidency of Huerta provides an especially poignant backdrop against which the movie makes its call for nonviolence. Huerta, after all, staged a military coup before arresting, torturing, and ultimately executing the duly elected president, Francisco Madero, and his vice president, José María Pino Suárez. Viewed in this light, Huerta represents one of the clearest examples of masculine violence that the film aims to contest through its own male protagonist who eschews the *machista* style of the film's president.

Given this fact, it is especially telling that Gapo's coming-of-age journey corresponds directly with his negotiation of his own masculinity. As Robert McKee Irwin explains, the term "masculinity" refers to "a collection of [learned] behaviors, attitudes, and attributes that men may or may not exhibit (but that, perhaps, they ought to)."[11] Gapo initially performs his gender by making and accepting dares, carrying out displays of courage, and playing with toy guns. While these activities are clearly coded as masculine, they also reflect a sort of childishness not related to true manhood. Indeed, throughout much of the film, Gapo searches for a path toward a proper adulthood. Manhood refers to a state or quality achieved after a rite of passage that allows an individual to be recognized as an adult rather than a child. Gapo's initial rite of passage is the Battle of Zacatecas, where he fights alongside Juan Escopeta and Villa's troops. That said, his most important initiation occurs when he confronts Juan Escopeta in the desert. Gapo's refusal to shoot his mentor challenges constructs of manliness that would emphasize violence and killing. In its place, he proposes that true men can be compassionate and merciful. In this way, Gapo's initiation into manhood calls into question machista notions of masculinity where, according to Víctor Macías González and Anne Rubenstein, power and status depend on a "vigorously defended gender hierarchy."[12] In the Revolutionary moment of the film, machista notions of masculinity revolve around firearms and violence.

The film thus reverberates with recent scholarship that has highlighted the problematic role that guns have played in constructing and contesting nationhood both in Mexico and throughout Latin America over the last century. Sophie Esch, for example, signals these weapons as "crucial artifacts and tropes for understanding narratives of insurgency and modernity."[13] This fact rings clear in *La revolución de Juan Escopeta*, where peasants, miners, and other previously disenfranchised actors demonstrate their agency and affirm their citizenship before an abusive state. In taking to arms, the characters of the film stand against systemic violence against the lower classes, a trait that characterized the Porfiriato against which these revolutionary characters rebel.[14] The characters of the film also oppose symbolic violence, which manifests itself in language against women and lower-class individuals.[15] The film ultimately reverberates with Esch's observation that, while revolutionaries aim to counter all these forms of violence, their movements "exert [their] own direct, indirect, and epistemic violence."[16] This is precisely the environment that Gapo confronts in his own experiences where violence and death follow people regardless of their political affiliations.

La revolución de Juan Escopeta and the Legacy of the Golden Age

The film references many aspects of the visual production related to the Mexican Revolution. As a matter of fact, the original idea for the story was inspired by "the drawing of a trio singing a corrido during the time of the Revolution" ["la representación de un trío cantando un corrido durante la época de la Revolución, realizada en caricatura"].[17] The animation shows detailed representations of the country's geographical features and the rich iconography of the armed phase, which were often explored in muralism and Golden Age cinema.[18] There was also a visible effort to re-create the local architecture in detail. For example, the animation team hired specialists to aid in the accurate depiction of the emblematic aqueduct of Zacatecas (see figure 3.1)[19] Moreover, some scenes of the animated feature employ techniques that typified the Golden Age. Figure 3.2, for example, shows the use of low-angle, diagonal composition, left alignment of the frame, and oblique perspective with multiple vanishing points, characteristic of the Fernández-Figueroa style.[20] Figure 3.1 employs similar techniques, in addition to "deep focus and [. . .] extended action in several planes," which are also distinguished features of the Fernández-Figueroa style.[21] Lastly, the diagonal position of the aqueduct accentuates the movement of the revolutionaries toward the building occupied by the federal troops. Of course, as an animated production, these visual elements are not shots in the traditional sense; rather, they are artistic recreations of many of the most popular cinematic styles of the Golden Age.

Golden Age film was also instrumental in the construction and negotiation of modern models of manhood that the film negotiates throughout.[22]

Figure 3.1. The animators render the emblematic aqueduct of Zacatecas. *Source:* Estrada, Jorge A., dir. *La revolución de Juan Escopeta*, 2011; Mexico City: Animex, 2012. BluRay.

Figure 3.2. A shot with oblique perspective and multiple vantage points that draws parallels to the Fernández-Figueroa Style. *Source:* Estrada, Jorge A., dir. *La revolución de Juan Escopeta*, 2011; Mexico City: Animex, 2012. Blu-ray.

The leading actors of the period—Jorge Negrete, Pedro Infante, and Mario "Cantinflas" Moreno—embodied three of the most prevalent types of masculinity to appear in the national cinema during those years. The former two were singer-actors who popularized the figure of the *charro* on the silver screen. Negrete's role as the violent Salvador Pérez, "El Ametralladora," in *¡Ay, Jalisco, no the rajes!* (1941) renewed the *ranchero* genre and aided in the construction of the stereotype of the Mexican macho.[23] Infante, in turn, "tended to enact roles along a spectrum of [. . .] masculinity, ranging from hard-drinking womanizers to tenderhearted, hardworking family men."[24] Infante's acting and singing skills, along with his charismatic personality, made him "the maximum embodiment of Mexican masculinity and the archetype of the working-class heterosexual male."[25] Lastly, the comedian Cantinflas embodied the *pelado*, a lower-class male with peasant origins who relocated to an urban area and used aggressiveness and homophobic jokes to affirm his masculinity and hide his inferiority complex.[26] His mestizo identity furthered the postrevolutionary state's cinematic celebration of mestizaje, and his humor helped blur racial conflicts. These representations of masculinity served multiple purposes: to shape and model constructs of national identity; to boost box office revenue; and to "ameliorate the threat of Revolutionary violence."[27]

La revolución de Juan Escopeta engages each of these constructs of masculinity through its different characters. Juan Escopeta is a multidimensional character: his past as an outlaw and a hitman illustrates an aggressive masculinity, but his transformation into a fatherlike figure to Gapo symbolizes his redemption—his own personal revolution evinced in the movie's title. Gapo's brother symbolizes the heroic masculinity of revolutionaries who justify their violent acts through idealism. This perspective helps to sanitize the depiction of Pancho Villa, who is shown very briefly in the movie during the sequence in Zacatecas. The animation also recycles and validates the masculine traits that Infante embodied in *Pepe el Toro* (1953) when Juan Escopeta takes care of the orphaned Gapo. Additionally, the animation critiques the violent masculinity of the *pelado*, represented by a nameless child bully who attacks Gapo twice, calling him *marica* [faggot] and provoking the protagonist to engage in physical confrontation. Unlike Juan Escopeta, this bully never achieves redemption; his violent and homophobic masculinity is decried as undesirable and unbecoming of a "good" Mexican.

An array of characters exemplifies numerous unhealthy articulations of masculinity throughout the film. For example, the federal troops that destroy Mineral de la Luz despite the fact that there are no revolutionaries in the town and its inhabitants (mostly women, children, and disabled individuals) present no risk to the federal government. Another problematic group is the revolutionary *Colorados*, whose motto, "shoot first, ask questions later" ["primero dispara, después averigua"], underscores a fundamental indifference to human life and human suffering.[28] Finally, the individual who most directly embodies this deviant masculinity is the villain, El Zopilote, who gleefully kills and tortures his victims, a fact evidenced when he purposefully shoots Juan Escopeta in both arms to make him suffer. It is especially interesting that Estrada would use an animated film to question and criticize negative examples of toxic masculinity. Although he could have filmed it in live action, Estrada—an enthusiast of animation—made a deliberate choice to produce it as an animated feature to take advantage of the potentialities of that medium.[29] Nevertheless, despite a context where animated films were among the most commercially viable genres in the domestic cinema, Estrada struggled to secure financing for his project.[30] Although the screenplay had been written years earlier, he was unable to find filming partners until the approximation of the centenary of the revolution and the bicentenary of independence.[31]

Ultimately, Animex Estudios decided to support Estrada. This looked like an excellent partnership on paper; the studio had demonstrated its interest in national (and nationalist) themes in previous productions like *La leyenda de la Nahuala* (2007) and *Nikté* (2009), both directed by Ricardo Arnaiz. However, when the partnership started, Animex was working on postproduction for *Nikté*. As such, the studio did not give Estrada's film top priority.[32] Furthermore, Animex's aesthetic leaned toward caricature with a childishness that undermined Estrada's vision.[33] Working on a different style demanded a time-consuming preproduction that delayed the movie's release.[34] Estrada and his coauthor, Alfredo Castañeda, also had to make concessions in how they presented the story. This entailed polishing the language and minimizing the violence.[35] Ricardo Arnaiz, the general director of Animex Studios, worried that graphic violence would alienate viewers; despite a growing market of adult animation, Animex usually targets children and adolescents.[36]

Nevertheless, given the movie's setting during the most violent conflict in Mexican history, it was unfeasible to make the film completely violence-free.[37] According to Estrada, "The film is not an apology of violence, but since it takes place during those years and we are going to talk about the Revolution, we had to include it" ["no es una apología de la violencia, sino que evidentemente como está situada en esa época y vamos a hablar de la Revolución, ni modo de no poner eso"].[38] That said, the film uses this violence to critique hypermasculine, old-fashioned, and overtly aggressive displays of masculinity. In this way, *La revolución de Juan Escopeta* is crafted to, on the one hand, reflect on the socioeconomic causes of violence and, on the other hand, to focus on the impacts of violence on communities, individuals, and especially children in Mexico. Gapo's coming-of-age experience is marked by orphanhood and violence, which are intrinsically connected to the negotiation of his own expressions of masculinity and citizenship. Interestingly, his experiences reverberate with anxieties in Mexican society that have emerged in light of the drug war, which had reached a crescendo when the movie came out in 2011.[39] It is reassuring, comforting, and even cathartic for the spectator to see victims of violence, such as Gapo, overcome trauma and grow up to be productive, nonviolent members of society.

Coming of Age: Child Protagonists, Trauma, and Revolutionary Violence

La revolución de Juan Escopeta is one of the few fictional depictions of the Mexican Revolution to have a child as the protagonist. One work that has significant similarities with Estrada's movie is Nellie Campobello's novel *Cartucho: Relatos de la lucha en el norte de México* (1931), the first narrative of the Revolution told from the perspective of a child and a novel that inspired Estrada.[40] Similar to *Cartucho*, the film is set in a mining town in northern Mexico that is overrun by revolutionary violence. In this way, the film reflects a referent similar to that of the novel where, according to Esch, firearms are depicted as "simultaneously empowering and traumatizing artifacts."[41] These weapons make revolutionary insurgents visible to the state and to Mexican society while at the same time leaving echoes of trauma to those who suffer and/or witness gun violence.[42] These arguments ring equally true when applied to Gapo's own fraught relationship with guns. *La revolución de Juan Escopeta* is also the second film set during the Revolution to have a child as the protagonist. Before that, *Marcelino, pan y vino* (José Luis Gutiérrez Arias, 2010), a remake of a classic Spanish film, had starred a child. While animation films commonly have young characters as protagonists, since the 2000s other cinematic genre movies starring children and adolescents as protagonists have become more frequent as well:[43] "In this increasingly postnational era, children and adolescents are appropriated to mediate issues of identity and difference, history, class and gender, as well as their place in discourses that question the construct of family and nation."[44] This appropriation happens because young protagonists can serve "as a 'screen' for adult anxieties and fears, particularly in films about civil violence or repression."[45] Geoffrey Maguire and Rachel Randall note that these cinematic productions tend to privilege the male perspective, often figuring boys as protagonists.[46] Despite several notable exceptions, this tends to hold particularly true in Mexico. As Irwin argues, "Mexico is protagonized by young men, and national unity is allegorized by male homosocial bonding."[47] In *La revolución de Juan Escopeta*, direct violence leads to the protagonist's orphanhood and subsequent exposition to and engagement with the overwhelming reality of a country taken by armed conflict. All these experiences of violence contribute to Gapo's coming of age, shaping his ideas about firearms, masculinity, and citizenship.

The film engages questions of violence from the opening scene, when Gapo and his friends play a game inspired by the Revolution. Some local boys pretend to take Gapo prisoner, stating, "Let us execute them, my general" ["Vamos a fusilarlos, mi general"]. With a red fabric blindfold covering their eyes, Gapo and another boy pretend to be "executed." As they enact their heroic deaths, the boys shout, "¡Viva la Revolución! ¡Viva México!" In doing so, they role play the bravery of countless revolutionaries who gave their lives and whose heroism they idealize and admire. This sequence dialogues with representations of executions inflicted by firing squads that abound in literary, photographic, and cinematic depictions of the conflict. Shortly afterward, when one of the children pretending to be "*federales*" pokes Gapo with his stick/pretend gun to check if he is "still alive," Gapo complains, "I'm already dead" ["pues ya estoy muerto"]. The bigger boy teases Gapo, saying "he is as much a faggot as his brother" ["es igual de marica que su hermano"], and they start fighting. To defend both his brother's honor and his own, Gapo tries to counter the boy's statement; Gapo lifts his own pretend gun but breaks it, making him angrier. The bully, who is older, taller, and stronger than Gapo, beats him up and leaves with his "soldiers." This opening scene shows examples of direct and epistemic violence. It foreshadows the pervasiveness of violence in Gapo's life and anticipates the actual encounter with the federales that happens later that day when Gapo witnesses his mother's death prior to his forced recruitment. This opening sequence also resonates with ideas of heroization, martyrization of revolutionaries, and finding honor in defeat and failure.[48] Despite being beaten up while defending his family's honor, Gapo's effort dignifies him and casts the other boy as a bully.

This opening scene challenges Octavio Paz's theorization of an idealized Mexican masculinity that never "cracks," never backs down.[49] It is important to note that the original publication in Spanish uses *rajarse*, which may be better translated as *to open*, and is more sexual and homophobic in nature than the verb *to crack*. Gapo "cracks" or "opens" when he cries and surrenders after the other boy slaps him. The bully dominates Gapo by sitting on him, an act that aligns him with Paz's famous *chingón*, while denoting Gapo as the *chingado* (see figure 3.3).[50] At one level, this scene alludes to a recurring depiction of masculinity from the Golden Age cinema that favors dominant actors as ideal representations of the Mexican macho. In doing so, it dialogues with Mexican cinematic representations of masculinity from the 1940s, which were highly influenced by the psychoanalytical examinations of Samuel Ramos and other intellectuals.[51] These traditional ideas of masculinity inform Gapo's concept of honor and explain why he takes offense and responds violently when the other boy calls both him and his brother *maricas*. At the same time, however, this scene invites a deeper interrogation of what constitutes appropriate masculinity. Speaking specifically on Paz's obsession with femininity and opening, Ben Sifuentes Jáuregui asserts that "suffering—or, more precisely, withstanding such suffering—makes a woman into a 'man.' This notion of bravery, of putting up with aversion,

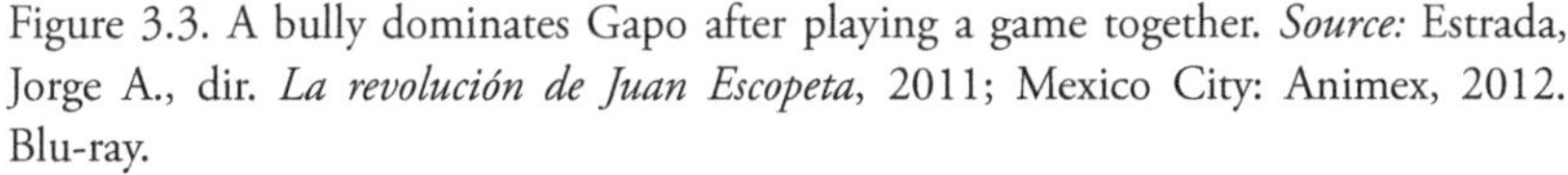

Figure 3.3. A bully dominates Gapo after playing a game together. *Source:* Estrada, Jorge A., dir. *La revolución de Juan Escopeta*, 2011; Mexico City: Animex, 2012. Blu-ray.

of withstanding pain or humiliation produces a shield (or another mask) of 'moral immunity' that covers up the wound to make women reach the same 'invulnerability' that 'we aspire to'—notice the implicit and tacit masculine 'nosotros.' "[52] Sifuentes-Jáuregui's observations apply equally to the violated male and, especially, to young boys like Gapo who are not allowed to enter into adult-male-dominated spaces as equals. Viewed in this light, this early scene foreshadows how Gapo will choose to suffer without fighting back. He will not engage in the violent masculinity of El Zopilote, the *Colorados*, and other masculine killers; nevertheless, he will articulate a valid—and even desirable—form of masculinity precisely because he chooses not to act violently when he could ethically do so. In this way, he absorbs the violence of others and seeks pacifist solutions to conflict.

In one of his first nights following his recruitment to the federal forces, Gapo begins to cry because he misses his mother. A soldier once again highlights Gapo's apparent subservience by calling him *marica* yet again. The soldier equates male emotion with emasculation, but the viewer quickly surmises that Gapo's sensitivity will ultimately allow him to recognize that he does not need weapons to become an ideal, revolutionary man. Certainly, Gapo will have to unlearn many ideas that he has internalized since childhood as he grows into an empathetic adult. As Héctor

Domínguez-Ruvalcaba asserts, "Mexican masculinity is an invention of modern colonialism, in which sensualizing means disempowerment."[53] As a result, Gapo himself associates his outward displays of emotion as testaments to his own weakness. More than anything, he wants a gun so that he can hide his emotion and exert power over others while hiding from his own feelings. Only after experiencing violence firsthand can he confront the colonizing discourses that have imposed a violent ideology upon him. In distancing himself from violence, Gapo ultimately implores the audience to seek and validate nonviolent articulations of masculinity as well.

Guns and Manhood: Overcoming Colonizing Masculine Discourse

Domínguez Ruvalcaba's association of Mexican masculinity with modern colonialism rings especially clear with regard to firearms, weapons that fascinate Gapo as the film begins. Indeed, Gapo's original conflation of masculinity with violence fits within Samanta Ordóñez's assertion that colonialist articulations of Mexican masculinity fit within a logic "with the purpose of masking violence and preserving the racial hierarchy."[54] Viewed in this light, the simple act of fetishizing weapons and seeking fulfillment through using them ensures that a domineering masculinity remains intact in Mexico regardless of who "wins" the war. As Esch argues, firearms are major phallic symbols of power that "were at the center of the revolutionary experience."[55] Not surprisingly, emblematic photos of revolutionaries often display men wearing cartridge belts and women wearing *rebozos*.[56] Indeed, firearms not only played a key role in the Revolution but in the conquest of the Americas as well. Viewed in this light, the firearm has been the quintessential tool of colonialism throughout the Americas since the earliest moments of the Contact Period. Clearly, these weapons have etched themselves into the Mexican and Latin American psyches in myriad ways. It is for this reason that Esch argues that firearms hold functional, economic, and spectral significance, alternating in their function as tools to kill, commodities with economic value, or echoes (the psychological and physical trauma they cause lingers even after the objects themselves are no longer physically present). Additionally, firearms also hold symbolic value as artifacts, tropes, and props with sociocultural, allegorical, and performative values.[57] Not surprisingly, Gapo views firearms through each of these lenses at different moments.

Gapo invokes the symbolic value of the firearm initially when he wishes to get a gun for himself. He believes that the act of holding a gun in his hands is enough to demonstrate his manliness. Nevertheless, the closer Gapo gets to using guns for their functional value, the more he becomes aware of their destructive potential.[58] Experiences of close contact with guns and gun violence—inflicted by both the government and insurgent groups—change the way Gapo relates to firearms. An important learning experience happens when Gapo and Juan Escopeta stop their journey to eat. Gapo says he has not brought anything with him and offers to hunt for food. Juan Escopeta seems surprised when Gapo says he can shoot but lends the boy his gun. Gapo plays with it at first like he used to do with pretend ones, but when he finally sees a rabbit, he is incapable of killing it. He aims for a while, and a close-up shows him breathing heavily as he tries, and ultimately fails, to pull the trigger. After the animal escapes, Juan Escopeta takes his gun back and says solemnly: "Anyone can say they can kill, but not everyone can actually do it" ["cualquiera habla, pero no cualquiera dispara"]. Although Gapo will understand these words later, this episode does not fully curtail his fascination with firearms. He still wants his own gun, and he finally gets one when Juan Escopeta kills a group of armed *Colorados* who have ambushed them. When Gapo finally gets the chance to live his dream of being a revolutionary combatant and fighting alongside Villa during the Battle of Zacatecas, he learns that he is not cut out to kill. As the federales shoot at them, Escopeta tells Gapo to return fire. However, the boy still cannot. He gallops to the line of fire and raises his weapon, but he never shoots, even though this means putting his own life at risk. In this way, Gapo's pistol holds a purely symbolic power; he does not use it to inflict violence, but it becomes a prop that inscribes the boy into the Revolutionary narrative.

The idea of using firearms as an artifact to express manhood also relates to their use as props for political participation: that is, citizenship. Indeed, "for many men the Mexican Revolution meant to turn a de jure citizenship into a de facto citizenship."[59] In this sense, revolutionaries used carbines, rifles, and other firearms as artifacts to affirm their political subjectivity. In her analysis of *Cartucho*, Esch argues that revolutionary "songs and novels tell a tale of peasants and other subalterns who take up arms [. . .] to affirm their presence as political subjects."[60] This reading holds true for *La revolución de Juan Escopeta* as well—both in the comic book and the animated feature film. In the comic book prequel to the film, we learn that Damián leaves Mineral de la Luz after standing up to the moral and physical abuses inflicted on himself and other miners.[61] He later joins the revolutionaries to fight for political and social changes that would benefit his fellow miners and other impoverished people. In the film, Jacinto Trujillo—a comrade of Damián—is one of the characters that voices his engagement in the insurgency as a means of political participation.

This idea of bellicose affirmation of citizenship is challenged as Gapo learns new ways to express and affirm his citizenship. Considering that citizenship implies rights and duties, political participation is an example of the latter (i.e., a means to contribute to society). By the end of the film, Gapo learns that he can contribute to Mineral de la Luz and Mexico in general through nonviolent means. This change in Gapo's perception, long alluded to, happens when he meets Damián's fellow fighters in the surroundings of Torreón. When Gapo finally arrives at Sierra del Sarnoso, where his brother is supposed to be hiding, he finds out that Damián is dead. Gapo calls out many times in front of his brother's grave, and Jacinto Trujillo comes to console the boy. He tells Gapo about Damián's prowess in the battlefield, but emphasizes that this was not what made Damián special: "Do you know what was the best thing about your brother? That he always made us laugh. When we were entrenched, having pissed ourselves out of fear, he would tell a joke [. . .] the troops appreciate that more than a boatload of carbines" ["Sabes lo que era el mejor de su hermano? Que siempre nos hacía reír. Cuando estábamos atrincherados, orinados de miedo, él contaba un chiste [. . .] eso la tropa lo agradece más que un montón de carabinas"]. Gapo then understands that what makes someone like his brother—and by extension, like himself—a hero is helping people.

The main ways in which Gapo shares his new ideas about violence, masculinity, and citizenship are storytelling and displays of compassion. For instance, on his way back home, Gapo stops at Trujillo's house to deliver some money that the revolutionary had asked him to give his family. When Gapo enters the house, he sees a baby crying out from pain due to an insect bite on his chest. He then rubs a medicinal ointment that he has received from Juan Escopeta on the baby's chest. It is an act of compassion for the baby's pain and for the overall plight of the mother who was left on her own taking care of three children while her husband fought in the war. When the children ask him about their father, Gapo tells them that Jacinto, like Damián, is brave and heroic. He then shares the story about how Damián would lighten the mood in moments of tension. By telling this story, Gapo makes the children feel closer to their father, while also honoring the memory of Damián. Upon returning to his hometown at the end of the movie, Gapo tells his friend, Timo, that Damián had sent him on a mission: "There is so much blood already [. . .] we have to help the people" ["ya hay mucha sangre [. . .] tenemos que ayudar a la gente"]. Here, Gapo shares with his friend what he has learned from his brief participation in the armed struggle.

Conclusion

In the end, Gapo's strategies to affirm his nonviolent masculinity and citizenship are the same as those of Nellie, the young female protagonist of *Cartucho*, who counteracts the traumas of war through "nonviolent" means like "compassion and storytelling."[62] No longer a tool for securing manhood or citizenship, Gapo now views firearms as agents of senseless destruction. This reflects his negative experiences both with government forces and with revolutionary groups like the *Colorados*. Through Gapo and Juan Escopeta's epic journey, *La revolución de Juan Escopeta* commemorates and dignifies the revolutionary gesture of taking up arms. That said, its representation of children also sheds light on the trauma caused by violence. Moreover, it displays and validates alternative, and most importantly, nonviolent ways to affirm one's masculinity and citizenship. Those ways are storytelling and displays of compassion.

Clearly, *La revolución de Juan Escopeta* suggests an array of new avenues from which to view twenty-first-century films about the Mexican Revolution. At one level, the film celebrates not only the conflict itself but the cinematographic traditions that developed in the ensuing decades. At a deeper level, however, the film contests many of the central tenets of revolutionary and postrevolutionary cinema. Rather than celebrate macho violence, it tells the story of a young boy who finds greater power in peace and empathy than in dominating others. In so doing, the film resists the colonial dynamics inherent to contemporary constructs of masculinity, thus suggesting a new paradigm altogether. The movie's approach to masculinity proves especially noteworthy given its status as an animated production ostensibly aimed at younger audiences. Indeed, animation provides a compelling lens through which to view the Revolution precisely because the genre has traditionally catered to children and families. Future research could follow in this chapter's footsteps to gauge how other animated films interface with overarching (bio)political structures of power. Such studies could interrogate discourses of violence in other examples of Mexican animation, or they could explore how other films about the Revolution—animated or not—approach that conflict. In either case, such scholarship will be indebted to this chapter's discussion of Estrada's film and the director's strategy for communicating an antibellicist ideal.

Notes

1. Unless otherwise indicated, all translations are by Sofia Paiva de Araujo.

2. Sergio de la Mora, *Cinemachismo: Masculinities and Sexuality in Mexican Film* (Austin: University of Texas Press, 2006), 7; Robert Mckee Irwin, *Mexican Masculinities* (Minneapolis: University of Minnesota Press, 2003), 117; Víctor Macías-González and Anne Rubenstein, "Introduction: Masculinity and History in Modern Mexico," in *Masculinity and Sexuality in Modern Mexico*, eds. Víctor Macías-González and Anne Rubenstein (Albuquerque: University of New Mexico Press, 2012), 2.

3. Brian L. Price, *Cult of Defeat in Mexico's Historical Fiction: Failure, Trauma and Loss* (New York: Palgrave Macmillan, 2012), 167.

4. Sophie Esch, *Modernity at Gunpoint: Firearms, Politics and Culture in Mexico and Central America* (Pittsburgh: University of Pittsburgh Press, 2018), 21–22, 26. For a discussion of another recent film that heavily criticizes those discourses that suggest that one can only achieve effective citizenship through firearms, see David S. Dalton's discussion of Julio Hernández Cordón's *Cómprame un revólver*. David S. Dalton, *Robo Sacer: Necroliberalism and Cyborg Resistance in Mexican and Chicanx Dystopias* (Nashville, TN: Vanderbilt University Press, 2023), chapter 5.

5. For a deeper discussion of the representation of cultural nationalism and the Revolution in twentieth-century cinema, see David S. Dalton, *Mestizo Modernity: Race, Technology and the Body in Postrevolutionary Mexico* (Gainesville: University of Florida Press, 2018), 100–107; de la Mora, *Cinemachismo*; Mónica García Blizzard, *The White Indians of Mexican Cinema: Racial Masquerade throughout the Golden Age* (Albany: State University of New York Press, 2022), introduction; Gilbert M. Joseph and Jürgen Buchenau, *Mexico's Once and Future Revolution: Social Upheaval and the Challenge of Rule since the Late Nineteenth Century* (Durham, NC: Duke University Press, 2013), 201; Zuzana Pick, *Constructing the Image of the Mexican Revolution: Cinema and the Archive* (Austin: University of Texas Press, 2010); Adela Pineda Franco, *The Mexican Revolution on the World Stage: Intellectuals and Film in the Twentieth Century* (Albany: State University of New York Press, 2019); Niamh Thornton, *Revolution and Rebellion in Mexican Film* (New York: Bloomsbury, 2015); Dolores Tierney, *Emilio Fernández: Pictures in the Margins* (Manchester: Manchester University Press, 2007); David M. J. Wood, "The Compilation Film of the Mexican Revolution: History as Catalogue and 'Monument,'" *Film History* 29, no. 1 (2017).

6. For a discussion of how *¡Vámonos con Pancho Villa!* showcases hypermasculine men who tie their masculinity to ideals of bravery and honor, see Charles Ramírez-Berg, *The Classical Mexican Cinema: The Poetics of the Exceptional Golden Age Films* (Austin: University of Texas Press, 2015), 73.

7. Vicente de Jesús Fernández Mora, "El nacionalismo cultural mexicano y sus contradicciones en la película *Vámonos con Pancho Villa*," *Fotocinema: Revista Científica de Cine y Fotografía* 14 (2017): 29–38.

8. Diego Zavala Scherer, "Mitificación/desmitificación en *Suertes, humores y pequeñas historias de la Independencia y la Revolución* (2010), proyecto de animación industrial en Jalisco, México, *El Ojo Que Piensa: Revista de Cine Iberoamericano* 3.

9. Ambriz noted that he struggled to find a studio willing to support his film. This may reflect, in part, his challenging aesthetic, but it also speaks to an overall exhaustion with films about the Revolution. See Alex Dudok De Wit, "*Revoltoso* is an Epic Stop-Motion Short from Mexico (Exclusive Online Premiere)," *Cartoon Brew*, May 20, 2020, https://www.cartoonbrew.com/cartoon-brew-pick/revolution-cubism-and-a-love-letter-to-cinema-revoltoso-is-an-epic-stop-motion-short-from-mexico-exclusive-online-premiere-192023.html, accessed 5/7/2023.

10. For a discussion about how contemporary Mexican cinema has had to cater to middle-class audiences, see Ignacio M. Sánchez Prado, *Screening Neoliberalism: Transforming Mexican Cinema, 1988–2012* (Nashville, TN: Vanderbilt University Press, 2014).

11. Irwin, *Mexican Masculinities*, xvii, xvii–xxi.

12. Macías-González and Rubenstein, "Introduction," 2.

13. Esch, *Modernity at Gunpoint*, 1.

14. Jürgen Buchenau, *The Last Caudillo: Alvaro Obregón and the Mexican Revolution* (Hoboken, NJ: Wiley-Blackwell, 2011), 18–20, 25; Ana Castillo, "The Underdogs: A Revolutionary Glimpse at a Mexican Novel," in *The Underdogs: A Novel of the Mexican Revolution*, by Mariano Azuela, translated by E. Munguia Jr. (New York: Signet Classics, 2008), vii. Esch, *Modernity at Gunpoint*, 46; Joseph and Buchenau, *Mexico's Once and Future Revolution*, 19–25; Paul H. Garner, *Porfirio Díaz. Profiles in Power* (New York: Longman, 2001), 197; Alan Knight, "The Myth of the Mexican Revolution," *Past and Present* 209, no. 1 (2010); Max Parra, "Afterword," *The Underdogs*, by Azuela, trans. Munguia Jr. (New York: Signet Classics, 2008), 163.

15. For a discussion on how violence tends to manifest linguistically against people from marginalized groups, see Gayatri C. Spivak, "Can the Subaltern Speak?," in *Colonial Discourse and Postcolonial Theory: A Reader*, ed. Patrick Williams and Laura Chrisman (New York: New York University Press, 1993), 76; Slavoj Zizek, *Violence: Six Sideways Reflections* (New York: Picador, 2008), 1.

16. Esch, *Modernity at Gunpoint*, 18.

17. Ostos, Carlos and Jorge Estrada, *La revolución de Juan Escopeta* (Mexico City: La Caja de Cerillos Ediciones, 2011), 10.

18. John Mraz, *Looking for Mexico: Modern Visual Culture and National Identity* (Durham, NC: Duke University Press, 2009), chapter 2, chapter 3.

19. Ostos and Estrada, *La revolución de Juan Escopeta*, 49.

20. For a discussion of the popular filmic techniques of the Golden Age, see Charles Ramírez-Berg, "The Cinematic Invention of Mexico: The Poetics and Politics of the Fernández-Figueroa Style," in *The Mexican Cinema Project*, ed. Chon A. Noriega and Steven Ricci (Los Angeles, CA: UCLA Film and Television Archive, 1994), 17–18.

21. Ramírez-Berg, "The Cinematic Invention of Mexico," 19.

22. For a discussion of how Golden Age cinema contributed to models of Mexican manhood, see de la Mora, *Cinemachismo*, 3; Jeffrey M. Pilcher, "The Gay Caballero: Machismo, Homosexuality, and the Nation in Golden Age Film," in *Masculinity and Sexuality in Modern Mexico*, eds. Macías-González and Rubenstein, 215.

23. Pilcher, "The Gay Caballero," 219–21.

24. Anne Rubenstein, "Theaters of Masculinity: Moviegoing and Male Roles in Mexico Before 1960," in *Masculinity and Sexuality in Modern Mexico*, ed. Macías-González and Rubenstein, 147–48. Interestingly, Infante played Salvador Pérez Gómez in *Ay, Jalisco*'s sequel, titled *El Ametralladora* (1943).

25. de la Mora, *Cinemachismo*, 15, 69–73; see also Joseph and Buchenau, *Mexico's Once and Future Revolution*, 153; Rubenstein, "Theaters of Masculinity," 148.

26. Samuel Ramos, [1934], *El perfil del hombre y la cultura en México* (Mexico City: Editorial Planeta Mexicana, 2001), 52–57; Pilcher, "The Gay Caballero," 216–25.

27. Pilcher, "The Gay Caballero," 217.

28. Ostos and Estrada, *La revolución de Juan Escopeta*, 10–13.

29. Ostos and Estrada, *La revolución de Juan Escopeta*, 10–13.

30. For a discussion of the commercial successes of Mexican animation, see the introduction in this book.

31. "Juan Escopeta muestra la Revolución." *El Siglo de Torreon*, October 19, 2009, https://www.elsiglodetorreon.com.mx/noticia/470743.juan-escopeta-muestra-la-revolucion.html; "La revolución de Juan Escopeta y sus batallas," *Informador.MX*, October 10, 2011, https://www.informador.mx/Entretenimiento/La-revolucion-de-Juan-Escopeta-y-sus-batallas-20111010-0201.html.

32. Ostos and Estrada, *La revolución de Juan Escopeta*, 15.

33. Ostos and Estrada, *La revolución de Juan Escopeta*, 21.

34. Paula Carrizosa, "La revolución de Juan Escopeta, un llamado para decir no a la violencia: Jorge Estrada," *La jornada de Oriente*, January 20, 2012, https://www.lajornadadeoriente.com.mx/noticia/puebla/la-revolucion-de-juan-escopeta-un-llamado-para-decir-no-a-la-violencia-jorge-estrada_id_2226.html.

35. Ostos and Estrada, *La revolución de Juan Escopeta*, 14.

36. Ostos and Estrada, *La revolución de Juan Escopeta*, 14; see also Cesar Huerta, "A 'Juan Escopeta' la consideraban violenta," *El Universal*, October 9, 2011,

https://archivo.eluniversal.com.mx/espectaculos/107977.html. For a discussion on adult-centered animation in Mexico, see Yunuen Ysela Mandujano Salazar in this book.

37. This is probably the reason why the film has different age restrictions in Retina Latina and Pantaya. In the latter, it has no age restrictions, but in the former, it is recommended for audiences aged fifteen years or older.

38. Huerta, "A 'Juan Escopeta' la consideraban violenta."

39. For a discussion of the Calderón administration's expansion of the Drug War, see *Raúl Diego Rivera Hernández, Narratives of Vulnerability in Mexico's War on Drugs*, trans. Isis Sadek (New York: Palgrave Macmillan, 2020), introduction.

40. Shortly after that, in 1937, Campobello would publish *Las manos de mamá*, which also addresses the Mexican Revolution through the perspective of a child. For a discussion of how Estrada read *Cartucho to* get a feel for the Revolution, see Ostos and Estrada, *La revolución de Juan Escopeta*, 12.

41. Esch, *Modernity at Gunpoint*, 51.

42. Esch, *Modernity at Gunpoint*, 45–48, 6–7.

43. Carolina Rocha and Georgia Seminet, "Introduction," in *Representing History, Class, and Gender in Spain and Latin America*, eds. Carolina Rocha and Georgia Seminet (New York: Palgrave Macmillan, 2012), 1; Geoffrey Maguire and Rachel Randall, "Introduction: Visualizing Adolescence in Contemporary Latin American Cinema—Gender, Class and Politics," in *New Visions of Adolescence in Contemporary Latin American Cinema,* edited by Geoffrey Maguire and Rachel Randall (New York: Palgrave Macmillan, 2015), 13–14.

44. Rocha and Seminet, "Introduction," 2.

45. Maguire and Randall, "Introduction," 8.

46. Maguire and Randall, "Introduction," 9. For an analysis of representations of childhood, loss of innocence, and adulthood in these movies, see Ignacio M. Sánchez Prado, "Innocence Interrupted: Neoliberalism and the End of Childhood in Recent Mexican Film," in *Representing History, Class, and Gender in Spain and Latin America*, eds. Carolina Rocha and Georgia Seminet.

47. Irwin, *Mexican Masculinities*, xiii.

48. For a discussion of the martyrization and heroization of revolutionaries, see Buchenau, *The Last Caudillo*, 3. For a discussion of finding honor in defeat and failure, see Price, *Cult of Defeat*, 2–5; Octavio Paz [1950]. *El laberinto de la soledad* (Mexico: Fondo De Cultura Economica, 1964), 31.

49. Octavio Paz, *The Labyrinth of Solitude: and the Other Mexico; Return to the Labyrinth of Solitude; Mexico and the United States; The Philanthropic Ogre*, trans. Lysander Kemp, Yara Milos, and Rachel Belash (New York: Grove Press, 2002), 29–30.

50. For a discussion of *chingón* and *chingado* in Paz's thought, see Paz, *El laberinto*, "Los hijos de la Malinche."

51. Américo Paredes, "The United States, Mexico, and Machismo," in *Folklore and Culture on the Texas-Mexican Border*, ed. Richard Bauman (Austin: University of Texas Center for Mexican American Studies, 1993).

52. Ben. Sifuentes-Jáuregui, *The Avowal of Difference: Queer Latino American Narratives* (Albany: State University of New York Press, 2014), 9.

53. Héctor Domínguez-Ruvalcaba, *Modernity and the Nation in Mexican Representations of Masculinity: From Sensuality to Bloodshed* (New York: Palgrave Macmillan, 2007), 3.

54. Samanta Ordóñez, *Mexico Unmanned: The Cultural Politics of Masculinity in Mexican Cinema* (Albany: State University of New York Press, 2021), 31.

55. Esch, *Modernity at Gunpoint*, 45.

56. Esch, *Modernity at Gunpoint*, 55, 60–63.

57. Esch, *Modernity at Gunpoint*, 6–7.

58. Arturo G. Aldama, "¡Todos somos Juan Escopeta!," in *La revolución de Juan Escopeta*, eds. Ostos and Estrada, 7.

59. Esch, *Modernity at Gunpoint*, 61.

60. Esch, *Modernity at Gunpoint*, 45.

61. Jorge Estrada and Alfredo Castañeda *La revolución de Juan Escopeta, el cómic* (Mexico City: Grupo Es Comic, 2011), https://issuu.com/escomic/docs/amx2.

62. Esch, *Modernity at Gunpoint*, 46.

Bibliography

Aldama, Arturo G. "¡Todos somos Juan Escopeta!" In *La revolución de Juan Escopeta*, edited by Ostos and Estrada, 6–8.

Arnaiz, Ricardo, dir. *La Leyenda de la Nahuala*. Morelia, Mexico: Animex Producciones, 2008. DVD.

———. *Nikté*. Mexico City: Animex Producciones, 2009. DVD.

Azuela, Mariano. *The Underdogs: A Novel of the Mexican Revolution*, translated by E. Munguia, Jr. New York: Signet Classics, 2008.

Buchenau, Jürgen. *The Last Caudillo: Alvaro Obregón and the Mexican Revolution*. Hoboken, NJ: Wiley-Blackwell, 2011.

Campobello, Nellie. *Cartucho and My Mother's Hands*. Austin: University of Texas Press, 1988.

Castillo, Ana. "The Underdogs: A Revolutionary Glimpse at a Mexican Novel." In *The Underdogs: A Novel of the Mexican Revolution*, by Mariano Azuela, v–vii.

Dalton, David S. *Mestizo Modernity: Race, Technology, and the Body in Postrevolutionary Mexico*. Gainesville: University of Florida Press, 2018.

———. *Robo Sacer: Necroliberalism and Cyborg Resistance in Mexican and Chicanx Dystopias*. Nashville, TN: Vanderbilt University Press.

de la Mora, Sergio. *Cinemachismo: Masculinities and Sexuality in Mexican Film*. Austin: University of Texas Press, 2006.

Domínguez-Ruvalcaba, Héctor. *Modernity and the Nation in Mexican Representations of Masculinity: From Sensuality to Bloodshed*. New York: Palgrave Macmillan, 2007.

Esch, Sophie. *Modernity at Gunpoint: Firearms, Politics and Culture in Mexico and Central America.* Pittsburgh: University of Pittsburgh Press, 2018.

Estrada, Jorge A., dir. *La revolución de Juan Escopeta.* Mexico City: Animex, 2012. DVD.

Estrada, Jorge, and Alfredo Castañeda. *La revolución de Juan Escopeta, el cómic.* Mexico City: Grupo Es Comic, 2011. https://issuu.com/escomic/docs/amx2.

Fernández Mora, Vicente de Jesús. "El nacionalismo cultural mexicano y sus contradicciones en la película *Vámonos con Pancho Villa.*" *Fotocinema: Revista Científica de Cine y Fotografía* 14 (2017): 19–42.

Fuentes, Fernando de, dir. *¡Vámonos con Pancho Villa!* Mexico City: CLASA, 2018. Internet Archive. https://archive.org/details/VmonosConPanchoVilla_201809.

García Blizzard, Mónica. *The White Indians of Mexican Cinema: Racial Masquerade throughout the Golden Age.* Albany: State University of New York Press, 2022.

Garner, Paul H. *Porfirio Díaz. Profiles in Power.* New York: Longman, 2001.

Gutiérrez Arias, José Luis, dir. *Marcelino, pan y vino.* Mexico City: LOB Films, 2010. DVD.

Guzmán, Martín Luis. *El águila y la serpiente.* Mexico City: Editorial Anáhuac, 1941.

Irwin, Robert Mckee. *Mexican Masculinities.* Minneapolis: University of Minnesota Press, 2003.

Joseph, Gilbert M., and Jürgen Buchenau. *Mexico's Once and Future Revolution: Social Upheaval and the Challenge of Rule since the Late Nineteenth Century.* Durham: Duke University Press, 2013.

Knight, Alan. "The Myth of the Mexican Revolution." *Past and Present* 209, no. 1 (2010): 223–73.

Macías-González, Víctor, and Anne Rubenstein, eds. *Masculinity and Sexuality in Modern Mexico.* Albuquerque: University of New Mexico Press, 2012.

Macías-González, Víctor, and Anne Rubenstein. "Introduction: Masculinity and History in Modern Mexico." In *Masculinity and Sexuality in Modern Mexico,* edited by Macías-González and Rubenstein, 1–21.

Maguire, Geoffrey, and Rachel Randall. "Introduction: Visualizing Adolescence in Contemporary Latin American Cinema—Gender, Class and Politics." In *New Visions of Adolescence in Contemporary Latin American Cinema,* edited by Geoffrey Maguire and Rachel Randall, 1–33. New York: Palgrave Macmillan, 2015.

Mraz, John. *Looking for Mexico: Modern Visual Culture and National Identity.* Durham, NC: Duke University Press, 2009.

Ordóñez, Samanta. *México Unmanned: The Cultural Politics of Masculinity in Mexican Cinema.* Albany: State University of New York Press, 2021.

Ostos, Carlos, and Jorge Estrada, eds. *La revolución de Juan Escopeta.* Mexico City: La Caja de Cerillos Ediciones, 2011.

Paredes, Américo. "The United States, Mexico, and Machismo." In *Folklore and Culture on the Texas-Mexican Border*, edited by Richard Bauman, 215–34. Austin: University of Texas Center for Mexican American Studies, 1993.

Parra, Max. “Afterword.” *The Underdogs: A Novel of the Mexican Revolution*, by Mariano Azuela, translated by E. Munguia, Jr., 163–71. New York: Signet Classics, 2008.

Paz, Octavio. [1950]. *El laberinto de la soledad*. Mexico City: FCE, 1964.

———. *The Labyrinth of Solitude; and the Other Mexico; Return to the Labyrinth of Solitude; Mexico and the United States; The Philanthropic Ogre*. Translated by Lysander Kemp, Yara Milos, and Rachel Belash. New York: Grove Press, 2002.

Pick, Zuzana. *Constructing the Image of the Mexican Revolution: Cinema and the Archive*. Austin: University of Texas Press, 2010.

Pilcher, Jeffrey M. “The Gay Caballero: Machismo, Homosexuality, and the Nation in Golden Age Film.” In *Masculinity and Sexuality in Modern Mexico*, ed. Macías-González and Rubenstein, 214–33.

Pineda Franco, Adela. *The Mexican Revolution on the World Stage: Intellectuals and Film in the Twentieth Century*. Albany: State University of New York Press, 2019.

Price, Brian. *Cult of Defeat in Mexico's Historical Fiction: Failure, Trauma and Loss*. New York: Palgrave Macmillan, 2012.

Ramírez-Berg, Charles. “The Cinematic Invention of Mexico: The Poetics and Politics of the Fernández-Figueroa Style.” In *The Mexican Cinema Project*, edited by Chon A. Noriega and Steven Ricci, 13–24. Los Angeles: UCLA Film and Television Archive, 1994.

———. *The Classical Mexican Cinema: The Poetics of the Exceptional Golden Age Films*. Austin: University of Texas Press, 2015.

Ramos Sr., Antonio, and Antonio Ramos Jr., dirs. *Tierra de Revolucionarios*. Guanajuato, GTO: Instituto Chihuahuense de Cultura/Juarez de Mis Recuerdos, 2010.

Ramos, Samuel. *El perfil del hombre y la cultura en México*. Mexico City: Editorial Planeta Mexicana, 2001.

Rivera Hernández, Raúl Diego. *Narratives of Vulnerability in Mexico's War on Drugs*, translated by Isis Sadek. New York: Palgrave Macmillan, 2020.

Robles Castillo, Aurelio, dir. *El Ametralladora*. 1943; Mexico City: Jalisco Films, 2007. DVD.

Rocha, Carolina and Georgia Seminet, eds. *Representing History, Class, and Gender in Spain and Latin America*. New York: Palgrave Macmillan, 2012.

Rocha, Carolina, and Georgia Seminet. “Introduction.” In *Representing History, Class, and Gender in Spain and Latin America*, ed. Carolina Rocha and Georgia Seminet, 1–32.

Rodríguez, Joselito, dir. *¡Ay Jalisco . . . no te rajes!*. 1941; Mexico City: Quality Films Mexico, 1964. VHS.

Rodríguez, Ismael, dir. *Pepe el Toro* 1953; Mexico City: Películas Rodríguez Cinematográfica Rodríguez, 2008. DVD.

Rubenstein, Anne. “Theaters of Masculinity: Moviegoing and Male Roles in Mexico Before 1960.” In *Masculinity and Sexuality in Modern Mexico*, eds. Macías-González and Rubenstein, 132–54.

Sánchez Prado, Ignacio M. "Innocence Interrupted: Neoliberalism and the End of Childhood in Recent Mexican Film." In *Representing History, Class, and Gender in Spain and Latin America*, ed. Rocha and Seminet, 117–34.

———. *Screening Neoliberalism: Transforming Mexican Cinema, 1988–2012*. Nashville, TN: Vanderbilt University Press, 2014.

Sifuentes-Jáuregui, Ben. *The Avowal of Difference: Queer Latino American Narratives*. Albany: State University of New York Press, 2014.

Spivak, Gayatri C. "Can the Subaltern Speak?" In *Colonial Discourse and Postcolonial Theory: A Reader*, edited by Patrick Williams and Laura Chrisman, 66–111. New York: New York University Press, 1993.

Tierney, Dolores. *Emilio Fernández: Pictures in the Margins*. Manchester: Manchester University Press, 2007.

Thornton, Niamh. *Revolution and Rebellion in Mexican Film*. New York: Bloomsbury, 2015.

Wood, David M. J. "The Compilation Film of the Mexican Revolution: History as Catalogue and Monument." *Film History* 29, no. 1 (2017): 30–56.

Zavala Scherer, Diego. "Mitificación/desmitificación en *Suertes, humores y pequeñas historias de la Independencia y la Revolución* (2010), proyecto de animación industrial en Jalisco, México." *El Ojo Que Piensa: Revista de Cine Iberoamericano* 3.

Zizek, Slavoj. *Violence: Six Sideways Reflections*. New York: Picador, 2008.

Chapter 4

Es un pájaro, es un avión

The Twenty-First-Century Animated Mexican Superhero

Vinodh Venkatesh

An axiom for the contemporary global mediascape is that superheroes are everywhere. From commercial cinema, and over-the-air television and web streaming, to bottom-up amateur YouTube productions, modern moving images are galvanized around the trope of the costumed hero whose actions in taking down the supervillain somehow speak to a broader sociocultural concern or horizon. It is thus unsurprising that in recent years in the Mexican context, the highest-grossing films per weekend belonged to a series of films from the Marvel and DC cinematic universes (MCU and DCEU respectively). A second axiom for the Mexican (and global box office, for that matter) is that animated films, such as *Coco* (2017) and *Toy Story 4* (2019), or films based on animated classics such as Disney's recent *The Lion King* (2019) and *Aladdin* (2019) come in a close second to their caped-and-cowled peers. Of course audiences can also enjoy the best of both worlds: Disney's *Incredibles 2* (number two in gross sales worldwide in 2018) is an animated film about superheroes.

The domination of the Mexican box office by Disney, Sony, Warner Bros., and other US-based producers is nothing new, and something that Ignacio Sánchez Prado has expertly traced in *Screening Neoliberalism: Transforming Mexican Cinema (1988–2012)* (2014). Yet also not new is the presence of superheroes in the Mexican moving-image imaginary; even a casual consumer of Mexican popular culture will be well aware of the presence of the figure in print and filmic media. General audiences and niche scholars have gone to cinemas in droves or sat in front of their television sets to revel in the adventures of such characters as Neutrón, La Sombra Vengadora, El Santo, Blue Demon, Mil Máscaras, Superzán, Kalimán, El Chapulín, El Aguila Descalzo, Chanoc, and La Mujer Murciélago, among many others.[1] Many of these characters first rose to fame in the comic book format, demonstrating that there was already in place a multilevel substrate of production and consumption for the superhero. Indeed two particular superheroes, that is, El Santo and El Chapulín Colorado, dominated the Mexican (and trans-Hispanic) imaginary of the superhero in television, cinema, and print mediums from the 1950s to early 1980s, becoming veritable cultural icons that have surpassed both their original narrative universes and mediums and the borders of the nation, transposed, circulated, and consumed as signs and signifiers in a global cultural economy.[2]

Their vitality, that is, the ubiquity of new productions and multimedia incarnations, however, fell to the wayside in the multifaceted crisis episteme of the *década perdida* of the 1980s that produced sharp austerity measures in cultural production. Sánchez Prado notes that the subsequent privatization of the cinematic ecosystem "led to major changes in the communities of spectatorship and in the social function of film."[3] Middle-class audiences who could maintain an industry had to now be drawn back into the cinema hall. Instead of the low-budget, kitschy films of El Santo and Co. that had little if any plot depth, audiences now had to be coaxed into screenings with films that reflected what Sánchez Prado considers a neoliberal structure of feeling, attracting viewers through "displacements in the ideologies and aesthetics of cinema brought about by the economic changes in production and distribution."[4] As a result, the industry favored the romantic comedy and other genres that appealed to the middle and upper classes, while a broader audience continued to consume whatever Hollywood produced. Fans of El Santo and the other spandex-clad men who fought monsters as an aside to grappling with each other in diegetic fight scenes in the ring, were now enthralled with the 1980s boom of the Hollywood action film and its muscled stars, and the subsequent rise of the superhero starting with the Batman films of the late 1980s and 1990s, in no short measure leading to the current state of ticket sales I outlined above.

Where are Mexico's superheroes today? With the exception of a handful of straight-to-DVD films (such as El Hijo del Santo's *Infraterrestre* [2001]), the Mexican superhero of yore has largely been relegated to the archive (the films and the television series from the glory days of the 1960s and 1970s now circulate on DVD, television reruns, and free streaming sites).[5] That is not to say, however, that there are no contemporary productions; indeed, Mexican superheroes have been resuscitated and reimagined through the second axiom I note above, that is, in the realm of animation. The following essay thus attempts to rescue the Mexican superhero within the contemporary mediascape dominated by X-Men, Avengers, and Dark Knights. Touching on issues of production, aesthetics, and reception, I identify and analyze recent animated productions such as *Santo vs. los clones* (2004), *Santos vs. La Tetona Mendoza* (2012), and *El Chapulín Animado* (2015), that—though not as successful as their serial antecedents—have attempted a resurrection of the trope in Mexican cinema and moving images. In doing so, I explore the production possibilities opened up by animation, as well as the circulatory drawbacks that it may pose. The reader will note that I am moving between cinema, television, and web series in this analysis, but the methodological route I suggest is informed by the very ontology of the superhero, as a complex trope whose genre is historically contingent on its seamless transition and translation between mediums and circuits of circulation/consumption. In other words, to talk of superheroes only within a discrete format or form (such as the cinema) is insufficient, and must instead defer to a multiformat data set to examine.[6] Linked to this idea is the notion that to cordon off animation to simply feature-length film is also insufficient since animation, as Suzanne Buchan argues, is "pervasive in contemporary moving image culture."[7] Commenting on its omnipresence, she ponders that "the expansion of animation in visual culture and its culture difference and distinctiveness puts into question whether we can be 'purists' with regard to what is deemed a subject for critical evaluation and analysis for film studies."[8] It is in dialogue with Buchan that I suggest that any evaluation of the contemporary animated superhero must be willing to address multiple formats and circulatory mechanisms.

Before moving on to our objects of study, it behooves us to come to an understanding of what animation is. Indeed, scholars have struggled to provide a succinct and universal definition for the term, or as Buchan observes: "Animation is an imprecise, fuzzy catchall that heaps an enormous and historically far reaching, artistically diverse body of work into one pot."[9] Research into animation as a definitive field of inquiry has its roots in the early 1990s, when several scholars such as Alan Cholodenko began to theorize animation both as an aesthetics and a praxis. Cholodenko notoriously claimed that "not only is animation a form of film but all film, film 'as such,' is a form of animation."[10] This idea parts from the notion that all film gives movement to the inanimate, that is, we are to consider the moving image as a movement of static images or frames that, through technological manipulation, are animated into life. While technically that may be true (though it is a theory that wanes as film becomes more and more digital), I tend to agree with Donald Crofton who views such ideas with skepticism; his "objections to the genealogy that animation begat cinema are that it may be largely semantics, deploying disingenuous definitions of animation and cinema."[11] Like Crofton, I believe Cholodenko's claim is a provocative one that was useful in kickstarting a broader critical inquiry into animation, but by itself is hollow in that it fails to account for an important distinction between what we typically conceive as animation and live-action film: the inanimate quality of the profilmic object coming to life through mechanical manipulation (as opposed, of course, to the filming of a live action profilmic subject such as a dog, cat, or person). Tom Gunning, in fact, historicizes this argument by noting that though all cinema has its roots in animation, "over time, the novelty of mechanical motion, so central to film's first reception, declined to the point where 'animation' became a specialized genre within cinema, referring to films that endowed the apparently inanimate (drawings or objects) with motion. Today the novelty of new media has once more foregrounded technological motion, as the 'moving image' asserts its priority over the more limited entity 'film.' "[12]

Keeping in mind these two schools of thought, Gunning suggests that "it might be useful to bisect our term animation into two related but separable meanings."[13] ("Animating" 40). Synthesizing Cholodenko's broad claim with Crofton's insistence on a more conclusive terminology, Gunning offers "animation"[1] as referring to "the technical production of motion from the rapid succession of discontinuous frames, shared by all cinematic moving images," while "animation"[2] is understood as "moving images that have been artificially made to move, rather than movement automatically captured through continuous-motion picture photography [. . .] not only displaying but also playing with the production of motion of animation."[14] He adds that while nonphotographic images are typical in the second definition, "photographs can also be animated."[15]

This detail is significant in the genesis of the Mexican superhero genre, as the source texts, that is, the comics on which the first Santo films were based, were an amalgam of photographic and nonphotographic images. First appearing in 1952, José Guadalupe Cruz's *El Santo, el Enmascarado de Plata* was a massive hit with a broad-based readership.[16] These comics "used photographed still images and captions to tell a story much like the drawn panels in traditional comic books and comic strips."[17] They were not *fotonovelas,* that is, comics composed of live-action photographs arranged to tell a story (for our purposes, analogous with live-action film), but rather used the technique of *fotomontaje* that combined photographs and drawings in a hybrid arrangement that transgressed the physics of the strictly photographic or drawn (following what Scott Bukatman calls cartoon physics).[18] I highlight this seemingly insignificant detail because it demonstrates that from the very beginning, the Mexican superhero is a pluri-aesthetic genre that conjugated together the live profilmic subject with the inanimate aesthetics of animation.

The combination of the animated and the live action was never quite achieved in the canon of El Santo films (though several secondary superheroes such as Superzán did resort to animated effects such as laser beams) but was integral to Roberto Gómez Bolaños's *El Chapulín Colorado* (1973–1979). Dressed in a characteristic red leotard and yellow shorts that accentuated his unequivocally nonmuscular body, the titular character appeared in over 256 episodes of a homonym television show that aired in more than seventeen countries. Indeed animation is present from the opening image of each episode, that is, the cartoon insignia of the superhero that greets the viewer as the narrative voice describes the protagonist's tongue-in-cheek strength, speed, and intelligence. The use of animation in the title screen visually links the program with the tradition of televised cartoons, apt for a wide range of audiences, but also suggests a playful disposition to what is to follow, even if the superhero and the recurring characters such as Super Sam often put forth a very much adult critique of the moment.

El Chapulín also brought into movement the aesthetics and poetics of the *fotomontaje* by using special effects (largely green screen techniques) that blur the lines between profilmic reality and animated fiction. One such example is the recurring scenes where El Chapulín is able to shrink in size, literally becoming a small grasshopper. While there is no use of drawing in these special effects, the fact that there are effects that manipulate the audience's perception of the real does gesture toward the affective reactions to the comics. In other words, the use of these visual techniques, in line with Crofton's animation, made visible the technologies of movement between the profilmic subject and the lens, thus posing a self-reflexive optics that foregrounds the possibilities to manipulate movement—to animate—the image. These scenes, though technologically complex for media standards at the time, however, do not exemplify Vivian Sobchack's observation that "animation has pushed cinema to its limits [. . .] so that what is animate and what is inanimate form a composite not easily discernible," as the unreality of the shrunken character is never posed as verisimilar.[19] Instead, the opening title screen sets the tone for viewership, reminding the reader that the physics and plot points to follow are more aligned with cartoons than with any attempt at representing reality. Instead, the presence of animation emphasizes the parodic ethos of the character vis-à-vis *mexicanidad* that was highlighted as a broader cultural trope in the transition years toward the *década perdida*.

That being said, all this is important in that it establishes the presence of animation (and its affects and technologies) in the beginnings and then heyday of the Mexican superhero, so much so that the current iteration of the trope in animated films and web and television series should come as no surprise. Animation in its multiple conceptualizations (and through its genealogy with the *fotomontaje*) is at the very core of the genre. Yet animation proper as a form and format never took off in Mexican cinema circles in the 1980s or 1990s, even though local superheroes faded while animation began to boom in North American studios. With reduced budgets and distribution channels (as the industry adapted to the northern hegemon), one would have thought that animated features would have provided some relief for local production of the superhero genre that had gained an unrivaled popularity from the 1960s onward. One could have imagined cartoon adaptations of the Santo films as being popular weekend programming for younger audiences, striking a nostalgic tone with parents who had flocked to theaters to view the latest film. Instead, and as Néstor García Canclini observes, "la relación con el mundo parecía más prestigiosa que el arraigo en lo local a medida que las comunicaciones se apuraban a traernos lo que se filmaba en Hollywood."[20]

It was only in the early twenty-first century that animation established a nascent footprint in the local mediascape in the shape of *Una película de huevos* (2006), which won an Ariel Award, and the *Leyendas* franchise headed by Ricardo Arnaiz (beginning with *La Leyenda de la Nahuala* [2007]).[21] This development comes at the tail end of what Cholodenko calls "an exponential leap of animation in [. . .] media, in the systems which deliver it and in its popularity."[22] The reference here, of course, is to the global ubiquity—or perhaps, super ubiquity—of characters, franchises, music, and storylines of Disney, Pixar, DreamWorks, and Studio Ghibli among many others into "an animation entertainment-industrial complex, one composed of networks proliferating ever increasing forms and experiences of animation, including through merchandising, licensing of character properties, marketing cross-promotions and tie-ins, studio stores, theme parks, [and] websites."[23] Certainly, animation today is no different than my earlier observation of the superhero genre, as it germinates and cross-pollinates across a variety of media and screens. The *Leyendas* franchise in fact demonstrates these characteristics over a sequence of five films and a Netflix web series, showcasing the local/global reach of Mexican animation to Spanish-language audiences.

The first foray of the Mexican superhero into the realm of animation occurs, however, before the success of *Una película de huevos*, in the shape of the Cartoon Network miniseries *Santo contra los clones* (2004).[24] Over the course of five short but interconnected episodes ("vignettes" would be a more accurate term given the relative brevity of each section), Santo faces some of his most famous adversaries, including mummies, wolf-women, vampires, and Frankenstein's monster. The miniseries was a sort of pilot for a potential complete season of episodes, but never gained traction and was simply aired as filler between the channel's regular programming.

The icon here is reimagined from the hypotext, adopting the recognizable aesthetics of the superhero. The opening credits foreground the title over flowing silver fabric as the camera zooms out revealing a caped Santo overlooking the national capital. Though Santo wore a cape in his films, it was usually only during the walk to the ring, cheered by the masses in the extended wrestling sequences, and not during his adventures fighting ghouls and supervillains. By recasting the protagonist through the familiar sartorial characteristics of the superhero, and within the kinesthetic tableau of his juxtaposition to the urban space he bears responsibility for, the animated series situates the *luchador* within the global mediascape of the superhero. This (poetic, aesthetic, epistemological) suture is subtle but important in that it familiarizes a figure that may be unfamiliar to younger viewers that never partook in the mixed media featuring El Santo. Included in this makeover are the genre conventions of a tech-savvy assistant crafting specialized tools and accouterments for the superhero, including boots to levitate, a laser watch, and an amphibious manta-ray submarine that is equally powerful in the air as it is underwater. As a result, the *luchador*'s abilities are a far cry from the reliance on *llaves*, *candados*, *quebradoras*, and, of course, divine intervention, that characterized the original character.

Presumably made for a younger audience (given the channel and the format of animation), the miniseries opens with a short scene of a man and woman sitting at a bar. The former orders another drink and then wonders aloud why men are always expected to take the lead in intimacy, and that he would prefer for a woman to come and "grab [him] by the hair" ["[le] agarrara [. . .] de las greñas]." His desire is met with indifference, as the female companion retorts: "Keep dreaming, son" ["sigue soñando hijo]." The camera then cuts to a shot of the congested highways of the city as a setting shot primed for the arrival of the *lobas* (themselves a possible reference to *Las lobas del ring*). The dialogue is lost among the action sequences to follow; yet this interchange between the man and woman, two modern denizens of Mexico City, is quite stark. His desire to be dominated stands in contraposition to the more sterile thematics that one would normally associate with child-friendly animation.

The opening sequence is short—consisting of less than fifteen seconds of runtime—but notable because it sets the series apart from the canon of Santo films that firmly held in place rigid expectations and representations of gender roles.[25] In fact gender and sexual norms were not contested in these films, but rather reified during a moment of social and sexual upheaval. The animated miniseries, however, is produced and screened in a different moment. Writing on the issues and themes seen in animated cinema in general, Jayne Pilling notes that "the changing climate in both sexual politics and sexual mores has put discussion of such matters firmly in the public domain"; a public domain saturated with animated media.[26] *Santo contra los clones* is thus produced and disseminated in a climate in which animated films are open to representing and working through individual and communal issues of gender and sexuality, even if the opening male's desires are quickly chastised.[27]

In the remaining vignettes, the miniseries rehashes many of the familiar plot points and tropes of the films, including a learned scientist who helps the protagonist, and a young female love interest (who is the daughter of said learned scientist). The series also makes explicit reference to the films when, in the second episode, the scientist indicates to El Santo that the bite marks left by mummies on their victims in the present day are the same as those found on El Santo when he fought them. The allusion here is, presumably, to two films made in 1970, *Santo en la venganza de la momia* and *Las momias de Guanajuato*. We can thus surmise that the superhero here is none other than the same one who defeated the monsters in the classic films. The fact that he does not age, furthermore, is another characteristic of the original Santo franchise as he is depicted as the leading man (always with youthful paramours) in films spanning three decades.[28]

Santo contra los clones was never developed into a longer season or feature-length film, even though the plot has an open ending. Given the superhero genre's reliance on reboots and reworking printed source material, an animated Santo film or series would have had plenty to work with. Perhaps the lack of commercially successful Mexican animation at the time, and the dominance of the US superhero and animation franchises in the box office produced understanding trepidation. Indeed, this hesitance will be proven quite correct with the commercial failure of the first feature-length animated superhero movie made in Mexico, *Santos vs. La Tetona Mendoza* (2012).

Based on Trino and Jis's popular 1980s comic book character, El Santos is a has-been hero who spends his days wrestling, while also frequently drinking, smoking marijuana, and unleashing a cacophony of flatulence. The film picks up after his divorce from La Tetona, as he and his competitor Peyote are challenged by the former to rid the streets of a horde of zombies. The film is a parody of the luchador films, issues in contemporary Mexican political and cultural production, globalization, and of a variety of cinematic genres, including ending credits that re-create the style of Bollywood. Counting on the voicework of well-known actors such as Daniel Giménez Cacho, Regina Orozco, José María Yazpik, Héctor Jiménez, and even Guillermo del Toro, the film is produced and screened after the boom in local animation (unlike *Contra los clones*, which was more experimental vis-à-vis the mediascape).

Like every other entry in the animated superhero genre, an understanding of the film requires an exploration of the hypotext. Writing on the genesis of the comics in the late twentieth century, Daniel Ribot observes that "*Santos vs la Tetona Mendoza* emerges from an underground comic tradition [. . .] [and] achieved national recognition well beyond the world of fanzines and underground comics, becoming a mainstay in the *Histerietas* Sunday cartoon supplement of the *La Jornada* newspaper."[29] The comic was an *objet* of the counterculture scene of the 1980s (that was in no part a product of the crisis episteme I highlighted above), and was part of "a growing market for material that challenged the status quo vis-a-vis the growing opposition to the government of the Partido Revolucionario Institucional (PRI)."[30]

The twenty-first-century film can thus be traced along two traditions. First, it follows in the footsteps of the Marvel and DC franchises by rebooting characters from the print format: that is, the moving image is anchored in a textual tradition whose intricate details and narrative universes may or may not be familiar to the audience. There is a segment of viewership that watches these films based on a rubric of adaptation (evaluating the portrayal of the Joker based on its fidelity to the print character from a particular issue, for example), while a separate demographic is familiar with these characters (due to their cultural ubiquity) but does not hold them in reference to earlier depictions. Second, the film builds on the ethos of the Mexican counterculture strip by flexing a polyvalenced critique of the social, political, and economic telos of the contemporary through an acerbic tone that leaves no stone unturned. The displacement of masculinity and other pillars of hegemony (including the law) are central to this critique, as are the frequent use of scatological puns and tasteless references that pull no punches. As a result, the film is very much an adult animated film not appropriate for younger audiences that have accounted for the popularity of Disney features such as *Frozen* (2013).[31]

Given that the film is an adaptation of a popular comic, and that local animation was already successful (*Las Leyendas* and Huevocartoon had spawned successful sequels), it is surprising that the film tanked at the box office (perhaps due to its very adult language and humor). In an interview with *El Norte* immediately after the release, Trino also expressed surprise but chalked up its unpopularity to the idea that the film "es específicamente una película con muchas referencias intelectuales, ya que la historieta salió de circulación hace más de una década."[32] Unlike the Anglo superheroes that continue to appear in comics and in other merchandising including clothing, Santos never gained mass-cultural appeal. One could suggest that the counterculture ethos behind the original strip had passed its expiration date in the twenty-first century, as Mexican politics had already come unshackled from the yoke of the PRI but were now governed by neoliberal tendencies instead. Perhaps the character and his localized critique were simply anachronic to a mass audience already awash in globalized cultural circuits. This is not to say that the character could not have been modernized for the present—and I think the creators were conscious of this by referencing Bollywood, as an example—as animation has a deep tradition of subversion. In fact, Esther Leslie argues in her "cartoon manifesto" that animation is always subversive: "Animation is subversive of nature, which has so often been mobilized as ideology. Animation is subversive of order, of logic, of stasis, of everything that would insist that things are so and must be so [. . .] Animation is subversive of itself—ever changing, ever shifting."[33]

Perhaps *Santos* should have taken the latter to heart—that is, it may have been a hit if it were only willing to engage in auto-ontological subversion.

Trino ends the interview with optimism, expecting to produce two more films in a Santos trilogy, "que seguramente tendrá mayor impacto en el público porque los jóvenes ya estarán familiarizados con los personajes."[34] The acknowledgment that the majority of younger adults were not familiar with the characters in 2012, ironically, is spot-on in identifying why this film never took off. Writing in 2020, no other Santos film has been made, even as Mexican animation has blossomed into a variety of genres and production circuits, and El Santo's cinema has experienced a renaissance of sorts due to its easy accessibility on YouTube and other online platforms. In a separate 2019 interview, Trino reveals that a streaming series is in the works, speaking to the cross-platform potential of the animated superhero genre. This should come as no surprise since the character first appeared in a seven-episode web series in 2003 (that was never mass circulated unlike *Contra los clones*), almost a decade before the feature-length film. Trino intimates that "ya otra película no aguanta porque no es de largo aliento, le va mejor en capítulos de 22 minutos sabrosos y bien armados," and that they plan to "adaptar al personaje para las nuevas generaciones con guionistas jóvenes."[35] (Angel). The creators' decision to target the streaming market, which with the boom of transnational services such as Netflix, with local production centers in the Spanish-speaking world including Mexico and Spain, speaks to the evolution of moving images (and animated moving images) into diverse circulatory channels, thus rendering simply a study of animated "cinema" insufficient.[36]

Perhaps more relevant in the 2019 interview is Trino's recognition of the need to rescript the character for a contemporary audience, which has been the case in the animated series of *El Chapulín Colorado*. *El Chapulín Colorado animado* premiered in 2015 first on a streaming platform and then later migrated to television. It followed *El Chavo animado*, also created by Roberto Gómez Bolaños, the star of both original homonym live-action shows. *El Chapulín animado* very much maintains the same poetics and ethos of the original television show (some of the episodes are even based on original storylines from the 1970s), and even recycles some of the character's most notable idiosyncrasies ("¡Síganme los buenos!," "No contaban con mi astucia"). In doing so, the series maintains key details that are familiar to older audiences yet are also easily assimilated by younger viewers who can laugh at the protagonist's bumbling heroics when he exclaims: "¡No panda el cúnico!" This dual key of viewership is analogously present in some of the dialogues and jokes, akin to the hypotext wherein adult audiences enjoyed a secondary discursive level superimposed onto the primary mode of humor. This characteristic opens up the series to a broader audience, not unlike such animated blockbusters like *Shrek* (2001) and *Toy Story* (1995) that were hits with multiple demographic segments.

What sets the digital series apart from the original television format, however, is the narrative and kinesthetic potentials opened up by animation. While the original show was relegated to studio shooting and relied on rudimentary special effects, the narrative world of El Chapulín is blown open as the superhero is freed from budgetary and production obstacles. As a result, the beloved character now enjoys enhanced powers and larger-than-life villains. This distinction is highlighted in the first two episodes of season 1. In the opener, "El anillo perdido," the action takes place in the closed space of a large mansion as El Chapulín comes to the rescue of a young mestiza maid who is accused of stealing a diamond ring owned by her rich, criollo *patrón*. The superhero intervenes and—with the help of his magic "pastillas de chiquitolina"—discovers that it was a private detective all along who was the thief. Older viewers of the first episode could easily confuse the plot for any number of similar escapades in the television series. This, however, is not the case in the second episode, "El gigantesco lagartosaurio," where a mad scientist creates a genetically modified monster that terrorizes the city.[37]

The "lagartosaurio" is made possible by the poetics of animation and would have been an impossibility in the original series with its limited production value. In subsequent episodes, El Chapulín fights giant robots and other supervillains that are easily rendered through tools of digital animation, where the only obstacle to representation is the imagination of the artist and not a production budget. The series, however, strikes a balance between these larger-than-life action sequences and duels between the superhero and villain with storylines that are based more closely on the original series. In the latter strain of narrative, the variety of characters addresses some of the concerns that really haven't changed in the almost forty-year difference in emission dates, such as the corruption of local politicians, the ineptitude of the police, and the prejudices of the *fresa* class vis-à-vis the layperson. Given its deft balancing of local and global, traditional and contemporary (super) villains, (and unlike say, *Santos vs La Tetona Mendoza*) *El Chapulín Colorado animado* has been the most successful animated superhero in Mexico.

The series' success suggests that there is a future for the animated superhero in the Mexican mediascape but that perhaps the genre is better suited for the small screen and not so much the traditional feature-length format (given the failure of *Santos* and the lack of any subsequent productions). It is important to note that in this corpus of moving images is the absence of any original characters, that is, new superheroes specifically imagined in the twenty-first century, as the works I trace above are all remakes and reboots of well-known characters and villains. In fact, there were suggestions of an animated Kalimán series or film, following the manga aesthetics of *Kalimán Regresa* (a late 1990s and early 2000s update of the famed 1960s radionovela, film, and comic book character), but this is still in the realm of speculation. The lack of new superheroes comes as no surprise (given the production dynamics of the Anglo power franchises), but perhaps it is exactly what is needed for the genre to be truly successful; a superhero liberated from the (cultural, political, social) baggage of the past and thus freer to engage with the globalized and transnational mediascape brought about by the neoliberal turn, a media ecosystem that shows no signs of waning.[38]

Notes

1. See Robert Cotter, *The Mexican Masked Wrestler and Monster Filmography* (Jefferson, NC: MacFarland, 2005); Doyle Greene *Mexploitation Cinema: A Critical History of Mexican Vampire, Wrestler, Ape-Man and Similar Films, 1957–1977* (Jefferson, NC: MacFarland, 2005); Raúl Criollo, José Xavier Návar, and Rafael Aviña, eds., *¡Quiero ver sangre! Historia ilustrada del cine de luchadores* (Mexico City: UNAM, 2013). Also see David Wilt's essential website, *The Films of El Santo*.

2. For a tracing of the genesis of the trope in Mexico and then its influence throughout the region in subsequent local iterations, see my book, *Capitán Latinoamérica: Superheroes in Cinema, Television, and Web Series* (Albany: State University of New York Press, 2020).

3. Ignacio M. Sánchez Prado, *Screening Neoliberalism: Transforming Mexican Cinema, 1988, 2012* (Nashville, TN: Vanderbilt University Press, 2014), 6.

4. Sánchez Prado, *Screening Neoliberalism*, 6.

5. Banished from local cinema halls, the luchador has had to resort to making homage films in the US instead—see the Mil Máscaras trilogy and the two films starring El Alambrista.

6. Testament to this claim is the inclusion of my book. See Vinodh Venkatesh, *Capitán Latinoamérica: Superheroes in Cinema, Television, and Web Series* (Albany:

State University of New York Press, 2020) in Sánchez Prado and Leslie Marsh's SUNY Series in Latin American Cinema. The reader may rightfully point out that I am omitting print superheroes in this essay, and they would be very much correct. Indeed, a more thorough study on the circulation of Mexican superheroes in media *and* print is needed, but unfortunately falls outside the scope of these pages.

7. Suzanne Buchan, "Introduction: Pervasive Animation." *Pervasive Animation*, ed. Suzanne Buchan (New York: Routledge, 2013), 1. Buchan adds that "as screens become part of everyday life—phones, laptops, pads, and future technologies to come—animation will increasingly influence our understanding of how we see and experience the world visually" (1).

8. Buchan, "Introduction," 2.

9. Suzanne Buchan, "Animation, in Theory," in *Animating Film Theory*, ed. Karen Beckman (Durham, NC: Duke University Press, 2014), 113.

10. Alan Cholodenko, "'First Principles' of Animation," In *Animating Film Theory*, ed. Karen Beckman (Durham, NC: Duke University Press, 2014), 98.

11. Donald Crofton, "The Veiled Genealogies of Animation and Cinema," *Animation* 6, no. 2 (2011): 94.

12. Tom Gunning, "Animation and Alienation: Bergson's Critique of the Cinématographe and the Paradox of Mechanical Motion." *The Moving Image* 14, no. 1 (2014): 2.

13. Tom Gunning, "Animating the Instant: The Secret Symmetry between Animation and

Photography," in *Animating Film Theory*, ed. Karen Beckman (Durham, NC: Duke University Press, 2014), 40.

14. Gunning, "Animating the Instant," 40.

15. Gunning, "Animating the Instant," 40.

16. Evan Lieberman, "Mask and Masculinity: Culture, Modernity, and Gender Identity in the Mexican *Lucha Libre* films of El Santo," *Studies in Hispanic Cinemas* 6, no. 1 (2009): 5; Anne Rubenstein, "El Santo's Strange Career," in *The Mexico Reader: History, Culture, Politics*, ed. Gilbert M. Joseph and Timothy J. Henderson (Durham, NC: Duke University Press, 2002), 572. Though I have listed 1952 as the date of print, several scholars contest this date, though the range of publication is 1951–1953.

17. Lieberman, "Mask and Masculinity," 5.

18. Bukatman suggests that animation gives "us a world that is ordered, but ordered differently: hence, cartoon physics," and that "cartoon physics has been with us for nearly as long as cartoons have existed, but it becomes important to write about now because its alternative universe of unnatural laws is threatened by the encroachments of the physics of the real world into the realm of animation in the digital age." See Scott Bukatman, "Some Observations Pertaining to Cartoon Physics; or, The Cartoon Cat in the Machine," in *Animating Film Theory*, ed. Karen Beckman (Durham, NC: Duke University Press, 2014), 302.

19. Vivian Sobchack, "Animation and Automation, or the Incredible Effortfulness of Being," *Screen* 50, no. 4 (2009): 382.

20. Néstor García Canclini, *Latinoamericanos buscando lugar en este siglo* (Buenos Aires: Paidós, 2002), 79.

21. See Elissa Rashkin's and Enrique Ajuria Ibarra's chapters in this book for studies related to these films.

22. Alan Cholodenko, "Introduction," in *The Illusion of Life 2: More Essays on Animation*, ed. Alan Cholodenko (Sydney: Power Institute, 2007), 20.

23. Cholodenko, "Introduction," 20.

24. Though *Santo contra los clones* is the first Mexican animated superhero production, it is not the first to recycle tropes from the *luchador* tradition. That honor belongs to *¡Mucha Lucha!*, aired on Kid's WB between 2002 and 2005. The series is set in California but freely uses Spanglish, acknowledging the multicultural impact and resonance of *lucha libre* for pan-Hispanic audiences. It is also the first animated series for children to be produced with Adobe Flash.

25. Even films starring female leads, such as *La Mujer Murciélago* (1968) and the series of *Las luchadoras*, always ended with male characters and sidekicks taking on primary roles of agency vis-à-vis the villain. In the former title, the heroine is rendered as a damsel in distress in the final shot where she leaps into the arms of her two male accomplices while a mouse scurries below her. See Venkatesh, *Capitán Latinoamérica,* chapter 2 for a greater discussion.

26. Jayne Pilling, "Introduction," in *Animating the Unconscious: Desire, Sexuality and Animation*, ed. Jayne Pilling (New York: Columbia University Press, 2012), 6.

27. Writing on the representation of gender and gender roles in Hollywood animated film, Sara Hare argues that not much has changed since the 1980s, which is troubling given the intrinsic role animation plays in providing "real-world models of behavior." See "Still No Jetpacks or Gender Parity: Animated Film from 1980–2016." *Journal of the Indiana Academy of the Social Sciences* 20, no.1 (2017): 51.

28. For a discussion of the agelessness of El Santo, see Carlos Monsiváis, *Los rituals del caos* (Mexico City: Ediciones Era, 1995); David S. Dalton, *Mestizo Modernity: Race, Technology, and the Body in Postrevolutionary Mexico* (Gainesville: University of Florida Press, 2018), 151.

29. Daniel Ribot, "*El Santos vs. Tetona Mendoza*: Wrestling with Mexico's Experimental Comic Book Narratives," *Studies in Latin American Popular Culture* 25 (2006): 49. See Ribot's article for a comprehensive analysis of the politics and circulation of the comic strip.

30. Ribot, "*El Santos vs. Tetona Mendoza*," 54.

31. That being said, the majority of these child-friendly animated films by the big studios also have a deep adult undercurrent, where double entendres and sly discursive and kinesthetic winks are easily perceived by an adult viewer.

32. Héctor Rosas, " 'Le ha ido más o menos'—Reconoce Trino que *El Santos vs. La Tetona Mendoza* no ha tenido el éxito esperado," *El Norte*, December 22, 2012.

33. Esther Leslie, "Animation and History," in *Animating Film Theory*, ed. Karen Beckman (Durham, NC: Duke University Press, 2014), 35.

34. Rosas, " 'Le had ido más o menos.' "

35. Mauricio Angel, "¿Tendrá *El Santos* su serie de TV?," *Reforma*, May 6, 2019, 2.

36. Both Debra Castillo and Jorge Ruffinelli have commented on the transformation of Latin American moving-image culture from the big screen to on-demand services consumed on smaller, mobile screens. See Castillo, "The New New Latin American Cinema: Cortometrajes on the Internet," in *Latin American Cyberculture and Cyberliterature*, ed. Claire Taylor and Thea Pitman (Liverpool: Liverpool University Press, 2007); Rufinelli, "De YouTube a la pantalla, de la pantalla a YouTube," *Nuevo Texto Crítico* 28, no. 51 (2015). See *Capitán Latinoamérica* for a broader discussion on streaming media and the superhero. Also see the critical success of such films as Alfonso Cuarón's *Roma* (2018) that was produced by Netflix.

37. Fans of the Santo films will quickly recognize the mad scientist/genetically engineered monster tandem, while viewers of the *Santo contra los clones* miniseries will appreciate the intertextual critique if the elevated highway built in Mexico City, supposedly to reduce traffic. Several episodes in the animated series pay homage to the *luchador* oeuvre, including "La maldición de Piesapestósotl" that revolves around an ancient Aztec curse.

38. I am here thinking of something along the lines of Netflix's *Super Drags* (2018), an animated Brazilian superhero series centered on three super drag queens who fight for LGBTQ rights. The theme of the show is universal, thus allowing for a greater circulation and consumption to even non-Lusophone audiences.

Bibliography

Angel, Mauricio. "¿Tendrá *El Santos* su serie de TV?" *Reforma*, May 6, 2019, 2.

Beckman, Karen, ed. *Animating Film Theory*. Durham, NC: Duke University Press, 2014.

Buchan, Suzanne. "Animation, in Theory." In *Animating Film Theory*, 111–30.

———. "Introduction: Pervasive Animation." In *Pervasive Animation*, edited by Suzanne Buchan, 1–21. New York: Routledge, 2013.

Bukatman, Scott. "Some Observations Pertaining to Cartoon Physics; or, The Cartoon Cat in the Machine," in *Animating Film Theory*, 301–16.

Castillo, Debra. "The New New Latin American Cinema: Cortometrajes on the Internet." In *Latin American Cyberculture and Cyberliterature*, edited by Claire Taylor and Thea Pitman, 33–49. Liverpool: Liverpool University Press, 2007.

Cholodenko, Alan. "Introduction." In *The Illusion of Life 2: More Essays on Animation*, edited by Alan Cholodenko, 13–95. Sydney: Power Institute, 2007.

———. " 'First Principles' of Animation." In *Animating Film Theory*, 98–110.

Cotter, Robert Michael. *The Mexican Masked Wrestler and Monster Filmography*. Jefferson, NC: McFarland, 2005.

Criollo, Raúl, José Xavier Návar, and Rafael Aviña. *¡Quiero ver sangre! Historia ilustrada del cine de luchadores*. Universidad Nacional Autónoma de México, 2013.

Crofton, Donald. "The Veiled Genealogies of Animation and Cinema." *Animation* 6, no. 2 (2011): 93–110.

Dalton, David S. *Mestizo Modernity: Race, Technology, and the Body in Postrevolutionary Mexico*. Gainesville: University of Florida Press, 2018.

García Canclini, Néstor. *Latinoamericanos buscando lugar en este siglo*. Buenos Aires: Paidós, 2002.

Greene, Doyle. *Mexploitation Cinema: A Critical History of Mexican Vampire, Wrestler, Ape-Man and Similar Films, 1957–1977*. Jefferson, NC: MacFarland, 2005.

Gunning, Tom. "Animating the Instant: The Secret Symmetry between Animation and Photography." In *Animating Film Theory*, 37–53.

———. "Animation and Alienation: Bergson's Critique of the Cinématographe and the Paradox of Mechanical Motion." *The Moving Image* 14, no. 1 (2014): 1–9.

Hare, Sara. "Still No Jetpacks or Gender Parity: Animated Film from 1980–2016." *Journal of the Indiana Academy of the Social Sciences* 20, no. 1 (2017): 50–63.

Leslie, Esther. "Animation and History," in *Animating Film Theory*, 25–36.

Lieberman, Evan. "Mask and Masculinity: Culture, Modernity, and Gender Identity in the Mexican *Lucha Libre* films of El Santo." *Studies in Hispanic Cinemas* 6, no. 1 (2009): 3–17.

Monsiváis, Carlos. *Los rituales del caos*. Ediciones Era, 1995. Kindle.

Pilling, Jayne. "Introduction." In *Animating the Unconscious: Desire, Sexuality and Animation*, edited by Jayne Pilling, 1–16. New York: Columbia University Press, 2012.

Ribot, Daniel. "*El Santos vs. Tetona Mendoza*: Wrestling with Mexico's Experimental Comic Book Narratives." *Studies in Latin American Popular Culture* 25 (2006): 49–71.

Rosas, Héctor. " 'Le ha ido más o menos'—Reconoce Trino que *El Santos vs. La Tetona Mendoza* no ha tenido el éxito esperado." *El Norte*, December 22, 2012, 10.

Rubenstein, Anne. "El Santo's Strange Career." In *The Mexico Reader: History, Culture, Politics*, edited by Gilbert M. Joseph and Timothy J. Henderson, 570–78. Durham, NC: Duke University Press, 2002.

Ruffinelli, Jorge. "De YouTube a la pantalla, de la pantalla a YouTube." *Nuevo Texto Crítico* 28, no. 51 (2015): 57–68.

Sánchez Prado, Ignacio. *Screening Neoliberalism: Transforming Mexican Cinema 1988–2012*. Nashville: Vanderbilt University Press, 2015.

Sobchack, Vivian. "Animation and Automation, or the Incredible Effortfulness of Being." *Screen* 50, no. 4 (2009): 375–91.

Venkatesh, Vinodh. *Capitán Latinoamérica: Superheroes in Cinema, Television, and Web Series*. Albany: State University of New York Press, 2020.

Wilt, David. *The Films of El Santo*. http://terpconnect.umd.edu/~dwilt/santo.html.

SECTION II

The Sixth Period

On Streaming and the Internationalization of Mexican Animation

Chapter 5

Politicized Web Praxis in Mexican Animated Short Films

Reality 2.0 (2012) and *Retrato Político* (2013)

Katherine Bundy

Animation in Mexico has enjoyed a long lifespan since the early twentieth century: one that largely mirrors and imitates the trends and techniques of animation produced just north of the border in Hollywood, California. While this parallelism and dialogue continue to the present moment in mainstream cartoons and animated films, the sphere of experimental animation in Mexico has expanded its access in both production and viewership beyond those with a privileged fine arts education due in large part to the expanding accessibility of the internet around the world. Rather than an industrial model of animation that translates to specialization and division in larger production teams, experimental animation often boils down to small collaborations and even "lone-wolf" individuals who are employing new techniques to create an experience for the viewer that is not readily found within mainstream cinema channels. Since animated cinema is consistently located at the crux of technological and cinematic innovation, it comes as no surprise that the evolution of the web itself plays a critical role in animation experimentation as a venue of online aesthetics, access, and participation since the advent of the internet in the 1990s.

The two short films analyzed in this chapter, *Reality 2.0* (Victor Orozco, 2012) and *Retrato político* (Güicho Núñez, 2013) are examples of animated short films that are born-digital online by curating web clips and images into visual narratives that are deeply engaged with denouncing corruption and narco-violence in Mexico surrounding the 2006 and 2013 elections. It just so happens that the years 2006 to 2013 fall within an era of the web that has been coined as the *Web 2.0* (also known as the "Participatory Web"). The so-called *Web 2.0* is largely characterized by "the cluster of technologies, devices, and applications that support the proliferation of social spaces on the Internet thanks to the increased broadband capacity, open source software, and enhanced computer graphics and interface."[1] This expansion of web access coupled with the shift in usership from search functionality during Web 1.0[2] toward networked participation in Web 2.0 both amplified and influenced cultural production and activities offline. In order to contextualize how animated short film can be digital-born and connect back to political discourses in Mexico, I will base my theory in internet and cyberculture studies to define *Web 2.0* in terms of usership and *cyberspace*.[3] In my close analysis of the two short films, I will connect the online engagement of *Reality 2.0* and *Retrato político* to theorizations of Latin American web praxis from Claire Taylor and Thea Pitman as well as David S. Dalton's term, *robo sacer*, which is an articulation of posthuman subjectivity grounded in Latin American cultural theory. In addition, my personal interviews with both animators in June of 2020 will aid in informing how their engagement with the Web 2.0 influenced their practices in experimental animation as well as within the content and impact of the short films themselves.

Web 2.0 and Cyberspace

As the beginnings of the World Wide Web in the 1990s promised global information accessibility, instant communication, and searchability, the dot-com bust of the early 2000s and the subsequent economic crash of 2008 meant that the businesses shaping the web at the time needed to undergo a revolutionary shift into the era known as *Web 2.0*, which is based on the following seven principles: (1) the Web as Platform; (2) Harnessing Collective Intelligence; (3) Data is the Next Intel Inside; (4) the End of the Software Release Cycle; (5) Lightweight Programming Models; (6) Software above the Level of a Single Device; and (7) Rich User Experiences.[4] Grant Blank and Bianca Reisdorf's interpretation of *Web 2.0* centers on the user's participation in platforms that is staged for collective contribution and promotion from users themselves. Keywords in their understanding of Web 2.0 usership include *network effects* ("the idea that some things are more valuable when more people participate") on *platforms* that are websites, apps, and social media spaces that allow for user-created content like photos, videos, blog entries, product and service reviews, or mashups.[5] Hence, their definition of Web 2.0 is "using the internet to provide platforms through which network effects can emerge."[6] Since the shift from Web 1.0 to Web 2.0 essentially began flipping the model of mass communication on the information superhighway to communication by the masses in participatory spaces, the network effects that take place on platforms in Web 2.0 carry powerful storytelling functions since many barriers of organization and collective action have been essentially removed.

The animated short films analyzed in this chapter engage with Web 2.0 characteristics in two distinct ways that are ultimately commenting on political realities in Mexico during the 2006 and 2012 elections. Orozco's *Reality 2.0* engages the Participatory Web by curating and rotoscoping web clips and computer screen recordings to narrate the online user's foray into Mexican narcoviolence in blogs, forums, and video-hosting platforms. Núñez's *Retrato político* came about through organizing a collaborative project on Facebook for individual users to modify the images of headless politicians that were then compiled into an animation unified by the soundtrack of a political speech mocking the corruption in Mexico.[7] Since both short films are *born-digital*, meaning that the material itself originates in a digital format rather than a digital conversion of analogue material, questions of impact between experimental animation's connection to expressions of the *real* go even deeper in examining how participants interact and share within the cyberspace of the Web 2.0, and how those politicized web practices are embedded within the content and production of Orozco's and Núñez's short films.

Alongside shifts from Web 1.0 to Web 2.0, debates of self-expression, influence, and censorship on the web circulated around the notion that what happens in cyberspace does not just remain in cyberspace as a separate virtual playground with no repercussions. Seeing this claim as false logic, John Marshall's interpretation of *cyberspace* insists that "cyberspace may be everywhere, but it is not uniform. Cyberspace is influenced by geopolitical, historical, developmental, and economic factors; by the expansion and intensification of capitalism; by access factors and by its use. Not only does the online world affect cyberspace, but cyberspace changes the way offline space is used."[8] Claire Taylor and Thea Pitman echo this sentiment regarding Latin

American online practices when they explain: "It is worth pointing out that Latin American cultural practice on the Internet does not do away with the concepts of locatedness. Granted, locality is re-worked and re-fashioned, and the nation-state no longer functions as the authoritative centre from which lettered culture is disseminated, as borders become transgressed and fragmented, by transnational flows. Nevertheless, varying degrees of locatedness adhere, which may include new forms of thinking communities, affiliations, and geographical connections."[9] While a geographical pinpoint could very well be traced back to a singular device, the connection between objects that are born-digital online and their association with the real can indeed be complicated to reconcile on social media platforms during Web 2.0. This ambivalence of locatedness with a web that was beginning to streamline across devices and platforms may play to the advantage of those who are denouncing corruption and violence in their immediate surroundings, diasporic communities, or even as an outsider. Early game-changing examples of harnessing Web 2.0 social media platforms for cyberactivism domestically and abroad include the uprisings and revolts during the Arab Spring in 2010–2012, the 15-M protests in Spain during 2011–2012, the Occupy movement in the United States in 2011, and, in Mexico, the #YoSoy132 movement[10] in opposition to the presidential election of Enrique Peña Nieto in 2012. These movements not only unified voices across national frontiers but managed to organize protest and dissent on the streets while still susceptible to the ever-shifting dynamics of real-time participation on and offline. The global impact of these earlier movements during Web 2.0 years began setting the stage for prolific cyberactivism that mobilized masses and affected legislation in subsequent years like the popularization of the hashtag movements like #MeToo and #BlackLivesMatter; and #NiUnaMenos and #MiPrimerAcoso in Latin America, just to name a few. While earlier stages of the web produced a "read-only" cyberspace between those who write code and those who search for and take in information, the network effects of Web 2.0 meant that the "read-and-write" web was fostering forms of democratic participation by those who were able to access the internet and create content.

The multidirectional channels of cyberspace and Mexican realities manifest in the two short films analyzed in this chapter in that both animators managed to harness the streams of content generation from the Participatory Web to curate a succinct political message about Mexican violence and political corruption. *Reality 2.0* resulted in an animated documentary that captured a sense of the web user's voyeurism and immersion online by rotoscoping found web footage whereas *Retrato político* actively called for user input on social media platforms to compile visual critiques of political corruption influenced by internet meme culture during #YoSoy132. While I would not argue that *Reality 2.0* and *Retrato Político* are themselves films that exist for the sole purpose of online activism, their engagement with blogs and social networks in the era of Web 2.0 highlight ways that animation portrays web practices that are entrenched with political critique.

Reality 2.0

In *Reality 2.0*, the connection to Mexico is formed by assembling web footage through a practice of remixing and curating user content that is tethered to the experience between real space and cyberspace. During the era of Web 2.0, digital cameras, camera phones, and mobile connectivity began gaining popularity around the world, albeit not unilaterally introduced.[11] With the introduction of video-hosting platforms like Vimeo in 2004 and YouTube in 2005, Web 2.0 users started to become content creators themselves—even those with little or no training in film production or editing. With content generating in troves along with the availability of software and tools to create social platforms from which to broadcast video within an instant, filmmaking itself had to pivot to incorporate the possibilities of new digital media and the user experience on the Participatory Web. Victor Orozco commented on the transformation of content generation in 2007 when he began to conceive of *Reality 2.0* as a project:

> There are not even aesthetic norms that come with it, people are making content on the fly [. . .] *como le sale de los huevos.* [. . .] They take the phone and shoot, that's it. There's no school for this since we're in a primitive moment of content generation. So that's what stood out for me. That transformation of content generation that I saw. Then I thought, 'okay what's my position as an artist?' If I've been robbed of my unique ability to create content, then by necessity I've become a curator. Therefore, with the work that conceptually defines my position as curator, I select material to then generate a new syntaxis of sorts but with content that is created by other people not just by me. (11:32–12:23)[12]

In the realm of animated cinema, the assemblage and animation of online-produced content points to a way for animation to produce a type of documentary, or an *anima-doc* (a term used by Orozco in our interview) that curates and enlivens footage and sound that otherwise might be buried, forgotten, or neglected. In fact, Orozco's website labels *Reality 2.0* as an animated documentary, pointing back to the style of the film, which comprises mostly live-action footage from online videos as well as screen-captures of web browsing that are traced over with animation (rotoscope method). Since Orozco was trained in documentary filmmaking in Hamburg, his investigations and collection of online clips preceded any sort of script or guide, and instead later came together as an animated documentary project as the material demanded.

Reality 2.0 is an example of how experimental animation borrows from the aesthetics and tools brought about from the Web 2.0 to reflect how narco-violence in Mexico and in cyberspace reflect the normalization of violence while simultaneously informing each other on and offline. The poetic narration throughout the film is told by a young Mexican man who arrives in Hamburg, Germany, and then intimately recounts insights about his homeland as a continual digital connection with current events there. On Orozco's website, he describes the film as an attempt to unsuccessfully separate his connection with Mexican current events once arrived in Germany: "It was autumn when I arrived in Germany. I thought that in this exotic country I could distance myself a little bit from Mexico, but I was wrong. Drug traffickers managed to take me back in a ruthless way. A short, animated documentary about the drug-related violence in Mexico."[13]

During the eleven-minute film, the viewer comes to understand that, while the protagonist of the film relocates to Germany (based on Orozco's move to attend film school in Hamburg), the content and history of his roots in Mexico continue to haunt him in the form of social media feeds, blogs, and forums dedicated to narco-violence and drug trafficking. The narrative voice explains that "I unwittingly transformed myself into a voyeuristic freak" (2:17) over a scene that features a video loading screen with a pixelated mouse curser clicking around the blank space. The voice-in-off continues: "but that allows me to immerse myself again in Mexican culture [. . .] but this time in an unconventional way" (2:21) that immediately precedes screen-capture footage of a YouTube page that plays a video called "Reaction to execution of Manuel Mendez Leyva."

While the web-savvy viewer would easily recognize the animated layout of YouTube and Web 2.0 features like the *reaction video* genre, the

Figure 5.1. *Reality 2.0* screenshot. *Source:* Orozco, Víctor, dir. *Reality 2.0.* Mexico: 2012. Online: https://orozcovictor.com/film/reality-2-0/.

amount of views displayed, and the panel of suggested videos on the side based on a taxonomy of tags and user behavior, the scene streams an execution by narco-traffickers that has been posted online.[14] As the viewer and the protagonist watch the video player, the horror and shock of a live-captured execution reaches the web user through the sound and subtitles from the YouTube video even though the actual footage is not shown. In this scene, both the viewer and the protagonist experience an event twice and thrice removed from the violent event that is framed within a cyberspace that had very few regulations at the time to censor or limit graphic content. The multilayered confrontation occurs as a mirror effect that distorts reality at every point of reflection since the viewer of the short film is face to face with the reactors to the execution posted online. In a purely directional sense, the viewer (sitting in for the narrator) becomes the object of disgust, seen as a voyeur or tourist in a corner of cyberspace that amplifies and normalizes violence in Mexican narco-warfare.

Curiously, the effect of projecting web voyeurism creates a type of closed-loop between filming, viewing, and web-usership. While many examples of cinematic voyeurism have played with this technique, the uncanny sensation of watching and being watched anonymously through screens is frequently evoked in the emerging film genres of Internet Horror and Desktop Cinema.[15] This effect of blurring web viewership and usership creates an implication that remote observation is a participatory act in itself that is not neutral or passive. The ability to "like," "share," and "comment" on nonsimulated violence and its shocking reactions convert a private encounter on a personal device into a public recognition of narcos as emboldened internet celebrities. The feedback loop between offline behaviors and online reactions exemplified in this scene reflects a posthuman order in which the technologization of the human is not a Terminator-like android but the ever-connected self that constructs worldviews and realities based on interactions and impulses available on the Participatory Web. N. Katherine Hayles makes this connection early on since she links the virtualization of materialism as disembodied information that seeks an embodiment in the posthuman.[16] In other words, the human who interacts closely with intelligent machines becomes implicated in a feedback loop of cognition in which machine-thinking and human-thinking inform the other. In the context of Mexico, the posthuman web user could be better articulated as a *robo sacer*, or a dehumanized, marginal human whose "identity is the way in which those in power signal certain individuals as less than human due to their relationship—or lack thereof—with technology."[17] Dalton explains that the *robo sacer* subjectivity is that of an oppressed technologized body that is not seeking to transcend race and class like the idealizations of Donna Haraway's postmodern cyborg, for example, but that the *robo sacer* is able to appropriate the same technological tools that repress them to later make themselves understood in communities online and/or outside of the national space.[18] In this sense, the *robo sacer* do not need to modernize themselves as mestizo, hybrid, or racially transcendent to access and use web technologies to their benefit.

From the standpoint of the Mexican *robo sacer* in *Reality 2.0*, the narcos themselves are performing *robo sacer* subjectivities who are reappropriating web tools and platforms to publicize their violence over figures of the state and the Mexican Drug War at large (politicians, police, betrayers). Considering that one of the essential genres of Web 2.0 was the weblog, the blog space was one of the main platforms that became weaponized by narcos[19] and infiltrated by shifty pirates and tourists[20] who were constantly negotiating truths and false claims of explicit narco violence. Orozco's description of the initial investigation that led to *Reality 2.0* describes his own tourism in a blog space that highlighted the brutality coming out of Mexico during that time in comparison to the relative peace of his life in Germany. He explained that he came upon the blog of a Spanish scholar who was writing their dissertation on the Zetas narco-trafficking group in

Mexico. Because of the number of mentions of the word, "Zetas" in the online text, the blog soon became the number-one search result on Google. In the comment section of the blog, users began to post their testimonies and local knowledge about Zetas in their region, and soon enough Zetas began to respond and ignite disputes until the comment section became a cyber-battleground for narcos. While many visitors of the site suspected that some of the so-called narcos were in fact trolls or pirates, one of the self-proclaimed narcos threatened the life of a named police chief. Orozco explained, "Well, the next day the police chief was cut to pieces [. . .] it actually happened. Then, another narco would respond in the comments and make a threat and it would happen. It was like being a witness to a war that started online in the craziest way and in the most unlikely place like a doctoral student's blog."[21] Orozco's fascination with the audacity of the narcos to publish intimate details of their personal life and acts of violence as a point of pride led him to other blogs like *El Blog del Narco* where he described the ease of geographically locating their posts and activities through applications like Google Earth. Orozco was not alone in his interest in narco spaces online; Emily Hind's work on *El Blog del Narco* (BDN) discusses the popularity of narco content in the form of blogs, Facebook pages, and YouTube communities during Web 2.0 years, explaining that at the peak of BDN, unique visits to the site were clocking in at around three million per month.[22]

The rest of the film goes on to remix found footage and sound online against a voiceover narration that calmly yet remorsefully describes the absorption of violence in Mexico as an explainable effect. A scene at the seven-minute mark animates a young boy playing a classic arcade game as the voice narrates: "The manipulation of fear by the Mexican government is similar to the one used by George Bush in his war against terrorism [. . .] and the drug trafficker's response has been similar to the one used by Al Qaeda" ["La instrumentalización del miedo por parte del gobierno Mexico se asemeja la utilizada por George Bush en su guerra contra el terrorismo. La respuesta del narco ha sido semejante a la que utilizó Al Qaeda"] (7:01–7:24). At the mention of Al Qaeda, the two-bit arcade game launches into a first-person shooter (FPS) game in which the player must mercilessly spray bullets into enemies on sight. The narration continues as the game mode switches to other FPS games with smoother and more sophisticated graphics, indicating an upgrade in experiential violence through gaming platforms: "Right now drug traffickers upload videos to YouTube where they interrogate, torture and execute hostages. In this media war, the drug traffickers express their feelings and their morale. They have developed their own aesthetic of horror. With this, they portray on the Internet their indisputable reality [. . .] this Reality 2.0 that is violently argued from the comfort of an Internet café" ["Ahora, los narcos suben a YouTube videos donde interrogan, torturan y ejecutan rehenes. En esta guerra mediática, el narco expresa sus sentimientos y su moral y han desarrollado su propia estética del horror. Con esto, retratan por Internet su realidad inobjetable, esa realidad 2.0 que se argumentan desde la comodidad de un cibercafé a chingadazos"] (7:24–7:45). The visual amplification of this commentary in *Reality 2.0* ropes in the viewer, gamer, web user, politician, and narco in the same arena as co-conspirators of violence both online and offline. The messaging is bleak since Orozco's narration suggests that the Mexican government's appropriation of fear tactics from their northern neighbor inspired the narco backlash in a form of domestic terrorism, which characterizes the militarization of the ongoing Mexican Drug War since 2006. By dropping the viewer in the first-person view of popular shoot-to-kill video games during this narration, *Reality 2.0* drives home the point that the new media genres like videogames that simulate terroristic violence exist seamlessly alongside web clips that show narcoterrorism take place. Again, the distorted mirror effect from this sequence that refracts real life and cyberspace, participant and voyeur, narco and politician is amplified by how animation can convey the surrealness and abstraction of web clips that are user generated and instantly shared in the era of Web 2.0.

While the gritty and wobbly animation style of *Reality 2.0* is meant to remix footage of "real" experiences in Mexico with metaphorical scenes that document the witnessing of narco-violence through the participatory web, the overall mood is that of nostalgia for the warmth and macabre essence of Mexico against the cold and scientifically rational zeitgeist of Germany. Again, the skill of curating sound, image, and animation style from web clips is the driving force of this anima-doc that contrasts the extreme violence occurring every day in Mexico against the calm security of Germany. The concluding narration declares this by elaborating on an early observation in the film about the prevalence of rabbits in Germany: "I've realized that the rats never evolved into rabbits in Germany. Instead, in Mexico, this surreal country, we managed to transform rabbits into rats" ["Me he dado cuenta que realmente las ratas nunca evolucionaron en conjeos en Alemania, sino que en Mexico, este país surrealista, nosotros hicimos que los conejos se transformaran en ratas"] (10:15–10:25).

Retrato Político

Six months before Enrique Peña Nieto's presidential election in Mexico on July 1, 2012, filmmaker and animator Güicho Núñez created a Facebook group named "Retrato Politico" with the concept that friends and users who were not necessarily artists or animators could participate in a collective protest against political corruption. The rules were simple: add a head onto a screen capture of a headless political figure. Núñez himself provided the images of political figures and removed their heads, and then uploaded the screen captures into albums in the Facebook group. The users would then download the image and add a head however they could whether through programs like Adobe Photoshop, Microsoft Paint, or even through printing, drawing, and re-scanning analogue to a digital image. At the time of launching the group, the project was not presented nor necessarily even conceived of as a short film, but as Retrato Político's Facebook group began to take on a life of its own, Núñez began rotoscoping the images and compiling them into a digital-born animated film with a Creative Commons license. Núñez revealed that he did not end up spending even one peso on the film itself, which also speaks to the spirit of the project as a cultural object that was open to the voluntary participation of the group members who contributed whatever they could with whatever was available to them (26:30).[23]

Retrato politico, a short film that runs at 2 minutes and 20 seconds, presents itself to the viewer as a political speech on a faulty television set, which curiously combines the web and television genres through animation. Looking as if the viewer were flipping through channels on a television set in Mexico, the first scenes are snippets of a melodramatic domestic dispute followed by another scene of the Pope setting a dove into flight. Then, the television settles on the headless politician who begins to deliver a speech to a crowd of constituents who applaud the deeply ironic and demeaning discourse. The speech begins with: "Countrymen and citizens, stupid jackasses. Dull conformist and sleeping people. Thanks to your attitude, ineptitude, and obedience, bunch of sheep, this country will still be shit." ["Compatriotas y ciudadanos, ibéciles de mierda. Pueblo dormido conformista y aburrido. Gracias a su actitud, ineptitud y obediencia, bola de borregos, este país seguirá siendo una mierda"] (0:15–0:36). After the first round of applause, the collage montage sets forth at a dizzying speed that challenges the viewer to quickly recognize the faces of popular culture icons, many of which stem from US cultural references like Mr. Burns from *The*

Simpsons, Ronald McDonald, the Terminator, Barbie, and Marilyn Monroe (see figure 5.2). As the devastatingly sarcastic political speech continues, the speed and changeability of the figurehead create an effect that is well-situated to simulate the hyper-speed of the neoliberal and capitalist nature of cyberculture propelled in large part by the US and the metropoles of Western Europe. The tone of this Trojan-horse effect echoes the fear that many internet theorists voice about online globalization as a charade for Western capitalist hegemony.[24] In these debates, local vs. global dichotomies tend to underestimate the antiglobalization mobilization of internet actors online, and, in the case of the Retrato Politico project, the participants that consciously illustrate the overlap between cultural and capitalist hegemony in (new) media genres.

The collective that Núñez curated for Retrato Político, is another example of *robo sacer* work that wields the technological tools to animate meme-like images that call out hypocritical "fine print" of political speeches and figureheads. The "beheading" of politicians to later modify them with existing images like celebrities, animals, and recognizable internet jokes draws upon online meme culture that functions as a string of interpretation and humor based on mimicry, remixing, and repackaging content. This attribute of memes "is highly compatible to the way that culture is formed in the so-called era of Web 2.0, which is marked by application platforms for facilitating user-generated content."[25] If the *Retrato político* viewer were

Figure 5.2. Screenshot from *Retrato olítico. Source:* Núñez, Güicho, dir. *Retrato politico* (Mexico: 2012). Vimeo. https://vimeo.com/61380043.

to be able to pause at any point in the montage, they could observe an individual frame contributed by a Facebook user that drives home the point that politicians are superficially serving public interests when in fact they are just another convenient pawn of neoliberal interests that perpetuates corruption and violence in Mexico. During the 2012 elections, this was a strong opinion surrounding Enrique Peña Nieto's candidacy perpetuated by the mass student protests of #YoSoy132 as his appearance was that of a handsome, well-spoken political figure that distracted from his affiliation with the authoritarian past of the PRI government. More than just the focus on Enrique Peña Nieto, the Yo Soy 132 movement was deeply concerned with Mexico's history of tensions between creativity and consumerism.[26] Mary Long argues in her text on #YoSoy132 that these tensions "echo international discussion about the implications of globalization for the rights of individuals to self-realization and also resonate within the historically recurring discussion of the importance of Mexican youth and their creative and intellectual projects as the agents of future national successes or failure."[27] The compilation of user-generated images in *Retrato politico* on social media reflects the posthuman strategies of the *robo sacer*, which activates an alternative democratic order of creative messaging and communication that are key demands of the online and offline organization of Yo Soy 132.

The speed of the montage in motion is key in *Retrato político* since viewers are only able to glimpse and instantly interpret some of the frames as they fly by, thereby creating an effect that asks the viewer to relate to the content in constant transformation and transition—a founding pillar of animation as a genre. During our interview, I asked Núñez about the particular ability of animation to express political critique, to which he replied: "I think that the biggest quality that animation has is the power to transform. I think that we can deform reality and mold it [. . .] make it what we want. This quality in animation is rebellious in and of itself" (18:00–18:25). Political rebellion is embedded in *Retrato político* not only through the curation and animation of user-modified images but also by the mobilization of the users themselves to contribute to a collective entity of protest in cyberspace. Taylor and Pitman describe similar practices of Latin American digital culture during Web 2.0 as processes that "play with the existing tools of digital technologies in an ambivalent fashion, at times playing with the accepted use of such tools, and at others, reformulating them in a tactical and partially resistant ways in the interstices of the (global, capitalist) system."[28] The ways in which the *Retrato político* project utilized Facebook as a platform to announce, inform, gather, cocreate, and assemble political expressions about Mexico's political corruption demonstrates how Web 2.0 practices can inform animation born in cyberspace, yet remain very much connected to real opinions and resistance grounded in physical place.

The acerbic political denouncement of *Retrato político* raises concerns of the collective's online anonymity in the era of Web 2.0 and the issue of accreditation as it began to circulate around film festivals in Mexico. At the end of the short film, Güicho Núñez's name appears as the director, followed by another frame that names all the contributors to the project. When I asked during our interview if he had any fears of retaliation after including his name and others' names, Núñez replied that he did consider the danger of including the names and so made sure to express to the contributors that he would include their Facebook usernames at the end and not pinpoint which user created which image. He did this to ensure that each user would see their voice credited in the production of the short film as a collaborative exercise of democracy and protest that would later be shown in film festivals with a varying degree of approval. Núñez described one animation festival in Mexico that did not screen *Retrato político* during the scheduled program because of some apparent technical errors, and that the organizers instead proposed to show the film during the award ceremony. On the night of the award ceremony, the film was not shown in the theater but rather on a projector in the street outside the venue with chairs set up for the public to view the film. Núñez speculated: "I'm not sure if it was exactly censorship, but the way that it happened made it so that the people in the street were the ones that were meant to see it, and not those in the film festival."[29] He then commented that it ended up being very satisfying for him to see the film screened for a true public out in the open since this was the objective of creating a collective film that critiqued the political landscape of Mexico during that time (14:30).

The dialogue that *Retrato político* facilitates between cyberspace and the streets of Mexico is not a unilateral conversation but rather a collective and pluralistic one with all of the messiness and shock value that comes with the ideas of the internet as a lawless global village. Indeed, animation was an invaluable tool for Núñez to assemble and communicate a born-digital short film made up of the voices of amateur content creators in Web 2.0. Therefore, the political significance that occurs through the animated sequence of internet art in *Retrato político* forces the viewer to allow the *remix-and-repackage* propeller behind the Participatory Web to generate work as a sum of parts rather than as an individual image posted by a singular user. The result of the collective political portrait ended up being "more of an entity than the project of the individual" (13:30).

Animated Short Film and Web 2.0: Inside Perspectives

In the global cinema and animation industry, short films are often perceived as the stepping-stones of career-bound animators who are experimenting and mastering new techniques, much to the dismay of experienced auteurs that prefer to work with the short format. Largely overshadowed and undervalued in comparison to feature-length films, the short format was actually responsible for cinema's world debut at the turn of the twentieth century. In fact, all films used to be short films, including the projects from the earliest days of hand-drawn animation techniques beginning with Emile Cohl's *Fantasmagorie* (France, 1908) and Latin America's claim to early animation, Cristiano Quirino's *El Apostol* (Argentina, 1919). In the first half of the twentieth century, animated short films habitually accompanied the live-action feature film as a form of preliminary entertainment that often played with comedic and musical tropes like Vaudeville. Now in the twenty-first century, the short film, much less the animated auteur short film, rarely enjoys screen time in mainstream cinemas.[30] As a result, animated short films are mostly showcased for select audiences during film festival programs. While mainstream animation has tended to follow the trajectory of the commercialized feature-length film, experimental animation auteurs have tended to maintain the short length format, which usually does not exceed a total running time of sixty minutes total.[31]

In the era of the Web 2.0, short films have found a new home on video-hosting websites and streaming platforms alongside other digital media such as web clips, music videos, fan-made tribute videos, vines, social media stories, among others. While the short format media object is dominant in the user experience on the Participatory Web, the great return of the short film might be too ambitious to declare in that short films are somehow still pigeonholed as singular narrative cultural objects that reside in "high art" spheres like film school exhibitions and film festivals for critical audiences. Experimental animated short films are arguably even more niched than live-action short films, and therefore usually find themselves in regional and international animation festivals and online archives or as a contender within the category of (experimental) animation in more broadly themed film festivals and collections. Nevertheless, the short film format has been ideal for animators who are embracing technologies that facilitate innovation and experimentation from their film school education or even as self-taught artists whose entire formation is thanks to Web 2.0 resources and tools that began to be integrated into Mexico and Latin America, albeit nonunilaterally compared to the metropoles of Western Europe and North America.

During my interviews with Núñez and Orozco, I asked them about how they envision the connection between short film and experimental animation in their careers, and both replied that the two genres are intimately connected. One reason being that funding for animation projects is easier to come by for short film since feature-length film proposals translate to more time, bigger teams, and more plentiful production resources.[32] Núñez also commented that he believes that there is a certain quality of animated short films that come along with smaller budgets. He explained, "We have to become much more creative to finish these projects, especially in the realm of experimental animation—it's harder to get grants but then it's actually easier to do the projects. I prefer the world of the animated short film above all because it represents all of the input and work of the whole team rather than a feature film that has to fill up time and to please the producers. I think that's why the short film genre will never die."[33]

The trajectory from film school formation to grant-funded projects to the industry might represent the typical path of hopeful filmmakers and professional animators. Yet the rise of digital animation techniques in the late twentieth century through the turn of the twenty-first century shifted the industry-bound animation by film school graduates to more and more self-taught individuals with access to technology, connectivity, and time to carry out a digital animation project. Through online tutorial videos, professional software for online purchase, "cracked"[34] software made available on forms and torrent-sharing sites, and low-cost online professionalization courses,[35] this DIY ("Do-It-Yourself") approach to learning and producing animation through digital tools and resources means that many web users are potentially a few steps away from becoming animators themselves.

In the case of directors Victor Orozco and Güicho Núñez, their approach to animation was almost entirely self-taught and consisted of these same autodidactic experimentations as more tools and methods became available during the years of Web 2.0. Having received degrees in design in Mexico, they both commented during our interviews that the curricula of film production preparation degrees in Mexico were and continue to be largely theoretical, and that more practical skills came about through assisting other filmmakers and apprenticing with animators who were more advanced in their projects. Núñez (2020) commented, "My experience in learning animation was coming from a place of frustration as to why others would not reveal their techniques and secrets, but then again you realize that everything you want to know is all out there. We are living in a moment in which anything that you want to ask about is online" (20:00). Orozco (2020) echoed the same sentiment as he described that the release of software and his curiosity to work out and experiment with new possibilities in those programs led him to progress with his animation skills and release more content. He recalled that he made his first film in the year 2000 because his Macintosh computer came loaded with the software like FinalCut and Flash. He continued, "I had no money to buy a camera or any other filmmaking equipment, so that computer opened my world and I started playing with Flash and made my first movie with that. [. . .] Then I started playing with other software and experimenting with that and, after 18 years, I'm still doing the same thing [. . .] discovering new things" (25:00–25:20). In the case of *Reality 2.0,* he recounted an instrumental update in his Adobe Photoshop software that allowed him to trace over video clips instead of only static images in the program. This formed the basis of his animation approach to *Reality 2.0*, which was animated largely through rotoscoping techniques on Adobe Photoshop.[36]

During the same decade as Web 2.0 development (c. 2004–2014), protest and public dissent against political corruption and narco-related violence in Mexico was expanding and culminating in new streams of dissidence and distribution through participatory platforms like blogs, forums, social network platforms, and video-sharing sites. Both films analyzed in this chapter demonstrate how *Reality 2.0* and *Retrato político* interweave Web 2.0 participation practices, user-created content, and interpretations of violence and political corruption through digital animation techniques and narration. In the case of directors Victor Orozco and Güicho Núñez, the possibilities to produce their short films with Web 2.0 features meant that they as animators could experiment with new techniques on the global web that mirrored and critiqued local and national politics that were grounded in physical space. By mining or crowdsourcing clips online and using rotoscoping techniques to animate and curate the content into visual narratives, both *Reality 2.0* and *Retrato político* are examples of digital-born animated short films that engage with the shifting norms of experimental animation that reflect usership and participation on the Web 2.0.

Notes

1. Manuel Castells, *The Rise of the Network Society* 2nd ed (Oxford: Blackwell, 2009), xxvii.

2. Web 1.0 is known as the "read-only" web since it is characterized by static web pages using Hypertext Mark-up Languages (HTML). Sites from Web 1.0 are only human-compatible and not machine-compatible, meaning that only the webmaster can update users and manage the site rather than machine intelligence. See Pranay Kujur and Bijoy Chhetri, "Evolution of World Wide Web: Journey from Web 1.0 to Web 4.0." *International Journal of Computer Science and Technology* 6, no. 1 (2015): 134.

3. For discussions of usership, see Grant Blank and Bianca C. Reisdorf, "The Participatory Web: A User Perspective on Web 2.0," *Information, Communication & Society* 15, no. 4 (2012). For a discussion of cyberspace, see John Marshall, "Cyber-Space, or Cyber-Topos: The Creation of Online Space," *Social Analysis: The International Journal of Social and Cultural Practice* 45, no. 1 (2001).

4. Tim O'Reilly, "What Is Web 2.0? Design Patterns and Business Models for the Next Generation of Software," *O'Reilly Media*, September 2005, https://www.oreilly.com/pub/a/web2/archive/what-is-web-20.html.

5. Blank and Reisdorf, "The Participatory Web," 538–39.

6. Blank and Reisdorf, "The Participatory Web," 539.

7. The elections of 2012 marked the return of the PRI (Partido Revolucionario Institucional) to power by the election of Enrique Peña Nieto, who was a candidate with a strong campaign based on marketing prowess. In terms of social mobilization as a result of the elections, student movements erupted in protest since they interpreted a PRI victory as a potential restoration of Mexico's long history of authoritarianism under the same party. See Juan C. Olmeda and María Alejandra Armesto, "Mexico: The Return of the PRI to the Presidency," *Revista de la Ciencia Política* 33, no. 1 (2013).

8. Marshall, "Cyber-Space," 94.

9. Claire Taylor and Thea Pitman, eds., *Latin American Cyberculture and Cyberliterature*, (Liverpool: Liverpool University Press, 2007), 11.

10. Yo Soy 132, or #YoSoy132 is also known as "the Mexican Spring," began in May of 2012 by 131 university students who were protesting the PRI (Partido Revolucionario Institucional) candidate, Enrique Peña Nieto and biased media coverage in his favor during the presidential elections. The phrase, "Yo Soy 132" refers to joining the 131 students in solidarity online and also through rallies and marches across Mexico. See Mary K. Long, " 'Yo soy': Public Protest, Private Expression. Contestatory Uses of Social Media by Contemporary Mexican Youth," in *Online Activism in Latin America*, ed. Hilda Chacón (New York: Routledge, 2018), 252.

11. Claire Taylor and Thea Pitman's introduction to *Latin American Cyberculture and Cyberliterature* explain that the most generous statistics as of September

2006 indicate that around 15.1 percent of Latin Americans had direct access to the internet compared to 69.1 percent of the United States population and 51.9 percent of the European Union population. See Taylor and Pitman, *Latin American Cyberculture and Cyberliterature*, 5.

Still, the massive increase of internet usage in Latin America and in Mexico after 2006 indicates a surge in internet participation in a web atmosphere that is largely shaped by neoliberal capitalist sentiments like a deregulated free market system. Hence, the techno-utopian dream of the global, postnational democracy of the web has since smoothed over the inequalities of access and the outdated inheritances of technologies between the so-called Global North and Global South.

12. Interview conducted over Zoom. All the quotations included from Victor Orozco and Güicho Núñez are my own translations since our interviews were conducted entirely in Spanish.

13. Víctor Orozco Ramírez, *Reality 2.0*, 2012. https://orozcovictor.com/film/reality-2-0/.

14. A reaction video is a user-uploaded clip that shows the faces of the viewer(s) as they watch other content that is usually of a shocking or comical nature.

15. Internet Horror and Desktop Cinema are genres that emerged in Web 2.0 years including the commercially successful *Unfriended* (2014), and the award-winning desktop film, *Searching* (2018). Since the COVID-19 global pandemic of 2020, screen-capture recording genres have crossed over heavily into the mainstream media experience including news broadcasts, commercials, and television programming.

16. N. Katherine Hayles, *How We Became Posthuman: Virtual Bodies in Cybernetics, Literature, and Informatics* (Chicago: University of Chicago Press, 1999).

17. David S. Dalton, *Mestizo Modernity: Race, Technology, and the Body in Postrevolutionary Mexico* (University of Florida Press, 2018), 183. Dalton's term is an articulation of Giorgio Agamben's term, homo sacer from *Homo Sacer: Sovereign Power and Bare Life* (1998). See David S. Dalton, *Robo Sacer: Necroliberalism and Cyborg Resistance in Mexican and Chicanx Dystopias* (Nashville, TN: Vanderbilt University Press), introduction.

18. For a discussion of Haraway's cyborg, see Donna Haraway, *Simians, Cyborgs, and Women: The Reinvention of Nature* (New York: Routledge, 2013), chapter 8.

19. One of the most popular narco blogs was *El Blog del Narco* (www.blogdelnarco.com) which spanned just over three years from March 2, 2010, through October 14, 2013. Emily Hind, "On Pirates and Tourists: Ambivalent Approaches to El Blog del Narco," in *Online Activism in Latin America*, ed. Hilda Chacón (New York: Routledge, 2018), 113.

20. Hind explains in her chapter on *El Blog del Narco* that "piracy can turn complacent and tourists can act out in contestatory manners, and thus pirates and tourists share unstable connotations." See Hind, "On Pirates and Tourists," 113.

21. Personal interview on Zoom, 14:30–16:09.

22. Hind, "On Pirates and Tourists," 113.

23. Interview via Zoom.

24. Castells, *The Rise of the Network Society*; Takis Fotopoulos, "Globalisation, the Reformist Left and the Anti-Globalisation Movement," *Democracy and Nature: The International Journal of Inclusive Democracy* 7, no. 2 (2001); Douglas Kellner, "Theorizing Globalization," *Sociological Theory* 20, no. 3 (2002).

25. Limor Shifman, "Memes in a Digital World: Reconciling with a Conceptual Troublemaker," *Journal of Computer-Mediated Communication* 18, no. 3 (2013): 365.

26. Mary Long's exemplifies the themes of Yo Soy 132 by reproducing the text of an event poster by the group from April of 2013: "#SomosCiudadanos NoConsumidores; Imagina, grita, brinca, mueve, llora, informa, sueña, comunica . . . #LosMediosSomosTodos; #ComunicoLuegoexisto; #TodosSomoselMensaje; #Los MediosSeránSocialesOnoSerán (#Somosciudadanos)." Long, " 'Yo soy,' " 253.

27. Long, " 'Yo soy,' " 253.

28. Claire Taylor and Thea Pitman, *Latin American Identity in Online Cultural Production* (New York: Routledge, 2013), 200.

29. Interview conducted via Zoom, 14:00.

30. An exception to this tendency is Pixar's frequent inclusion of animated short films that appear before their feature films in theatres. The award-winning short, *Luxo Jr.* (1986) was a game-changing animated short as its protagonist became emblematic as the jumping lamp that playfully stomps out the the letter "i," in Pixar before turning its light toward the audience.

31. Cynthia Felando, *Discovering Short Films: The History and Style of Live-Action Fiction Shorts* (New York: Palgrave Macmillan, 2015), 12.

32. Zoom interview, 26:30.

33. Zoom interview, 29:00.

34. "Cracked" software refers to professional software and programming that is made available for free (illegally) whereas that same software would normally be purchased officially.

35. Domestika.org is an example of low-cost online courses that are highly detailed and available for many levels of experience. Many of the courses are for specific topics of animation like motion design and 3D techniques. For example, one course might cost less than twenty US dollars, and are often taught by Spanish speakers from Mexico, Spain, and Southern California with subtitling available in English.

36. Zoom interview, 27:00.

Bibliography

Blank, Grant, and Bianca C. Reisdorf. "The Participatory Web: A User Perspective on Web 2.0." *Information, Communication & Society* 15, no. 4 (2012): 537–54.

Castells, Manuel. *The Rise of the Network Society*, 2nd ed. Oxford: Blackwell, 2009.

Chacón Hilda, ed. *Online Activism in Latin America*. New York: Routledge, 2018.

Dalton, David S. *Mestizo Modernity: Race, Technology, and the Body in Postrevolutionary Mexico*. Gainesville: University of Florida Press, 2018.

———. *Robo Sacer: Necroliberalism and Cyborg Resistance in Mexican and Chicanx Dystopias*. Nashville: Vanderbilt University Press, 2023.

Haraway, Donna. *Simians, Cyborgs, and Women: The Reinvention of Nature*. New York: Routledge, 2013.

Hayles, N. Katherine. *How We Became Posthuman: Virtual Bodies in Cybernetics, Literature, and Informatics*. Chicago: University of Chicago Press, 1999.

Hind, Emily. "On Pirates and Tourists: Ambivalent Approaches to El Blog del Narco." In *Online Activism in Latin America*, edited by Hilda Chacón, 113–27. New York: Routledge, 2018.

Felando, Cynthia. *Discovering Short Films: The History and Style of Live-Action Fiction Shorts*. New York: Palgrave Macmillan, 2015.

Fotopoulos, Takis. "Globalisation, the Reformist Left and the Anti-Globalisation Movement.' *Democracy and Nature: The International Journal of Inclusive Democracy* 7, no. 2 (2001): 233–80.

Kellner, Douglas. "Theorizing Globalization," *Sociological Theory* 20, no. 3 (2002): 285–305.

Kujur, Pranay, and Bijoy Chhetri. "Evolution of World Wide Web: Journey from Web 1.0 to Web 4.0." *International Journal of Computer Science and Technology* 6, no. 1 (2015): 134–38.

Long, Mary K. " 'Yo soy': Public Protest, Private Expression. Contestatory Uses of Social Media by Contemporary Mexican Youth." In *Online Activism in Latin America*, edited by Hilda Chacón, 252–72. New York: Routledge, 2018.

Marshall, John. "Cyber-Space, or Cyber-Topos: The Creation of Online Space." *Social Analysis: The International Journal of Social and Cultural Practice* 45, no. 1 (2001): 81–102.

Nuñez, Güicho. 2020, June 5. Interview by author via Zoom.

———. 2013. "Retrato Político / Political Portrait." Uploaded in 2013. Vimeo video, 2:20 min. https://vimeo.com/61380043.

O'Reilly, Tim. "What Is Web 2.0? Design Patterns and Business Models for the Next Generation of Software." O'Reilly Media, 2005, September 30. https://www.oreilly.com/pub/a/web2/archive/what-is-web-20.html. Accessed October 18, 2020.

Olmeda, Juan C., and María Alejandra Armesto. "Mexico: The Return of the PRI to the Presidency." *Revista de la Ciencia Política* 33, no. 1 (2013): 247–67. https://scielo.conicyt.cl/pdf/revcipol/v33n1/art12.pdf. Accessed October 18, 2020.

Orozco, Victor. 2020, June 8. Interview by author on Zoom.

———. 2012. "Reality 2.0." https://vimeo.com/39942381. Accessed October 18, 2020.

———. *Reality 2.0*. Victor Orozco Ramirez, 2012. https://orozcovictor.com/film/reality-2-0/. Accessed October 17, 2020.

Shifman, Limor. "Memes in a Digital World: Reconciling with a Conceptual Troublemaker." *Journal of Computer-Mediated Communication* 18, no. 3 (2013): 362–77.

Taylor, Claire, and Thea Pitman, eds. *Latin American Cyberculture and Cyberliterature*. Liverpool England: Liverpool University Press, 2007.

Taylor, Claire, and Thea Pitman. *Latin American Identity in Online Cultural Production*. New York: Routledge, 2013.

Chapter 6

The Impact of Anime in Mexico-Centered Adult Animation and Global Mexican Representation

Yunuen Ysela Mandujano-Salazar

In Mexico, the 1990s were a decade culturally marked by the boom of Japanese animation—commonly known as anime—among young urban generations. Far from a unique phenomenon, this occurred throughout Latin America, the United States, and other Western countries that were importing and broadcasting numerous titles of anime with considerable success. The global impact of anime by the turn of the century was such that economic and cultural analysts talked about it as part of a potential Japanese cultural invasion and a tool of cultural diplomacy.[1] Although actual policies from Japan were not behind the promotion of anime until the decade of 2010 with the Cool Japan strategies, what is undeniable is that the organic popularity that anime has gained since the 1990s manifested in the emergence of global subcultures of dedicated fans who called themselves *otaku,* a term that is now recognized as a synonym for fans of anime and manga, or Japanese comics.[2]

The popularity of Japanese media content in Mexico was supported during the first decade of the twenty-first century by the widening access to the internet among young generations in urban regions, which allowed them to be part of worldwide fan communities that shared—mostly illegally—anime episodes subtitled or dubbed by themselves, and information about their favorite series. Through said means, Mexican fans of Japanese culture and anime like myself had access to more content than those offered by Mexican open and pay television.

The impact of anime among the generations of Mexicans who have been exposed to it during the last three decades can be traced by the emergence of undergraduate and graduate theses exploring *otaku* groups and culture around the country.[3] These have been interested in exploring the practices, narratives, and identity construction of *otaku* communities. However, it remains to be analyzed how anime has impacted the Mexican creators who consumed anime and were inspired either by the style and narrative tools of Japanese productions or by the possibilities of animation aimed at any kind of audience to create their own.

Thus, in this chapter, I aim to explore the influence that anime has had on Mexican creators and the development of adult animated productions related to Mexico that are taking Mexican culture and representation to the global market. I begin with a brief review of the history of anime in Japan. Then, supported by documental analysis, I reconstruct how anime reached the United States and Mexico and, with the widening access to the internet, how online communities of fans formed and exchanged Japanese content that solidified the popularity of anime in North America; I also rely on my own experience and on anecdotal evidence that I have collected throughout my career as a Mexican scholar of Japanese studies. From there, the discussion moves to anime productions in Mexico based on an anime aesthetic. The chapter ends with a discussion of the context of production and main representations of *Onyx Equinox*[4] and *Seis Manos/Six Hands*,[5] where I conclude that anime has inspired young Mexican creators to produce an animation that aims to enrich global representations of their country.

Anime in Japan

Japanese society seems to favor the production of drawings to leave proof of history and express the social likes, anxieties, and expectations of an epoch, usually featuring a mix of real and supernatural elements that were part of folklore.[6] Anime was an evolution of manga—Japanese-style comics—and, even today, most animated titles are adaptations of successful manga stories. It was in the early twentieth century when the first short animated films appeared in Japan. Some were foreign productions and others were created locally. In both cases, they were called *senga eiga*.[7] During the first half of the twentieth century, when Japan was immersed in militaristic imperial campaigns and nationalism was being pushed by the government, cinema—including animated films aimed at both the young and adults—was strictly regulated and scrutinized by educators and ideologues to reflect the national ideology that was being widely advocated at the time.[8] Although this certainly limited the themes of those first animations, the ideological power of the genre—especially among young audiences—was clear from the beginning.[9]

Immediately after the end of World War II, most previous anime productions were destroyed, as they were considered dangerous nationalistic propaganda tools by the Allied forces that supervised Japan's reconstruction. In this context, occupying forces imposed new restrictions on the topics of cinema: Japanese films should be about topics that facilitated the configuration of a pacific, democratic society.[10] In any case, animation was expensive and Japanese creators and society could not afford to invest in it.

Nevertheless, in the 1960s, amid a growing economy, the popularization of television sets in homes, and a society that desired to leave behind the terror of war, Japanese animation took off, prompted by the foundation of important production houses like Toei Animation in 1956 and Mushi Productions in 1961—this by the hand of Osamu Tezuka, considered the father of contemporary anime.[11] Tezuka produced numerous amateur manga while studying medicine; in the 1960s, Toei Animation asked him to write the script and codirect an animation called *Saiyuki* [*Going to the West*], marking the beginning of his professional career in this genre.[12] In 1963, the first animated television series from Tezuka's studio was broadcasted in black and white: *Tetsuwan Atomu* or—as it is known in Western countries—*Astro Boy.* After this title, he produced many others in color, among the most famous outside Japan: *Jungle Taitei* (*Kimba the White Lion*) in 1965 and *Ribbon no Kishi* (*Princess Knight*) in 1967. These animations were very popular in Japan and soon attracted the attention of foreign distributors who took them to other Asian countries, Europe, and the American continent.[13] Tezuka developed distinctive aesthetics, and an artistic and production style that would become characteristic of Japanese animation from then on.

With the success of Tezuka, numerous popular manga titles were turned into animated series or movies. This gave a further boost to manga in Japan, and both genres soon became widely popular in postwar society.[14] In the following years, other talented artists nurtured the development of Japanese animation. In 1985, Hayao Miyazaki and Isao Takahata established their own production company, Studio Ghibli. From this studio, in the 2000s, the world would get enormously acclaimed titles such as *Spirited*

Away, Howl's Moving Castle, and *Ponyo*. Between 1961 and 1990, more than seven hundred animated series and movies were produced in Japan, covering a wide range of topics, and priming a wide array of the audience to enjoy the country's distinctive animation.[15]

Anime, as it came to be known globally, established itself as a genre of visual media that included more subgenres than realistic cinema and television, most of the time mixing some supernatural element within the stories. Contrary to the dominant perception in Western countries of animation being for children or presenting only fantastic, innocent, or comedy themes, in Japan, the adult audience eagerly consumed animation. As a result, anime included all kinds of topics and issues, even those considered taboo or difficult to portray in other types of media. Different subgenres of anime emerged for housewives, working men, teenage boys, teenage girls, children, and older people, focusing on all types of themes such as history, science fiction, sports, food, family life, romance, sexual adventures, violence, pets, children, and so on.[16]

The passion for anime and manga among some people in Japan gave place to the phenomenon of the *otaku*, a word originally used to refer politely to another person or another person's home. Because manga and anime artists had to spend most hours confined to their offices, which usually were in their homes, the word began to be used to refer to them. Afterward, manga and anime fans began to call themselves *otaku* as well.[17] When anime became popular around the world, non-Japanese fans adopted the word to identify themselves and their communities.[18]

The Popularization of Anime across the Pacific and the Emergence of Borderless Online *Otaku* Communities

Although several successful anime series were exported to the United States and Latin America between the 1970s and 1980s, most of these were not recognized as Japanese by the audience and were considered typical cartoons aimed at children. They were, using Iwabuchi's notion, culturally odorless; they did not refer specifically to Japanese society or culture.[19] Titles such as *Heidi*, *Remi*, *Candy Candy*, and *Princess Knight* were children or teenager-focused stories about European or American characters with corresponding sceneries and contexts. Others showed futuristic worlds that, during their translation, lost the original Japanese names and the stories were completely Westernized—as in the case of *Voltron* and *Robotech*. Hence, although the design of the characters was distinctively different from that of American animation, for the American and Latin American children and teenagers of the time it may have been difficult to identify its origin. There is a lack of academic references on the impact of anime on those first-exposed audiences but anecdotal evidence suggests that Mexican youngsters who watched those titles on open television during the 1970s and early 1980s thought they were watching American cartoons. In my own research on anime fandom communities in Mexico, I have heard many people say that Japan was hardly in their imaginary as they consumed anime in their childhood. At the time, open television, radio, and newspapers were the only media accessible to them and, with the entertainment content controlled by a couple of national-level media corporations—one private (Televisa) and one public (Imevisión)—their imaginary of the world was built by Mexican productions and those imported from the United States.

This changed during the 1980s as US cinema began to popularize and express admiration for Japanese culture following the heavy investment of Japanese corporations in Hollywood (i.e., Sony, Matsushita, and JVC/Victor).[20] Successful movies like the original *Karate Kid* saga (1984–1994) and *Bloodsport* (1988) were focused on Japanese martial arts and traditional cultural elements. Other popular US films presented almost negligible references, either with admiration or fear, to the technological advancement of the Asian country. We see this, for example, in *Back to the Future III* (1990), *Gremlins* (1984), *Die Hard* (1988). Through Hollywood, the popularization of Japan's traditional cultural elements—as viewed by the United States—grew in the Western world, including Mexico. During the late 1980s and early 1990s, I repeatedly watched these movies with family and friends on open television in Mexico, because the main broadcaster at the time—Televisa—dedicated the slot of Saturday afternoons on one of its channels to popular American movies with different themes every week. These Hollywood-produced images of Japan and its culture were, perhaps, the earliest that fed my imaginary of the Asian nation.

In the 1990s, the importation and broadcasting of numerous "*nihon-seikusai*" (trans. Japaneseness-smelling) products—borrowing another Iwabuchi's notion—exposed new generations of American and Mexican audiences to anime.[21] These audiences began calling anime by its name, and they—myself included—became interested in its cultural specificity. At that time, the television signal of Televisa and Televisión Azteca (Imevision between 1985 and 1993, then privatized) easily reached all urban regions in Mexico. Both companies had timeslots dedicated to children's content and, during the first half of the 1990s, both broadcasted some groundbreaking anime.

In 1992, then-Imevision premiered *Saint Seiya* (in Mexico, *Caballeros del Zodiaco*). This was a story about teenage warriors who had to fight epic battles to save the world. Although most of the story is developed in other parts of the world and is based on Greek mythology, some references are made to Japan and there are a few Japanese characters. Most importantly, however, it was explicitly promoted as Japanese animation. This anime was remarkably popular among children and teenagers, particularly boys. This popularity prompted the production of diverse merchandise and marketing campaigns from products directed to young people who began to use the characters. On the other hand, in 1994, the FIFA World Cup was to be celebrated in the United States. Soccer is the most popular media sport in Mexico, and having the World Cup so close was the perfect context for Televisa to broadcast *Captain Tsubasa* (in Mexico, *Supercampeones*), which was a story about Japanese children who dream of becoming professional soccer players. Contrary to *Saint Seiya,* this anime was completely focused on 1980s Japan, showing sceneries of big and small cities, the lifestyle, customs, and people of the Asian country. The Mexican version respected that background, although it Westernized the names of the characters. These two anime were very popular among early-1990s Mexican youngsters, and both broadcasters soon increased their offer of Japanese animation with titles that were being already introduced in the United States and Europe: *Dragon Ball, Sailor Moon, Ranma ½,* and *Inuyasha,* and later *Naruto, Cowboy Bebop, Yu-Gi-Oh, One Piece, Death Note,* and *Pokémon,* among many others. These anime were big commercial successes launched with official licenses by American and Mexican television studios and accompanied by the selling of official merchandise in these countries. Japanese videogames—particularly those related to Nintendo and Sony—became also highly popular.

In Mexico, both television corporations dedicated special timeslots and even TV shows to talk only about anime, Japanese videogames, and the anime conventions that were increasingly appearing throughout the neighboring country to the north. However, the undeniable popularity of anime among children and teenagers in Mexico caused a negative reaction among some sectors of society. Mexican broadcasters imported anime titles and, because they were animations, they marketed them as family content, broadcasting them at times when children watched television, regardless of the topics and original intended audience in Japan. Some of the titles were certainly aimed at older teenagers and a more mature audience for their violence and sexual content. The cultural ignorance of the broadcasters and the general population caused some conservative sectors to accuse anime and video games of being even diabolic—because of the constant supernatural elements they involved—and harmful to children.[22]

During that same decade, the internet opened a new channel of communication for fans of anime around the world, which would benefit also Mexicans. As the internet became accessible to common people in advanced economies, Western teenagers and young adult fans of Japanese culture, anime, and manga began to create networks with Asian and Western expatriates in Japan to share Japanese content that was not yet available outside that country. Beyond playing a key role in the diffusion of anime throughout the Western world, these online communities also challenged the idea that animation was only for children. Indeed, most of the active members were older teenagers and young adults. Non-Japanese fans adopted the label of *otaku* to identify themselves on the internet and at comics conventions around the world, which began to have distinguishable sections for fans of Japanese content.[23] Soon, non-Japanese *otaku* communities, online and offline, grew, shared information, and recorded content officially available only in Japan and in the Japanese language. These multinational, multicultural, and multilingual communities worked to create subtitles in English, Chinese, Spanish, and other languages for the benefit of fans around the world. As Newitz noticed very early, the phrase "Subtitled by fans for fans. Not for sale or rent" could be found in most of the Japanese content that circulated illegally at conventions, in video rental stores, and among fan clubs outside Japan.[24] When the video-sharing technology for the internet evolved and the domestic connection speed in different countries allowed it, the fan-subbed anime inundated *otaku* communities that united people from all over the world.

One of the most relevant *otaku* communities was Crunchyroll, which was started in 2006 by college students at the University of California as a piracy site run by donations that shared anime and Japanese drama series and movies subtitled by fans. It became one of the main sites for fans of Japanese content outside Japan to watch titles not officially released in their countries. In a couple of years, after gathering some resources, it was turned into an official online distributor of numerous Japanese anime, dramas, and movies subtitled in English. Bought by Sony in 2021, it has become a producer and distributor of original "anime" giving the chance for non-Japanese artists who grew up watching and admiring anime to share their own hybrid creations.[25]

Another of the big names behind the anime boom in the United States was a company called Viz, founded in 1986 by Seiji Horibuchi, a Japanese immigrant involved in the business of cultural products. Interested in publishing manga in English, Horibuchi approached the director of one of the largest Japanese publishing firms—Shogakukan—and got the startup capital to launch Viz Communications in California.[26] In the 2000s, the company became Viz Media through various strategic mergers with Japanese manga and anime publishers and producers. Through this means, it became one of the major anime, manga, and Japanese film distributors in the United States and around the world.[27]

Anime influenced Gen-X and millennial fandom in the United States in such a way that numerous animations and live-action movies have been produced in this country that either take elements of anime aesthetics or directly make live adaptations of Japanese stories. These are then shown on streaming services or network channels. Titles such as *The Powerpuff Girls, Teen Titans, Ultimate Spider-Man*, and *Batman: The Brave and the Bold*, to name a few, are inspired by the artistic style of anime. Live-action adaptations of Japanese manga/anime can be found in *Dragon Ball Evolution, Death Note, Ghost In The Shell*, and *Pokémon Detective Pikachu.*[28]

These developments in the United States market of Japanese content and *otaku* communities encouraged the popularity of Japanese media products among Mexican teenagers and young adults during the 1990s and 2000s. The increasingly available access to the internet in urban areas helped Mexican *otaku* to feed their interest through the online *otaku* communities that were greatly shaped by American fans. At the beginning of the 1990s, as a Mexican middle-class teenager living in a mid-sized urban region, I depended on what the mainstream media in my country offered of Japanese content. Nevertheless, at the end of the decade, when I first got my personal computer connected to the internet via a phone modem, I would wake up daily at 4 a.m.—when the connection was relatively faster and free—to search for anime news, images to print, fanfiction, and so on, that I could share and exchange with other friends at school, who also got internet access at home or went to internet cafes increasingly popular at the time. By the mid-2000s, my friends and I exchanged home-burned CDs with new anime that was being released in Japan and we had found subbed in English or Spanish in *otaku* communities. At the same time, as pay television became widely available in urban areas, the licensed offer of anime of all genres increased and was broadcasted over and over. Some old titles, such as *Remi, Heidi,* and *Candy Candy* were shown again on open television, this time visibly identified as anime. This was the golden age of Japanese animation in Mexico.

Young Mexican anime fans, following the American and European trends, began to identify as *otaku* and the first conventions and anime clubs began to appear around the country, normalizing them as a subculture. Anime/manga became a reason for Mexican and other Spanish-speaking *otaku* to exchange information and form communities based on their likes of a particular title or genre, also inspiring the scholars' interest in their identity formation and community sense and interactions—in person and through virtual communities that trespassed national and ethnic borders.[29] Since then, numerous undergraduate and graduate theses in Mexico on self-identified *otaku* have tried to unveil personal and group identity construction processes, stereotypes, and stigmas, and highlight the intercultural element that is at the base of all *otaku* outside Japan.[30]

By the second decade of the century, anime consumption among teenagers and adults became normalized and the *otaku* subculture remains strong in Mexico into the present. Japanese animation changed the perception among Mexican people that cartoons were a genre meant only for children. Moreover, it is undeniable that, as in the case of the United States, in Mexico, anime also impacted many talented people who would go on to produce animations in their home country. Because of their passion for anime, these aspiring artists began drawing, or liking to draw, and, after consuming anime, they saw their style influenced somehow by Japanese animation. This is what happened to Sofía Alexander, the creator of *Onyx Equinox*. Furthermore, as anime became mainstream around the world, Mexican creators began collaborating with international studios or distribution companies. As a result, the hybridization of Mexico-focused stories and anime aesthetics has become more common, as in the case of *Seis Manos*.

American Animation and Mexico-Inspired Stories

In 2017, Pixar and Disney successfully exploited Mexican scenarios and characters in the CG animated children's story *Coco*.[31] In another text, I have argued that this movie's representation of Mexican people and culture and the reiterative narrative of authenticity around its promotion are problematic because Hollywood builts a discourse on what Mexico and Mexican people are and should be, imposing those ideas even on Mexicans.[32]

Despite a seemingly positive tone, they nurtured stereotypes and limited the imaginaries that circulate throughout the world. For a Mexican society that is changing and experiencing a rupture of traditional values, the movie feels indoctrinating and propagandistic.[33] Nevertheless, the success of this family-oriented animated movie seemed to open the door to more diverse animated productions focused on Mexico.

In July 2019, at the Anime Expo in the United States, Netflix—the giant streaming site—announced a new series for the fall that it labeled as anime and that would be set in 1970s Mexico: *Seis Manos* or *Six Hands*; the production was from Viz Media and Powerhouse Animation Studios. This would be the first adult-oriented animation centered in Mexico and intended for a global audience. It was not that Netflix asked for a Mexico-centered series, but a succession of events opened the door for a production that had Mexican people and culture as main themes in a format that was inspired by anime.

According to the diverse interviews that creators Brad Graeber and Álvaro Rodríguez have given to the media, they had been working on the idea for many months and were pitching it around without response. However, in late 2017, when they took it to Viz Media, the company became interested in producing it and, when this company took it to Netflix, the streaming corporation quickly decided to add it as part of its original "anime" series.[34] Interestingly, it was around this time when *Coco* was breaking all records at the box office in Mexico.[35]

Graeber is a Texan executive and producer of Powerhouse Animation who has said that anime influenced him by showing that animation can be for all demographics and for representing adult themes without losing the opportunity to add supernatural or fantasy elements. Accordingly, when most American animation continued to be made for children and it became common practice to use CG—as in the case of *Coco*—he wanted to make 2D adult animation.[36] On the other hand, Rodríguez is a Mexican American screenwriter who was born and bred in southern Texas. Although he also grew up watching anime, he was more interested in and influenced by traditional cinema and television in which he worked before.[37] Graeber had wanted to produce an original adult animation for Powerhouse, and, when he met Rodríguez, they developed the idea of a supernatural action story situated in 1970s Mexico that mixed Shaolin, drug mafia, and Mexican mysticism elements. They invited Daniel Domínguez—a Latinx writer of Puerto Rican descent who had experience working in animation—to join them, and *Seis Manos* took form.[38] Netflix released the story of eight episodes in October 2019, leaving the door open for further seasons.

One year later, in November 2020, Crunchyroll, the now Sony-owned online streaming site of anime and other Japanese and Asian content, premiered *Onyx Equinox,* an original adult anime of action, violence, fantasy, and drama centered on Mesoamerican cultures that had as its main character an Aztec boy, Izel. The anime was created by Mexican illustrator Sofía Alexander. Alexander was born and grew up in Cancún, part of the Mexican Caribbean and a place that belonged to the ancient Maya civilization, which still hosts many important archeological sites. In diverse interviews, she stated that her grandfather had Indigenous roots and that he transmitted pride in their culture to her and her brothers and sister. As a result, Mesoamerican cultures were always a theme of interest for her.[39] In 2007, when she was in college, Alexander took inspiration from *Lord Of The Rings'* magical epic world and her likes of anime/manga own epic stories like *Rurouni Kenshin, Wolf Rain* and Japanese videogames like *The Legend of Zelda* to develop a comic strip about an Indigenous boy whose sister is offered in a ritual sacrifice and begins the quest to save the living from a blood-thirsty Aztec god.[40] By her senior project, in 2011, this story and characters had evolved, and she was close to signing a contract to turn it into a comic. Ever since her childhood watching anime, however, her dream had been to see one of her stories and illustrations become an animated series. In 2018, she approached an executive producer of Crunchyroll to offer her the story of *Onyx Equinox* and began working to transform it into an original anime series of twelve episodes.[41]

Alexander has constantly declared that she had a direct influence on the style, aesthetics, and format of anime for *Onyx Equinox.* In mid-2021, the Annecy International Animation Film Festival—perhaps the largest event dedicated to animation in the world—hosted a panel about the influence of anime on international creators. In this, along with other creators, she shared that she had been exposed to anime as a child—*Dragon Ball, Saint Seiya*—and that it was *Cardcaptor Sakura* that inspired her to draw in that style, without even realizing that these were Japanese animations. As she grew up, she began to appreciate the wide range of topics in anime—not just for children—and how they portrayed Japanese cultural elements. This further inspired her as a creator because she wanted to share some of her heritage in a way that would be attractive for everyone to watch (Baron 2021; Campbell 2021). She began reading a lot of manga and, initially, wanted to be a comic book artist. When she learned about storyboarding in college and worked as a freelancer storyboard artist on some American productions, however, she realized she could become an animator and create the stories she wanted in the anime style she liked.[42]

In Crunchyroll, Alexander worked with Japanese animator Kuni Tomita as her supervising director, who had worked in big anime titles like *Candy Candy, Battleship Yamato,* and *Akira.* This gave *Onyx Equinox* more legitimacy as an original anime. Nevertheless, its essence is hybrid. Alexander did not just want to do any anime; she wanted to create a magical story that had as many authentic Mesoamerican elements and mythologies as possible. So, she did her research, got an anthropologist and archeologist as a consultant, and another Mexican artist, Mónica Robles, to collaborate on the project.[43] She said that one of her objectives was for the audience—Mexican and otherwise—to know more about those cultures. She hoped that her animation would spark greater interest in pre-Columbian cultures while at the same time showing a different representation of Mexicans and their diverse cultures than those usually shown in Hollywood.[44]

Mexican Representation in American "Anime"

Seis Manos follows the story of Isabella, Jesús, and Silencio (nickname) in the (fictional) small traditional town of San Simón in 1970s Mexico. They are young people who became orphans when they were children and were taken by a Chinese immigrant, Chiu, who trained them in martial arts and Chinese philosophy. Silencio's real name is unknown; he lost the ability to talk after a drug lord known as El Balde cut his tongue off when he was a child after also killing his parents. He was taken by Chiu and grew up along with Isabella and Jesús peacefully until people related to El Balde appeared and, using supernatural abilities, killed Chiu. The three orphans try to avenge the death of Chiu. El Balde and his allies turn out to be also a kind of cult; they venerate Santa Nucifera—a statue that resembles the Santa Muerte—and receive supernatural powers by the consumption of something that appears to be a drug but turns out to be tears and saliva of the mother of El Balde, a witch that is trapped inside the statue of Santa Nucifera. In their quest for justice, the orphans meet a local policewoman named García and an African American DEA (US Drug Enforcement Agency) agent named Brister who has traveled to Mexico in search of El Balde. There is also a group of Catholic priests who turn out to be drug dealers, a *curandera,* and townspeople.

This series has a mixed aesthetic of Japanese anime and American action animation similar to that of DC productions. It is in the complex and supernatural story development, graphic violent images, and adult themes where anime influence is most evident. *Seis manos* has the atmosphere of Quentin Tarantino, Jackie Chan, and Bruce Lee movies, but it also combines traditional mainstream and underground Mexican elements. It shows an environment that is certainly common in rural towns of the center and south of Mexico: a central Catholic church and plaza, Indigenous and mestizo people distinguishable by their traditional or Western clothes, a street market, and images of saints and the Virgen de Guadalupe (figure 6.2).[45] Domingo, one of the town boys, a character that is important in the first episode, is shown wearing the Mexican national soccer team uniform. These accurate rural representations are somehow exacerbated by more stereotypical elements such as the mariachi environmental music or the colorful *papel picado* that are shown as part of daily life.

The very Mexican ambiance of the town San Simon contrasts with the Chinese style of the house of Chiu, where Isabella, Jesus, and Silencio live and practice kung fu. Regarding this, the creators have said in interviews that they were inspired by the migration of Chinese people who arrived in Mexico in the 1970s.[46] The music is one of the elements that emphasizes each culture or their hybridization. In every scene that focuses on the town square, the imagery shown in figure 6.1 is accompanied by loud mariachi

Figure 6.1. San Simón's central plaza and church. *Source:* Graeber, Brad, and Álvaro Rodríguez, creators. *Seis manos*. Season 1, Episode 1, "Toppled." Bulliner, Willis, dir. 2019. Streaming, Netflix, 2019.

Figure 6.2. The house of the curandera with an image of the Virgen de Guadalupe and papel picado mixing images of Saints and Death. *Source:* Graeber, Brad, and Álvaro Rodríguez, creators. *Seis manos.* Season 1, Episode 3, "Night of the Wolves." Willis Bulliner, dir. 2019. Streaming: Netflix, 2019.

music; by contrast, every scene at Chiu's house has a musical motive with woodwind sounds that suggest an Asian feel. More importantly, the opening piece of every episode mixes strings and trumpets with woodwind instruments and certain motives that evoke mariachi, Western, and Chinese traditional music in an epic-sounding theme.

The Mexican characters are portrayed quite accurately considering that the story developed exclusively in a small rural town, and they are supposed to be locals: all characters are brown and have different hair textures, corporality, and styles. Female characters are strong physically and emotionally. An orphan girl is shown taking care of herself and the other children against the mafia men that have them trapped; policewoman García rejects the explicit machismo of the African American Brister; Isabella is the leader of the group. Interestingly, the Mexican male characters, although apparently of the *macho* type—violent, physically strong, drunk, etc.—do not show the explicit ideological sexism that Brister expresses.

On the other hand, *Onyx Equinox* is a very typical *shonen* (boy) anime. As an animation for an adult audience, it shares the supernatural, violent, and gore elements with *Seis Manos,* but it is completely developed in a pre-Hispanic epoch and, accordingly, unlike the mestizo characters in the other production, here all characters belong to the different Mesoamerican

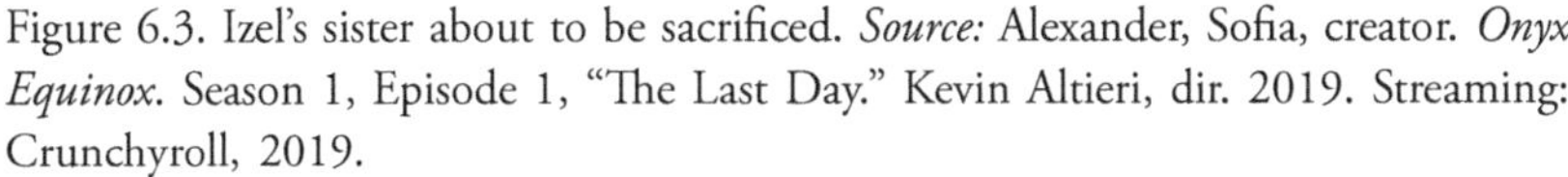
Figure 6.3. Izel's sister about to be sacrificed. *Source:* Alexander, Sofia, creator. *Onyx Equinox*. Season 1, Episode 1, "The Last Day." Kevin Altieri, dir. 2019. Streaming: Crunchyroll, 2019.

ethnic communities of past centuries. The story focuses on Izel, a teenage boy who, after his sister is killed in ritual sacrifice, is chosen by the god Quetzalcoatl to show the god Tezcatlipoca that a human can close the doors of the underground and save the world.

Like many Japanese *shonen* anime protagonists, Izel tends to be less than a hero and has many weaknesses that he eventually overcomes. Along with the supporting human characters, his adventures show many elements of Mesoamerican mythologies. While the human characters' personal histories or personalities are not particularly well developed, the gods are at the heart of the story, showing elements that follow Mesoamerican mythologies. Also, although the drawing of the scenery is quite rough and lacks details, the representation of cultural artifacts, sites, and people seem respectful of the archaeological evidence and evokes what could be living in that time and place in history. An important element is the scores accompanying the scenes, which help evoke the Mesoamerican Indigenous ambiance by emphasizing the sounds of flutes, conches, drums, and feminine vocalization; the opening theme is actually sung in Mayan.

Alexander and her team put great effort into trying to show the richness of these Indigenous cultures. However, they ended up taking many liberties that resulted in some anachronistic errors, for example, mixing

Figure 6.4. A market in the world of Onyx Equinox. *Source:* Alexander, Sofia, creator. *Onyx Equinox*. Season 1, Episode 1, "The Last Day." Altieri, Kevin, dir. 2019. Streaming: Crunchyroll, 2019.

cities that were not contemporary by more than a few centuries like Monte Alban—which existed between the fifth century BCE and the eighth century CE—and Tenochtitlan, founded in the fourteenth century CE.

The reception of both series among Latin American *otaku* was mixed. In their YouTube channels, many expressed that these animations should not be called anime because they do not have a pure anime aesthetic nor are they produced by Japanese animators or studios. They also derided, in both cases, the low quality of the animation and the mix of Japanese and American styles in the designs; however, they have generally praised the focus on their culture and the representation of Mexican people and cultural elements. All are comments on the relevance of having Latin American cultures represented in animations that have a global reach and that are created by Latin Americans.[47] Thus, although these animations have caused mixed reactions, their success can be viewed precisely in their success at triggering debates on Mexican representation as the main topic for animation.

Conclusion

Many Mexican—and Latin American—audiences are tired of being represented in global media productions by Hollywood stereotypes. After the success of *Coco* (and, more recently, *Encanto*), through the new streaming platforms, and inspired by anime's popularity among adult audiences around the world, creators of Mexican origin are finding in animation a place to promote new representations and narratives about Mexico. These homegrown animations build on international trends, but they also result in more realistic representations. Even the supernatural elements of the stories tend to be firmly grounded in Mexican traditions and mythology.

Coco was a family animation that certainly rescued very traditional cultural elements and family values, but, as most children-oriented animations, it was very simplistic and the dichotomic characters—hero and villain—produced a story that felt more like an idealization of Mexican culture and people. By contrast, *Seis manos* and *Onix Equinox,* as adult-oriented stories, exploit the complexity of human nature and Mexican society and culture, showing not black and white characters, but gray ones, and a society that is also complex, not monolithic.

Seis Manos, although centered in a small town, showed that Mexico is not a country of only mestizo and Indigenous Mexicans. Rather; the country also boasts immigrants from other places that bring their own cultural elements and result in the hybridization of practices, ideologies, and cultures. Isabella, Jesús, and Silencio, as mestizo children raised by a Chinese immigrant, grew up to be adults who followed some Daoist ideas and practices but sometimes recurred in Catholic and Indigenous witchcraft practices. The characters are also nuanced and sometimes ambiguous. Even the heroes have dark sides. Mexican society is not idealized: the presence of the drug mafia is acknowledged as an integral part of the society. *Onyx Equinox* and its representation of three different Indigenous cultures and mythologies, as well as the showing of cruel original practices, like the human sacrifices, is also a positive element for a more realistic and complex representation that challenges Hollywood's black-and-white portrayal of Mexico and its people.

The presence in the industry in the United States of talented Mexican creators who grew up watching anime can continue to nurture the recent trend of animation focused in Mexico and, through this, the enrichment of Mexican representations around the world.

Notes

1. Douglas McGray, "Japan's Gross National Cool," *Foreign Policy*, no. 130 (2002): 55–54; Roland Kelts, *JAPANAMERICA: How Japanese Pop Culture Has Invaded the US* (New York: Palgrave Macmillan, 2007), 37; Susan J. Napier, *ANIME*

from Akira to Princess Mononoke. Experiencing Contemporary Japanese Animation (New York: Palgrave), 3–38.

2. Yunuen Mandujano, "The Politics of Selling Culture and Branding the National in Contemporary Japan: Economic Goals, Soft-Power and Reinforcement of the National Pride," *The Scientific Journal of Humanistic Studies* 9 (2013): 31–41.

3. For example, Laura Ivonne Castillo Quiroz, "Cosplay, Jugando a Ser Otro: El Uso Del Disfraz En La Construcción Sociocultural de Las Comunidades Otaku En México (Tesis de Licenciatura). Ciudad de México" (BA thesis, Instituto Nacional de Antropología e Historia, 2015); Rosario Barba González, "Otaku Mexicanos. El Análisis de La Cultura Participativa de Aficionados a Las Narrativas Transmediales Japonesas" (PhD diss., Universidad Autónoma de Aguas Calientes, 2017).

4. Created by Sofia Alexander, released November 21, 2020, on Crunchyroll.

5. Created by Brad Graeber and Álvaro Rodríguez, released October 3, 2019, on Netflix, Viz Productions.

6. Brigitte Koyama-Richard, *Mil Años de Manga* (Barcelona: Sociedad Editorial Eleca, 2008).

7. Frederick S. Litten, *Animated Film in Japan Until 1919* (Norderstedt: Books on Demand, 2017), 27–41.

8. Daisuke Miyao, "Before Anime : Animation and the Pure Film Movement in Pre-War Japan," *Japan Forum* vol. 14, no. 2 (2002): 194.

9. David Desser, "From the Opium War to the Pacific War: Japanese Propaganda Films of World War II," *Film History* 7, no. 1 (1995): 45–46.

10. Donald Richie, *Cien Años de Cine Japonés* (Madrid: Jaguar ediciones, 2004).

11. Nobuyuku, Tsugata, "A Bipolar Approach to Understanding the History of Japanese Animation," in *Japanese Animation,* ed. Masao Yokota and Tze-yue G Hu (Jackson: University Press of Mississippi, 2013), 25–32; Stefan Riekeles, *AnimeArchitecture: Imagined Worlds and Endless Megacities* (London: Thames & Hudson, 2020).

12. Frederik L. Schodt, *Manga! Manga! The World of Japanese Comics* (Tokyo: Kodansha International, 1983).

13. Tezuka Productions, "About Tezuka Osamu," Tezuka Osamu Official. Tezuka Productions, March 22, 2022, https://tezukaosamu.net/en/about/.

14. Yoshihiro Yonezawa, "El Anime La Cultura Pop de La Animación Japonesa," *NIPPONIA,* no. 27, December 15, 2003, https://web-japan.org/nipponia/nipponia27/es/feature/index.html.

15. Antonio Horno López, "Animación Japonesa: Análisis de Series de Anima Actuales" (doctorate's thesis, Universidad de Granada, 2014).

16. Kelts; Napier.

17. Takahashi Sasaki, *Otaku Bunkaron [Culture of Otaku]* (Tokyo: Goshi Gaisha Icon, 2011).

18. In the 1980s, Japanese amateur artists used anime and manga conventions to present their works with some risky themes: homosexuality, sexual violence, sexual relations of adult men with very young women, etc. Gradually, a stereotype of the

enthusiastic fans of manga and anime developed, and *otaku* became a synonym for weirdos. It is worth noting that, in contemporary Japan, the use of *otaku* has expanded to identify people who are extremely—sometimes obsessively—enthusiastic fans of any celebrity or hobby, not just anime and manga.

19. Koichi Iwabuchi, *Recentering Globalization: Popular Culture and Japanese Transnationalism* (Durham and London: Duke University Press, 2002).

20. Aljean Harmetz, "Japanese Invest in 2 Hollywood Production," *The New York Times,* December 25, 1989, https://www.nytimes.com/1989/12/25/movies/japanese-invest-in-2-hollywood-productions.html; Nina J. Easton, "Japanese Firm in $100-Million Hollywood Deal," *Los Angeles Times,* August 21, 1989, https://www.latimes.com/archives/la-xpm-1989-08-21-ca-726-story.html.

21. For a discussion of *nihonseikusai,* see Iwabuchi, 23–50.

22. See Josue Romero Quiroz, "Influencia Cultural del Anime y Manga Japonés en México" (BA thesis, Universidad Autónoma del Estado de México, 2012); Mario Javier Bogarín Quintana, *Otakus Bajo El Sol. La Construcción Sociocultural Del Fanático de Manga y Anime En Mexicali* (Mexicali: Universidad Autónoma de Baja California).

23. Annalee Newitz, "Anime Otaku: Japanese Animation Fans Outside Japan," *Bad Subjects,* no. 13 (1994): 1.

24. Newitz, 2.

25. Alex Mateo, "Sony's Funimation Global Group Completes Acquisition of Crunchyroll from AT&T (Updated)," *Anime News Network,* August 9, 2021, https://www.animenewsnetwork.com/news/2021-08-09/sony-funimation-global-group-completes-acquisition-of-crunchyroll-from-at-t/.176073; Chris Morrison, "Crunchyroll, for Pirated Anime Content," *VentureBeat,* September 6, 2007, https://venturebeat.com/2007/09/06/crunchyroll-for-pirated-anime-content/.

26. Tomohiro Oikawa, "Weekend Beat: Cashing in on over-the-Counter Culture," *Asahi.com,* September 1, 2007, https://web.archive.org/web/20080316125943/http://www.asahi.com/english/Herald-asahi/TKY200709010077.html; VIZ, "About VIZ," *VIZ,* Accessed April 16, 2022, https://www.viz.com/company-about.

27. Rafael Antonio Pineda, "Entrevista: Sofía Alexander Comporta los Secretos de Onyx Equinox," *CINE PREMIERE,* November 20, 2020, https://www.cinepremiere.com.mx/sofia-alexander-onyx-equinox-entrevista.html.

28. Reuben Baron, "The Makers of Wolfwalkers, We Bare Bears and More Discuss Anime's Global Influence," *CBR.Com,* June 23, 2021, https://www.cbr.com/annecy-anime-global-influence-wolfwalkers-we-bare-bears/; Samuel Edwards, "How Anime Influenced Western Animation—Inspired Traveler," *Inspired Traveler,* October 11, 2021, https://www.inspiredtraveler.ca/how-anime-influenced-western-animation/.

29. Federico Manuel Álvarez Gandolfi, "Acercarse a los otakus: Reflexiones sobre el abordaje de las derivas identitarias del consumo fan de manga/animé en el contexto de una cultura de convergencia," *Avatares de la Comunicación y la Cultura,* no. 13 (2017): 1–9.

30. See, for example: Barba González; Bogarín Quintana; Castillo Quiroz; Romero Quiroz.

31. Created by Lee Unkrich, Jason Katz, Matthew Aldrich, and Adrian Molina.

32. See Yunuen Ysela Mandujano-Salazar, "Coco: El Discurso de Autenticidad y la Reproducción de Estereotipos a través del Mito de la Mexicanidad," in *Más Alla Del Mundo de Ensueño: Desenmascarando Los Mensajes de Las Películas y Su Significación Social,* ed. Yunuen Ysela Mandujano-Salazar, (Ciudad Juárez: Universidad Autónoma de Ciudad Juárez, 2021), 13–30. See also Molly Todd's chapter in this book.

33. Mandujano-Salazar, 26–27.

34. Zac Bertschy, "Interview: The Creative Team Behind Netflix's Seis Manos," *Anime News Network*, October 2, 2019, https://www.animenewsnetwork.com/interview/2019-10-02/the-creative-team-behind-netflix-seis-manos/.151771; John Schwarz, "Seis Manos Q&A: Brad Graeber (SEIS MANOS Showrunner, Co-Creator and Executive Producer) and Alvaro Rodriguez (SEIS MANOS Writer and Co-Creator)," *Bubbleblabber*, October 1, 2019, https://www.bubbleblabber.com/seis-manos-qa-brad-graeber-seis-manos-showrunner-co-creator-and-executive-producer-and-alvaro-rodriguez-seis-manos-writer-and-co-creator/.

35. Nancy Tartaglione, "Pixar's "Coco" Is Otherworldly In Mexico, Becomes #1 Movie Ever," *Deadline*, November 15, 2017, https://deadline.com/2017/11/coco-pixar-mexico-highest-grossing-film-all-time-box-office-record-1202209221/.

36. Schwarz.

37. He is a cousin of Robert Anthony Rodríguez, a Mexican American filmmaker known for his Mexico-related films, like *Machete, El Mariachi, Desperado,* and *Once Upon a Time in Mexico.* Álvaro Rodríguez worked with him on some of this as a screenwriter and composer.

38. Dave Trumbore, "Seis Manos Creators on How the Mexicanime Series Made Castlevania Possible," *Collider*, May 30, 2020, https://collider.com/seis-manos-season-2-creators-interview/.

39. Kiara Halls, "Onyx Equinox Creator Sofia Alexander Talks Representation, On- & Off-Screen," *CBR.Com,* November 29, 2020, https://www.cbr.com/interview-onyx-equinox-creator-sofia-alexander-latinx-representation-on-off-screen/; Ross Locksley, "Interview with Sofia Alexander," *UK Anime Network*. November 20, 2020, https://www.uk-anime.net/articles/Interview_with_Sofia_Alexander.html; Gustavo Pineda, "Entrevista: Sofía Alexander Comparte Los Secretos de Onyx Equinox," *CINE PREMIERE,* November 20, 2020, https://www.cinepremiere.com.mx/sofia-alexander-onyx-equinox-entrevista.html.

40. Darinka Rodríguez, "Onyx Equinox, La Historia Animada Con Un Niño Indígena Como Protagonista," *Lo Mejor de Verne,* November 19, 2020, https://verne.elpais.com/verne/2020/11/19/mexico/1605764156_646252.html.

41. Ramin Zahed, "New Trailer/Q&A: Sofía Alexander Reanimates Mesoamerican Myths in Onyx Equinox," *Animation Magazine*, October 29, 2020, https://

www.animationmagazine.net/streaming/new-trailer-qa-sofia-alexander-reanimates-mesoamerican-myths-in-onyx-equinox/.

42. See Locksley.

43. Rachael Harper, "Onyx Equinox: Interview with creator Sofia Alexander," *SciFiNow*, December 15, 2020, https://www.scifinow.co.uk/tv/onyx-equinox-interview-with-creator-sofia-alexander/.

44. See Halls.

45. For a discussion of the fluidity of Indigenous and mestizo racial identities, see David S. Dalton, *Mestizo Modernity: Race, Technology and the Body in Postrevolutionary Mexico* (Gainesville: University of Florida Press, 2018), introduction.

46. Kate Sánchez, "Interview: "Seis Manos," Representation, and Animation with Alvaro Rodriguez," *But Why Tho?*, September 25, 2019, https://butwhythopodcast.com/2019/09/25/interivew-seis-manos-representation-and-animation-with-alvaro-rodriguez/.

47. See, for example, Alfrely, "El Nuevo Anime Mexicano Onyx Equinox Resumen y Opinión," YouTube, December 3, 2020, https://youtu.be/7KW4S OwyeIc; BlackLightJack, "Onyx Equinox Sucks (Part 1)," YouTube, February 12, 2022. https://youtu.be/hpSylx6Z_PA; Dacollector, "Onyx Equinox ¿Vale La Pena Verlo?," YouTube, November 24, 2020, https://youtu.be/-SeySSusPSU; Fuera de Foco, "Crítica/Review: Seis manos—el primer anime en México," YouTube, October 5, 2019, https://youtu.be/x9ip2p8Ip10; La Zona Cero, "Seis Manos Crítica#43," YouTube, October 4, 2019, https://youtu.be/R_Lp3rDlR5o.

Bibliography

Alexander, Sofia, creator. *Onix Equinox*. Released November 21, 2020, on Crunchyroll. Crunchyroll Studios.

Alfrely. "El Nuevo Anime Mexicano Onyx Equinox Resumen y Opinión." YouTube, December 3, 2020. https://youtu.be/7KW4SOwyeIc.

Álvarez Gandolfi, Federico Manuel. "Acercarse a los otakus: Reflexiones sobre el abordaje de las derivas identitarias del consumo fan de manga/animé en el contexto de una cultura de convergencia." *Avatares de la Comunicación y la Cultura,* no. 13 (2017): 1–9. https://ri.conicet.gov.ar/handle/11336/76253.

Barba González, Rosario. "Otaku Mexicanos. El Análisis de La Cultura Participativa de Aficionados a Las Narrativas Transmediales Japonesas." PhD thesis, Universidad Autónoma de Aguascalientes, 2017. http://bdigital.dgse.uaa.mx:8080/xmlui/handle/11317/1390, 2017.

Baron, Reuben. "The Makers of Wolfwalkers, We Bare Bears and More Discuss Anime's Global Influence." *CBR.Com,* June 23, 2021. https://www.cbr.com/annecy-anime-global-influence-wolfwalkers-we-bare-bears/.

Bertschy, Zac. "Interview: The Creative Team Behind Netflix's Seis Manos." *Anime News Network,* October 2, 2019. https://www.animenewsnetwork.com/interview/2019-10-02/the-creative-team-behind-netflix-seis-manos/.151771.

BlackLightJack. "Onyx Equinox Sucks." YouTube, February 12, 2022. https://youtu.be/hpSylx6Z_PA.

Bogarín Quintana, Mario Javier. *Otakus Bajo El Sol. La Construcción Sociocultural Del Fanático de Manga y Anime En Mexicali.* Mexicali: Universidad Autónoma de Baja California, 2012.

Castillo Quiroz, Laura Ivonne. "Cosplay, Jugando a Ser Otro: El Uso Del Disfraz En La Construcción Sociocultural de Las Comunidades Otaku En México." BA thesis, Instituto Nacional de Antropología e Historia, 2015. https://mediateca.inah.gob.mx/repositorio/islandora/object/tesis%3A2489.

dacollector. "Onyx Equinox ¿Vale La Pena Verlo?" YouTube, November 24, 2020. https://youtu.be/-SeySSusPSU.

Desser, David "From the Opium War to the Pacific War: Japanese Propaganda Films of World War II." *Film History* vol. 7, no. 1 (1995): 45–6. Accessed March 2, 2020. https://www.jstor.org/stable/3815159.

Easton, Nina J. "Japanese Firm in $100-Million Hollywood Deal." *Los Angeles Times,* August 21, 1989. https://www.latimes.com/archives/la-xpm-1989-08-21-ca-726-story.html.

Edwards, Samuel. "How Anime Influenced Western Animation—Inspired Traveler." *Inspired Traveler,* October 11, 2021. https://www.inspiredtraveler.ca/how-anime-influenced-western-animation/.

Fuera de Foco. "Crítica/Review: Seis manos—el primer anime en México." YouTube, October 5, 2019. https://youtu.be/x9ip2p8Ip10.

Graeber, Brad, and Álvaro Rodríguez, creators. *Seis Manos.* Directed by Willis Bulliner. Released October 3, 2019, on Netflix. Powerhouse Animation Studios and Viz Productions.

Halls, Kiara. "Onyx Equinox Creator Sofia Alexander Talks Representation, On- & Off-Screen." *CBR.Com,* November 29, 2020. https://www.cbr.com/interview-onyx-equinox-creator-sofia-alexander-latinx-representation-on-off-screen/.

Harmetz, Aljean. "Japanese Invest in 2 Hollywood Productions." *New York Times,* December 25, 1989. https://www.nytimes.com/1989/12/25/movies/japanese-invest-in-2-hollywood-productions.html.

Harper, Rachael. "Onyx Equinox: Interview with Creator Sofia Alexander." *SciFiNow,* December 15, 2020. https://www.scifinow.co.uk/tv/onyx-equinox-interview-with-creator-sofia-alexander/.

Horno López, Antonio. "Animación Japonesa : Análisis de Series de Anime Actuales." Doctorate's thesis, Universidad de Granada, 2014. http://hdl.handle.net/10481/34010.

Iwabuchi, Koichi. *Recentering Globalization: Popular Culture and Japanese Transnationalism.* Durham and London: Duke University Press, 2002.

Kelts, Roland. *JAPANAMERICA: How Japanese Pop Culture Has Invaded the US.* New York: Palgrave Macmillan, 2007.

Koyama-Richard, Brigitte. *Mil Años de Manga.* Barcelona: Sociedad Editorial Eleca, 2008.

La Zona Cero. "Seis Manos Crítica#43." YouTube, October 4, 2019. https://youtu.be/R_Lp3rDlR5o.

Litten, Frederick S. *Animated Film in Japan Unitl 1919.* Norderstedt: Books on Demand, 2017.

Locksley, Ross. "Interview with Sofia Alexander." *UK Anime Network,* November 20, 2020. https://www.uk-anime.net/articles/Interview_with_Sofia_Alexander.html.

Mandujano, Yunuen. "The Politics of Selling Culture and Branding the National in Contemporary Japan: Economic Goals, Soft-Power and Reinforcement of the National Pride." *The Scientific Journal of Humanistic Studies* 5, no.9 (2013): 31–41. https://www.academia.edu/5407709/The_Politics_of_Selling_Culture_and_Branding_the_National_in_Contemporary_Japan_Economic_Goals_Soft-power_and_Reinforcement_of_the_National_Pride.

Mandujano-Salazar, Yunuen Ysela. "Coco: El Discurso de Autenticidad y La Reproducción de Estereotipos a Través Del Mito de La Mexicanidad." In *Más Alla Del Mundo de Ensueño: Desenmascarando Los Mensajes de Las Películas y Su Significación Social,* edited by Yunuen Ysela Mandujano-Salazar, 13–30. Ciudad Juárez: Universidad Autónoma de Ciudad Juárez, 2021. https://elibros.uacj.mx/omp/index.php/publicaciones/catalog/book/190.

Mateo, Alex. "Sony's Funimation Global Group Completes Acquisition of Crunchyroll from AT&T (Updated)." *Anime News Network,* August 9, 2021. https://www.animenewsnetwork.com/news/2021-08-09/sony-funimation-global-group-completes-acquisition-of-crunchyroll-from-at-t/.176073.

McGray, Douglas. "Japan's Gross National Cool." *Foreign Policy,* no. 130 (2002):44–54.

Miyao, Daisuke. "Before Anime : Animation and the Pure Film Movement in Pre-War Japan." *Japan Forum* 14, no. 2 (2002):191–209. http://doi.org/10.1080/09555800220136356.

Morrison, Chris. "Crunchyroll, for Pirated Anime Content." *VentureBeat,* September 6, 2007. https://venturebeat.com/2007/09/06/crunchyroll-for-pirated-anime-content/.

Napier, Susan J. *ANIME from Akira to Princess Mononoke. Experiencing Contemporary Japanese Animation.* New York: Palgrave, 2001.

Newitz, Annalee. "Anime Otaku: Japanese Animation Fans Outside Japan." *Bad Subjects,* no. 13 (1994): 1–12.

Oikawa, Tomohiro. "Weekend Beat: Cashing in on over-the-Counter Culture." *Asahi. Com,* September 1, 2007. https://web.archive.org/web/20080316125943/http://www.asahi.com/english/Herald-asahi/TKY200709010077.html.

Pineda, Gustavo. "Entrevista: Sofía Alexander Comparte Los Secretos de Onyx Equinox." *CINE PREMIERE,* November 20, 2020. https://www.cinepremiere.com.mx/sofia-alexander-onyx-equinox-entrevista.html.

Pineda, Rafael Antonio. "Viz VP: Company Saw 70% Growth in 2020 U.S. Market." *Anime News Network,* March 4, 2021. https://www.animenewsnetwork.com/news/2021-03-04/viz-vp-company-saw-70-percent-growth-in-2020-u.s-market/.170213.

Richie, Donald. *Cien Años de Cine Japonés.* Madrid: Jaguar ediciones, 2004.

Riekeles, Stefan. *Anime Architecture: Imagined Worlds and Endless Megacities.* London: Thames & Hudson, 2020.

Rodríguez, Darinka. "Onyx Equinox, La Historia Animada Con Un Niño Indígena Como Protagonista." *Lo Mejor de Verne,* November 19, 2020. https://verne.elpais.com/verne/2020/11/19/mexico/1605764156_646252.html.

Romero Quiroz, Josue. "Influencia Cultural del Anime y Manga Japonés en México." Undergraduate's thesis, Universidad Autónoma del Estado de México, 2012. http://hdl.handle.net/20.500.11799/214.

Sánchez, Kate. "Interview: "Seis Manos," Representation, and Animation with Alvaro Rodriguez." *But Why Tho?,* September 25, 2019. https://butwhythopodcast.com/2019/09/25/interivew-seis-manos-representation-and-animation-with-alvaro-rodriguez/.

Sasaki, Takashi. *Otaku Bunkaron [Culture of Otaku].* Tokyo: Goshi Gaisha Icon, 2011.

Schodt, Frederik L. *Manga! Manga! The World of Japanese Comics.* Tokyo: Kodansha International, 1983.

Schwarz, John. "Seis Manos Q&A: Brad Graeber (SEIS MANOS Showrunner, Co-Creator and Executive Producer) and Alvaro Rodriguez (SEIS MANOS Writer and Co-Creator)." *Bubbleblabber,* October 1, 2019. https://www.bubbleblabber.com/seis-manos-qa-brad-graeber-seis-manos-showrunner-co-creator-and-executive-producer-and-alvaro-rodriguez-seis-manos-writer-and-co-creator/.

Tartaglione, Nancy. "Pixar's "Coco" Is Otherworldly In Mexico, Becomes #1 Movie Ever." *Deadline,* November 15, 2017. https://deadline.com/2017/11/coco-pixar-mexico-highest-grossing-film-all-time-box-office-record-1202209221/.

Tezuka Productions. "About Tezuka Osamu." *TEZUKA OSAMU OFFICIAL.* Accessed March 22, 2022. https://tezukaosamu.net/en/about/.

Trumbore, Dave. "Seis Manos Creators on How the Mexicanime Series Made Castlevania Possible." *Collider,* May 30, 2020. https://collider.com/seis-manos-season-2-creators-interview/.

Tsugata, Nobuyuki. "A Bipolar Approach to Understanding the History of Japanese Animation." In *Japanese Animation,* edited by Masao Yokota and Tze-yue G Hu, 25–32. Jackson: University Press of Mississippi, 2013. http://doi.org/10.14325/mississippi/9781617038099.003.0003.

Unkrich, Lee, Jason Katz, Matthew Aldrich, and Adrian Molina, creators. *Coco.* Los Angeles: Walt Disney Studios, 2017.

VIZ. About VIZ. *VIZ.* Accessed April 16, 2022. https://www.viz.com/company-about.

Yonezawa, Yoshihiro. "El Anime—La Cultura Pop de La Animación Japonesa." *NIPPONIA,* no. 27. December 15, 2003. https://web-japan.org/nipponia/nipponia27/es/feature/index.html.

Zahed, Ramin. "New Trailer/Q&A: Sofía Alexander Reanimates Mesoamerican Myths in "Onyx Equinox." *Animation Magazine,* October 29, 2020. https://www.animationmagazine.net/streaming/new-trailer-qa-sofia-alexander-reanimates-mesoamerican-myths-in-onyx-equinox.

Chapter 7

The Day of the Dead

Mexican Gothic and Animated Cinema

Enrique Ajuria Ibarra

Mexico celebrates death, but it does so ambiguously. Mexican culture views death with fear, acceptance, and joy; the result of an amalgamation of beliefs about the relation between life and any possible afterlife. It is a strange, paradoxical approach that may baffle foreigners: a mixture of the macabre, tinted with color and sweetness. Stanley Brandes argues that the "view of death" in Mexican culture "appears highly contradictory" but that it reflects common universal patterns of "expressing an ambivalent response to death, a simultaneous fascination with and repugnance from it."[1] He emphasizes that these are cultural manifestations through which feelings about death are projected.[2] Claudio Lomnitz claims that the celebration of death in Mexico is the result of early twentieth-century national policies, with the idea of death "perfectly impersonating the formula of cultural hybridity, of mestizaje, that constituted the core of Mexico's cultural revolution ["una personificación perfecta de la formula de la hibridación cultural, el mestizaje, que constituía el corazón de la revolución cultural de México"]."[3] Lomnitz rejects Octavio Paz's (and other intellectuals') "romantic" view on death in Mexico as a traditional symbol of harsh social realities that has been reproduced in the arts and the media[4] from an essentialist point view.[5] Instead, he claims that the celebration of death is political, "a paradigmatic image of mestizaje ["una imagen paradigmática del mestizaje"]" that resulted in an "aesthetic project and a formulation of ["proyecto estético y una formulación de"]" social and cultural parameters "effectively mediated by the State ["una mediación efectiva del Estado"]."[6] In its filmic representation, the festivity of the Day of the Dead may lure the audience into thinking about joyful celebrations, which leads us to consider the intricacies of this particular cultural phenomenon even further when these visual narratives address the topics of community and family unity. Such is the case of three recent animated films whose plots are primarily set against the backdrop of the Day of the Dead holiday in Mexico.

The Book of Life (2014), directed by Jorge R. Gutiérrez, tells the romance of Manolo and María, from the town of San Ángel. Their destiny is set by a wager between La Muerte (Lady Death) and the lord of the underworld, Xibalba. Manolo ends up visiting the land of the dead and reunites with his past relatives as he strives to get back to the land of the living and save his town from the bandit Chakal and his gang. Pixar's *Coco* (2017), directed by Lee Unkrich and Adrian Molina, became the highest-grossing film in Mexico that year, according to CANACINE. In this film, young Miguel belongs to a family of shoemakers, but his real passion is to play music. Strictly forbidden by his grandmother, the boy decides to steal a guitar from the mausoleum of celebrated singer Ernesto de la Cruz. Because he trespasses a tomb, he is whisked into the land of the dead, where he meets his past relatives. In an attempt to get back home, it is revealed that de la Cruz poisoned and stole the songs of Miguel's real great-great-grandfather Héctor, who is running the risk of being completely forgotten by his daughter Coco—Miguel's great-grandmother—and disappearing from the land of the dead forever.

These two productions are characterized by their rich and elaborate representation of this Mexican holiday, and for the imaginative and colorful portrayal of the land of the dead. The films emphasize the celebratory nature of this festivity by infusing both the realm of the living and the dead with vivid scenarios. They are accompanied by lively soundtracks that feature mariachi musical arrangements, which help highlight the Mexican cultural background and setting, reflecting on their narrative content since the protagonists of these two films are aspiring musicians. Also, *Coco* particularly references *alebrijes*, which have become staple pieces of artwork in Mexican popular culture, and it could be suggested they are an indirect inspiration to the film's lavish settings. Both films also display a notoriously Hispanic production team and cast, not only acknowledging American multicultural society but also paying homage to the relevance of the Day of the Dead for

Hispanic American communities in the United States as a matter of cultural inheritance. Furthermore, *The Book of Life* was produced by Mexican director Guillermo del Toro and features the voices of Mexican actors, such as Diego Luna, Kate del Castillo, Héctor Elizondo, and Ana de la Reguera. Even though this is an American film, it recognizes transnational cooperation between Mexicans and Americans and notices more complex cultural references associated with Hispanics in the United States. For Laura Fernández, *The Book of Life* "is a lighthearted attempt at showcasing Mexican culture, something that is lacking in mainstream American culture." She praises that, even though Gutiérrez's film draws on " 'stereotypical' iconography" about Mexico, it "is not afraid to showcase its inherent Latinidad," which can also be found in the United States.[7] These films have been acclaimed for their positive representation of cultural elements of the other and for their celebratory and well-crafted narratives. As Fernández claims, films like *The Book of Life* facilitate the discussion of plural cultural backgrounds that define the varied population of the United States.

A third animated film, Carlos Gutiérrez Medrano's *Día de Muertos*, also focuses on the Day of the Dead and was released in 2019. Unlike the previous two, which were produced in Hollywood for international and Mexican audiences, this latter one was produced in Mexico for a primarily domestic audience, but the successes of the US-produced films lie in the background for this one.[8] Metacube, the production company based in Guadalajara, had plans to distribute the film in 2017, but decided to postpone it for a year because of Pixar's competition. Once again, they had to delay the release once more because *Coco* reopened in 2018 in Mexican cinemas to continue with its unprecedented financial success.[9] Nevertheless, and despite its delayed release, *Día de muertos* managed to become the sixth-highest-grossing Mexican production in 2019, according to the data provided by the *Statistical Yearbook of Mexican Cinema* of that same year.[10] Ironically, the production company owed at least some of this success to *Coco* for opening a market for films dedicated explicitly to the Day of the Dead. The plot revolves around Salma, an orphan girl who lives with her grandmother and her cousins Pedro and Jorge. Ever since she was a little girl, she has always wanted to meet her deceased parents, but her attempts to bring their spirits back from the land of the dead by setting up an altar on Día de Muertos ends up in disaster. Supernatural forces always seem to be around her desperate attempts. Even though her grandmother has forbidden her to learn anything from her parents, she spends the rest of her childhood and adolescence trying to figure out who they were. Her research leads her to accidentally set free an old wizard named Professor Morlete. She learns from him that her parents were witches who helped Morlete stop death so he would never lose his beloved wife. This villain makes use of Salma's sensibility and unleashes her magical powers. Like her parents, Salma realizes her mistake and prevents Morlete from fulfilling his wish. Ultimately, Salma understands the value of family unity in life and the remembrance of those who have passed away.

These three films all have plotlines that revolve around the notions of family union and memory. Their protagonists are bound to tradition, and their conflicts focus on their commitment to themselves as individuals or as part of a larger family and their inherited social and cultural practices. They foreground the relevance of the Day of the Dead as the time to remember relatives who passed away. The idea of being completely forgotten puts the souls of the land of the dead at risk of disappearing completely, as is the case in *Coco*, or of being sent off to Xibalba's Land of the Forgotten, as occurs in *The Book of Life*. In these stories, ghosts take on a different meaning, not as a haunting but rather as acts of celebrated return. This notion of spectral return points to a different sense of temporality in relation to life and death. Jacques Derrida claims that "the specter is the future, it is always to come, it presents itself only as that which could come or come back," but he also warns about the anxiety of the perilous return of the thing of the past.[11] The films' reliance on the Mexican holiday as the backdrop to their stories encourages viewers to rethink life, death, and what lies after death with a restructuring of remembrance that, according to Derrida, can have the political potential for better-being because "being-with specters would also be, not only but also, a politics of memory, of inheritance, and of generations."[12] Inscribed as a combination of cultural understandings of death, the Day of the Dead prompts us to appreciate the return of the dead by means of symbolic offerings and enlivened memory.

Although the Day of the Dead may sound disturbing or macabre, these animated films are very celebratory, which goes hand in hand with the attitude toward death in Mexican culture. It is thus difficult to assert if this festivity should be considered Gothic. The Gothic is often characterized by its "ornateness, hyperbole," and "violent exclamation,"[13] linked primarily with the supernatural, terror, and horror. Although the idea of the return of the dead—as well as the exuberant celebration of this reunion with the living—could be aligned with this brief description, it is necessary to point out that the Day of the Dead is not perceived negatively; instead, it is considered positive. Thus, the fearful and claustrophobic return of the past that Chris Baldick claims is characteristic of Gothic fiction[14] is difficult to articulate with this holiday. Nevertheless, the themes of death and the past that are cyclically remembered are commercially appropriated, and could be associated with the recent rise of a more happy, contemporary Gothic.

Since these films are giving a wider audience outside Mexico a sense of what the Day of the Dead is, then it is necessary to ask ourselves if a Gothic approach is useful at all. Inés Ordiz and Sandra Casanova-Vizcaíno have noticed the absence of the term "Gothic" in Latin America, which they consider "connected to issues of identity, nationhood, and the global market,"[15] as the region has embraced more fully other terms such as "the fantastic" and "magic realism." Nonetheless, Ordiz and Casanova-Vizcaíno also encourage us to think of the Gothic as a malleable form that can "evolve in various ways, adapting to different socio-historical contexts and becoming a dark and complex response to different processes of modernity as experienced in different parts of Latin America."[16] This incorporation of the term, considering it an aesthetic and a critical approach, responds to ever-growing dynamics of global marketing. The positive response to these films may not necessarily focus on the contradictory fusion of terrifying, supernatural elements with happiness and celebration. If this is the case, it is therefore necessary to rethink any possible connections between the Mexican holiday and the Gothic. As such, these films may not be Gothic per se, but they do contribute to a revised look at death and remembrance in contemporary global culture.

Rather than looking at a list of Gothic features in these animated films, it is more sensible to understand if (1) a Gothic reading is appropriate for these texts, and (2) if it does, what can Gothic reveal about its structure and content. Catherine Spooner argues that we need to understand the "relentless adaptive" nature of Gothic, which always finds "new outlets and hybrid forms," but also insists that "it is less interesting to investigate what Gothic is than what it does."[17] Thus, in order to understand certain happy and celebratory dynamics of contemporary Gothic, we must ask ourselves: what does Gothic do in terms of perception of other cultural traditions about death, and also, how does Gothic help narrate stories about family and identity with the holiday of the Day of the Dead as a backdrop? The emphasis on the return of the specter—seen as a contradictory affront to linear, progressive time—reveals its political nature as it "seeks to counteract erasure, silencing, and forgetting that eschews melancholic attachment to loss."[18] The impact it has on identity, both individual and communal, forces to reconsider remembrance as both festive and revelatory of past deeds, whether painful or joyful. In this sense, for a film such as *The Book of Life*, it may be difficult to point out particular and essential Gothic features, but Gothic may still disclose itself through narrative structure in terms of kinship, identity, villainy, and deceit. Conversely, the Mexican film *Día de muertos* acknowledges national and customary celebrations, so it is able to delve deeper into the ambiguous fear Mexicans have of death. Of these films, the latter is more Gothic; its narrative uses motifs more explicitly to reveal an insistent anxiety about the end of life and the loss that cannot be overcome. Only by cheating death can this be overturned, but with dark and disastrous results.

Death and the Family

In *The Book of Life*, Manolo yearns to be a musician, but his father forces him to follow the family's traditional profession of bullfighting. The film foregrounds the importance of tradition and obedience as key factors that allow families to thrive together. This, along with the notion of remembrance, rounds up the idea of strong kinship, one which is centrally pinned down by the festivity of the Day of the Dead itself. The film includes lavish sequences in the cemetery, where people make offerings and altars to remember their relatives who have passed away. Living relatives honor their family plots while the spirits of the dead linger around, called back to the land of the living for one night. The grim location changes mood with bright warm colors to match the *cempasúchil* (marigold) bouquets laid on every tomb. Far from being a sober holiday, the scenes in the cemetery attempt to associate it with a more festive mood.

A year later, a more commercially successful film would portray the Day of the Dead in this same fashion. The opening chase sequence from the twenty-fourth installment of the James Bond movie franchise, *Spectre* (2015), directed by Sam Mendes, takes place in Mexico City during this holiday too. A fade-in introduces the audience to a panning shot of floats bearing skeletons driven through downtown Mexico City. Subtitles clearly confirm to the audience that this is the Day of the Dead. People stroll down the street wearing black costumes, flowers, masks depicting skulls, and several groups of people are dressed as *catrines* and *catrinas*.[19] The sound of mariachi music, as well as the traditional song "Llorona," further emphasizes the scene's festive mood. In this Bond film, what could be considered a macabre setting for a celebration is quite carnivalesque.

Carnival refers to, in Mikhail Bakhtin's words, feasts "linked externally to the feasts of the Church"; that is, a sort of "people's second life, organized on the basis of laughter" to commemorate or celebrate "breaking points in the cycle of nature or in the life of society and man," such as "death and revival."[20] What is depicted as the background for Bond's action sequence looks more positive than gloomy, where a holiday dedicated to the dead brings about colorful and joyful costumes and ornaments for people to revel in and laugh with. In his comparative study on Halloween in the United States and the Day of the Dead in Mexico, Brandes describes the Mexican holiday as "colorful—some would say carnivalesque," with "ritual performances and artistic displays," as well as "humorous" takes on the theme of death itself.[21] Brandes's view reminds us of Bakhtin's notion of carnival: this ambiguous, nonofficial suspended time of celebration, in which exaggerated assumptions provide some sort of relief in contrast to official rituals and ceremonies that remind people of life and death. For Brandes, the Day of the Dead keeps this contradiction but also displays cultural concerns and significations towards the absence of life in everyday social practices.

Spectre's carnivalesque setting has provided the grounds for a new commercial look at the Day of the Dead. Before *Spectre*, *The Book of Life* provided a fresh, contemporary look at this traditional Mexican holiday for foreign audiences by means of fiction. Instead of being depicted in an atmosphere traditionally associated with grief, loss, and death, a more festive mood is being portrayed that can end up exoticizing this local holiday. Likewise, the films have prompted a reconsideration of its potential commercial possibilities. For instance, Mexico City now holds an annual parade during the week of the Day of the Dead. In a BBC News article, the executive director of the Mexican Tourist Board, declared that, with the success of *Spectre*, there would be expectations from locals and tourists surrounding the celebration of the holiday, particularly "a big parade."[22] I attended it in 2019, and listened to the presenters describe it as "traditional." The overall mood closely resembled the one depicted in the James Bond film. Additionally, Chapultepec Park hosted a Mictlán, a spectacle titled "Celebrating eternity ["Celebrando la eternidad"]," with night tours of the site heavily ornamented and alluding to the Day of the Dead. This leads us to question the relationship between tradition and commercial celebration, bound by a contemporary global culture that becomes interested in, borrows, and makes use of local associations with gloom, terror, and horror for consumption.

Spooner claims that, in contemporary Gothic texts, "products, imagery and artefacts can no longer be regarded as almost universally gloomy and miserable, or even scary and horrid." Instead, she argues that Gothic texts are noticeably more celebratory and often combine comedy and romance. Thus, "contemporary Gothic can increasingly be described as comic, romantic, celebratory, gleeful, whimsical or even joyous."[23] In our times, Gothic has become a more visible aspect of popular culture, with recognized features and intertextual associations that help expand its conventions. Gothic is not necessarily terrifying or macabre, eliciting anxiety; now, Gothic motifs have become so familiar that they are seen in a different light. It is no longer just a matter of fear but also a matter of recognition that prompts more positive associations between the dark and the supernatural and everyday experiences.

This approach to contemporary Gothic responds to its worldwide recognition, itself the result of global media outreach and shared narrative experiences. For Glennis Byron, the idea of global Gothic forms not only responds to the outreach of what is typically known as "Western Gothic" but also of "a growing awareness that the tropes and strategies Western critics have associated with the gothic, such as the ghost, the vampire and the zombie, have their counterparts in other cultures, however differently these may be inflected by specific histories and belief systems."[24] This global exchange, Byron notes, is not solely commercial but has prompted scholars to rethink and reconsider tropes associated with terror, horror, and the supernatural in different local cultures and their links to identity and anxiety. She proposes that the term "globalgothic" suggests an encounter of cultural manifestations that are the result of global production and dissemination. When combined, these terms also monstrify the idea of globalization itself.[25] Under these circumstances, the recent animated films whose setting focuses on the Day of the Dead may be considered part of these postmillenial media culture dynamics. Here, the celebratory nature of this Mexican holiday is used to reconsider the idea of death as a grim experience. Likewise, it demonstrates the avid hunger to incorporate other cultural traditions for commercial purposes, no matter how respectful the approach is, such as *Coco*.[26]

Despite its heavy use of motifs related to death and the supernatural, *The Book of Life* focuses more on the typical narrative structure of the hero's journey, with Manuel ending up in the land of the dead by the wager played between La Muerte and Xibalba. These creatures contain godlike features and personalities, changing the course of the story with their own tricks. Xibalba wants to rule the land of the dead—the colorful and joyful place that contrasts with the depressive world of the forgotten, which he governs. As the protagonist, Manuel decides to travel to the land of the forgotten in search for the delegated Muerte, in order to let her know that Xibalba cheated on the wager. The hero must then face the challenge of fighting the spirits of all the bulls his family has killed in order to return to the land of the living to save the town of San Ángel from a horde of raiding bandits, and win the hand of his love interest María. The intervention of divine beings in this film defers any perception of horror and foregrounds that despite death, family, love, and union prevail with the aid of remembrance. The film suggests that the Day of the Dead reconsiders the experience of loss to highlight the importance of living memory. More than a mournful haunting, the return of the spirits of the deceased for a single day is a welcoming action that extends the notion of life through remembrance.

In *The Book of Life*, the association between family, kinship, and memory is transgressed by murder and deceit. With these two aspects in mind, a Gothic approach can disclose perceptions of family and spiritual haunting during the Day of the Dead. For Agnes Andeweg and Sue Zlosnik, family is one of the key features in Gothic fiction. They claim that "sociocultural figurations of the family are negotiated" in the Gothic and that its "figurations of kinship both contest and reinforce orthodox notions of the nuclear family."[27] Through the Gothic, the idea of family and what constitutes it may be challenged or transformed. It reconsiders and questions the insistence of tradition and opens up the possibility of contemplating other forms of family structures. Although *The Book of Life* points out that the preservation of family can only work by adhering to tradition, it also suggests that remembrance keeps a vital role in the constitution of individual and domestic identity. Haunting is restructured around the acceptance or the rejection of the death, with the celebration of the return of those who are worth remembering and the total obliteration of those who are not kept in their living relatives' minds.

If there is a haunting in this film, it would rather be the risk of oblivion represented by the souls in Xibalba's realm (figure 7.1). The dead are able to maintain an afterlife as long as their living relatives keep remembering them through the annual celebration of the Day of the Dead. The border between life and death becomes blurry, in temporal and metaphysical terms, and this is due to the potential of memorization, a sort of specter too, according to Derrida,[28] which defines the future ontology of the subject who has passed away. *The Book of Life* illustrates such spiritual reunion in the town's cemetery, and when Manolo enters the land of the dead, he is able to recognize past relatives in the afterlife. His reaction is not of fear of the spirits, but rather of surprise that he does not need to wander alone in this realm. Thus, souls in the film are not the frightening type. According to

Figure 7.1. The souls that inhabit Xibalba's realm. *Source:* Gutiérrez Medrano, Carlos, dir. *Día de muertos*, 2019; Mexico City: Zima Entertainment/Videocine Distribución, 2020. DVD.

Peter Buse and Andrew Stott, haunting, that is, a ghost's "capacity to return," which is "indispensable" to understand our sense of time, "is not necessarily a happy event."[29] Yet, *The Book of Life* mediates the presence of ghosts in a more welcoming and comic way through an idealized popular celebration. These ghosts act as a source of extended vitality through memory. People can live beyond their physical existence as long as someone in the land of the living remembers them, keeping them in constant connection with the present. A Gothic understanding of these aspects in the narrative helps us reconsider what social and cultural dynamics are being worked through in terms of the perception of death.

Witchcraft and Haunted Castles

Incidentally, the Mexican production *Día de muertos* is the most Gothic of these films. Clearly designed to cash in on the recent commercialization of the Day of the Dead in US cinema, particularly through *Spectre*, it creates a more autochthonous popular representation of the holiday by Mexicans for Mexicans. While *Coco* and *The Book of Life* justify the fair and respectful use of imagery associated with the Mexican holiday, *Día de muertos* already assumes knowledge about the social values about the dead and their significance within the framework of the yearly celebration. It makes use of elements like *altares de ofrendas* and a land of the dead to identify its thematic backdrop. Likewise, there is an element of questioning the subject's identity in terms of family, but the film moves beyond kinship and tradition to delve into the protagonist's own fears about having no relatable past. The film incorporates several recognizable Gothic motifs that take the ritual and cultural experience beyond its lush, denotative aspects. In this sense, *Día de muertos* adheres more closely to the "negative aesthetics" that, according to Fred Botting, "informs gothic texts."[30] The antagonist's desire to fool death and live eternally seeks to eliminate the painful process of mourning and the rituals of remembrance, putting the balance of life and death at perilous risk. Morlete is intent on fulfilling a fantasy of never having to experience loss. This works as a transgression, which according to Botting is characteristic of Gothic fictions. Morlete's transgressive acts make us aware of "boundaries and taboos, both of their existence and the consequences of breaking them."[31] They are catalysts to address the fears of death that are hermetically sealed with the appearance of a joyful celebration.

As such, the film incorporates elements of terror and horror that challenge the positive assumptions of the holiday, in order to glimpse at its potential negative implications. For David Punter, this is related to the "plethora of unresolved issues to do with the past, with that extraordinary, singular past which is Mexico's, a past compounded of the traces of the indigene, of conquest, of the feudal, of successive dictatorial tyrannies."[32] The celebration hides concerns that have to do with cultural identity, whether collective or individual, and this is where *Día de muertos* delves into the perils of bringing back the dead into the realm of the living.

One of the key features that puts the relationship between life and death at stake in this film is witchcraft. Morlete's fear of death turns him into a self-centered individual whose only intent is to never lose anything or anyone he considers his. His characterization can be closely associated with that of a Gothic villain: he uses (and psychologically abuses) Salma for his own personal ends by revealing her past and turning her against her own living family. Morlete is able to bend Salma's will so he can benefit from her anger. Morlete is deceitful and cruel, thus disclosing a personality that is typical of antagonists in Gothic fiction. The dynamic between female protagonist and male villain results in an unleashing of darkness that does not depend entirely on one single character, but, as Helene Meyers suggests, in the relation between "the figure of the Gothic villain-hero" and the "heroine's relation to him." This results in situations and conflicts in a world that "is presented as a confusing and dangerous place for women."[33]

Likewise, an important setting in the film is the abandoned castle. By means of her research, Salma knows that she might be able to unravel the secret of who her parents were by visiting the castle. The building stands on a small island in the middle of a lake close to the town. It features a distinctive nineteenth-century European architectural style, which adds to the strangeness of Salma's mystery.[34] Accompanied by Jorge and Pedro, Salma explores it in the middle of the night. The group walks through a dark forest where they encounter a secret door on the castle grounds. Here, they find a small axolotl, which Jorge claims is an animal linked to the realm of the dead. When the axolotl jumps back through one of the holes on the locked door and opens it, a long shot reveals that it bears the shape of a skull that slightly resembles Aztec depictions of the god of the underworld, Mictlantecuhtli (figure 7.2). Hidden behind shrubbery, it suggests that the place has not been tended to for a long time. Additionally, it stands on the side and under the main bulk of the castle, a secret entrance that reveals itself to the characters. The passageway links Salma's and her cousins' present with something long forgotten. Once inside, the characters wander through an ancient pre-Hispanic-like temple with columns resembling skulls and skeletons as well as more carvings of skulls on its walls. On the altar, there is a book that contains a pre-Hispanic codex. Salma is able to read it, revealing her inherent magic powers. She immediately understands that the big tree behind the altar, called a *ceiba*, is a permanent link between the lands of the living and the dead. Its roots go deep under the earth providing a physical and mystical connection that must be respected.

This castle scenario in itself features several familiar Gothic motifs: a still-standing remnant of the past, its abandonment giving it a brooding

Figure 7.2. The hidden door beneath the castle resembling the god Mictlantecuhtli. *Source:* Gutiérrez Medrano, Carlos, dir. *Día de muertos*, 2019; Mexico City: Zima Entertainment/Videocine Distribución, 2020. DVD.

and terrifying appearance, with secrets kept (both natural and supernatural) inside its walls.[35] At the same time, its architectural structure departs from the castles found in European Gothic fiction by acknowledging that the base and root of this European-style building has been built on top of a previous (conquered) civilization. This in turn reveals the complex cultural and historical constitution of Mexicanness, which is the result of a stacking up of different traditions, artfully combined to denote an amalgamation of cultural elements, in this case related to death. In its structure, the castle's disassociated but linked architectural styles form the basis for an attempt to connect not only time but also differing cultural understandings of time itself, life, and death in a presumably hybrid mode. For Antonio Alcalá González and Ilse Bussing López, this provides a way to better understand what Gothic does in Latin American literature and culture. It is "a hybrid that incorporates local and foreign traditions,"[36] reminding us of the double "cultural heritage" of the region,[37] itself in constant struggle because it is haunted by the past that gave rise to this complex identity.

Gothic in this film seeks to acknowledge again aspects that are both structural and symbolic. On the surface, it represents the celebration and respect for death inherent in Mexican culture. Underneath it all, there are elements that, when revised once more, reveal darker and more negative intentions toward death, based primarily on the fear of the end of life on behalf of the antagonist. This is further linked to Salma's quest to know who her parents were, thus appropriately making her a Gothic heroine whose identity involves confronting her own sense of morality when she is manipulated by a selfish man who longs to keep his past relationship alive.

The film is not Gothic because of its formal elements but due to how it highlights a conceptualization of dark and brooding aspects surrounding the Day of the Dead, based on disclosing secrets, the fear of death itself, and the horror of breaching the limits set out by life and death. The Day of the Dead honors this balance, but Morlete's desire to break it threatens existence and nonexistence—and the value of memory as the keeper of kinship through past, present, and future. These ulterior character motives drive the narrative in this Mexican film. Rather than pay homage to well-known and familiar rituals and traditions, *Día de muertos* discloses a persistent anxiety derived from the ambiguity toward death in Mexican culture. The plotline delves deeper into instances of personal identity and puts specific cultural attitudes toward family and kinship into question. Well-kept secrets anger Salma and lead to her malpractice of magic, with negative consequences for the town and its inhabitants. When Morlete gains the powers of death, he decides to open a rift that brings in revenants, both good and evil, into the realm of the living. All this to fulfill his own personal desire. The result is a world that risks becoming undead. When Salma tries to save the town, she understands that the Day of the Dead does not involve mourning, but rather remembrance.

When a traditional holiday turns dreadfully dark, it exposes the terror of the undead and the horror of demonic specters in the mundane world. The Day of the Dead is not Gothic itself; rather, the treatment of this Mexican festivity in this film explores anxieties surrounding loss and mourning. The return of the not-living is tinged with supernatural and macabre aesthetics manifested visually, in the form of animation that discloses cultural fears about opening up a hermetic cultural attitude toward life and death. This is what Gothic does. It lays bare a series of beliefs that are manifested during a traditional celebration and questions what lies beneath them and how this affects identity and systems of signification. While *The Book of Life* and *Coco* pay their respects to the Mexican holiday, they also recognize cultural diversity both within the United States as well as with its southern neighbor. Structures of kinship and deceitful villains may provide a marginal Gothic line in their plotlines, but they do not take part in dark or macabre imaginings that would make them fully Gothic.

On the other hand, the Mexican film *Día de muertos*' very conscious attempt to provide a more terrifying story by means of dark magic and villainy allows for a combination of celebration and fear when characters disobey cultural assumptions toward death. In the end, Salma realizes and reinforces her sense of kinship, identity, and belonging, but only by baring herself to supernatural powers and actions that force her to think about her actions and their consequences in her hometown. To describe the Day of the Dead as Gothic would be an error; instead, it is more appropriate to understand that Mexican Gothic always looks at the complex constitution of Mexican identity and its ambiguous approach to death by going deeper into anxieties and fears that lie under this traditional, and seemingly happy, holiday.

Notes

1. Stanley Brandes, «Is There a Mexican View of Death?," *Ethos* 31, no. 1 (2003): 130.

2. Brandes, 133.

3. Claudio Lomnitz, *Idea de la muerte en México* (Mexico: Fondo de Cultura Económica, 2006), 43.

4. Lomnitz, 25.

5. Lomnitz, 54. For Paz's problematic understanding of the Day of the Dead, see Octavio Paz, *El laberinto de la soledad/Postdata/Vuelta a El laberinto de la soledad* (Mexico: Fondo de Cultura Económica, 2004), 51–71.

6. Lomnitz, 49.

7. Laura Fernández, "Canta y No Llores: Life and Latinidad in Children's Animation," in *The Routledge Companion to Latina/o Popular Culture*, ed. Frederick Luis Aldama (New York: Routledge, 2016), 74.

8. This is not the first time an animated Mexican film has set a narrative during the Day of the Dead. *La leyenda de la Nahuala* (2007), created by animation company Animex, also tells the story of an orphaned boy in the early nineteenth century who lives the colonial city of Puebla, who, on the Day of the Dead, unleashes the evil spirit of La Nahuala. Motifs similar to *Día de muertos* can be instantly recognized, such as the search for family origins, religion, haunted houses, and the search for immortality. The film spawned a series of sequels produced by Ánima Estudios, with each one addressing a horror-related Mexican folk legend, as is the case of *La llorona*, the mummies of Guanajuato, *el chupacabras*, and *el charro negro*.

9. Vicente Gutiérrez, "Día de muertos no le tiene miedo a Coco," *El Economista*, October 16, 2018, https://www.eleconomista.com.mx/arteseideas/Dia-de-muertos-no-le-tiene-miedo-a-Coco-20181016-0150.html.

10. *Anuario estadístico de cine mexicano 2019 / Statistical Yearbook of Cinema* (Mexico: Secretaría de Cultura / Instituto Mexicano de Cinematografía, 2020).

11. Jacques Derrida, *Specters of Marx: The State of the Debt, the Work of Mourning and the New International* (New York: Routledge, 1994), 48.

12. Derrida, xviii.

13. David Punter, *The Literature of Terror: A History of Gothic Fictions from 1765 to the Present Day. Volume 1: The Gothic Tradition*, 2nd ed. (London: Longman, 1996), 9.

14. Chris Baldick, *The Oxford Book of Gothic Tales* (Oxford: Oxford University Press, 1992), xix.

15. Inés Ordiz and Sandra Casanova-Vizcaíno, «Introduction: Latin America, the Caribbean, and the Persistence of the Gothic», in *Latin American Gothic in Literature and Culture*, ed. Sandra Casanova-Vizcaíno and Inés Ordiz (New York: Routledge, 2018), 2.

16. Ordiz and Casanova-Vizcaíno, 5.

17. Catherine Spooner, *Post-Millenial Gothic: Comedy, Romance and the Rise of Happy Gothic* (London: Bloomsbury, 2017), 10.

18. Alberto Ribas-Casasayas and Amanda L. Petersen, «Introduction: Theories of the Ghost in a Transhispanic Context», in *Espectros: Ghostly Hauntings in*

Contemporary Transhispanic Narratives, ed. Alberto Ribas-Casasayas and Amanda L. Petersen (Lanham, MD: Bucknell University Press, 2016), 6.

19. A *catrina* is an illustration of a skeleton dressed in traditional Mexican clothing. It became immensely popular by illustrator José Guadalupe Posada. This figure has become an icon during the Day of the Dead as an elaborate impersonation of Death itself. For more information about *catrinas*, see Paco Zavala, "Cumplió Cien años "La Catrina" Imagen Creada por José Guadalupe Posada," *La Prensa San Diego*, February 17, 2012. https://laprensa.org/cumplio-cien-anos-la-catrina-imagen-creada-por-jose-guadalupe-posada.

20. Mikhail Bakhtin, "Folk Humor and Carnival Laughter," in *The Bakhtin Reader: Selected Writings of Bakhtin, Medvedev and Voloshinov*, ed. Pam Morris (London: Arnold, 1994), 198–99.

21. Stanley Brandes, «The Day of the Dead, Halloween, and the Quest for Mexican National Identity», *The Journal of American Folklore* 111, no. 442 (1998): 360.

22. "México: James Bond inspira un desfile del Día de los Muertos," *BBC Mundo*, October 29, 2016, https://www.bbc.com/mundo/noticias-37813219.

23. Spooner, *Post-Millenial Gothic: Comedy, Romance and the Rise of Happy Gothic*, 3.

24. Glennis Byron, "Introduction," in *Globalgothic*, ed. Glennis Byron (Manchester: Manchester University Press, 2013), 3.

25. Byron, 4–5.

26. Molly Todd's chapter in this edited collection pays particular attention to the ethics of representation of Mexican culture in this Pixar film. The relationship between Gothic and commercial interests has not been overlooked. For more information, see Catherine Spooner, *Contemporary Gothic* (London: Reaktion Books, 2006).

27. Agnes Andeweg and Sue Zlosnik, "Introduction," in *Gothic Kinship*, ed. Agnes Andeweg and Sue Zlosnik (Manchester: Manchester University Press, 2013), 2.

28. Derrida, *Specters of Marx*, 36.

29. Peter Buse and Andrew Stott, "Introduction: a Future for Haunting," in *Ghosts: Deconstruction, Psychoanalysis, History*, ed. Peter Buse and Andrew Stott (Basingstoke, UK: Macmillan, 1999), 8.

30. Fred Botting, *Gothic*, 2nd ed. (London: Routledge, 2014), 1.

31. Botting, 9.

32. David Punter, *The Gothic Condition: Terror, History and the Psyche* (Cardiff: University of Wales Press, 2016), 171.

33. Helene Meyers, *Femicidal Fears: Narratives of the Female Gothic Experience* (Albany: State University of New York Press, 2001), 18.

34. The incorporation of foreign architectural styles in Latin America helps re-localize the Gothic experience as it shifts and reverses the notions of the local and the foreign, the familiar and the threatening, and the present and the past. For more information about this strategy in the play *Las manos de Dios*, by Guatemalan-born Carlos Solórzano, see David S. Dalton, "Liberation and the Gothic in Carlos Solórzano's

Las manos de Dios," in *Latin American Gothic in Literature and Culture*, ed. Sandra Casanova-Vizcaíno and Inés Ordiz (New York: Routledge, 2018), 84–95.

35. A subsequent scene shows the characters at the main entrance of the castle where two gigantic statues of armor guard the door. Both statues become animated and prevent Salma and her cousins from entering the castle. This is a slight nod to what is considered the first Gothic novel, whose narrative conflict starts when Manfred's son Conrad is crushed by a giant helmet on the day of his wedding to Isabella. For more information, see Horace Walpole, *The Castle of Otranto: A Gothic Story* (Oxford: Oxford University Press, 1982).

36. Antonio Alcalá González and Ilse Bussing López, "Introduction», in *Doubles and Hybrids in Latin American Gothic*, ed. Antonio Alcalá González and Ilse Bussing López (New York: Routledge, 2020), 3.

37. Alcalá González and Bussing López, 10.

Bibliography

Alcalá González, Antonio, and Ilse Bussing López. "Introduction." In *Doubles and Hybrids in Latin American Gothic*, edited by Antonio Alcalá González and Ilse Bussing López, 1–15. New York: Routledge, 2020.

Andeweg, Agnes, and Sue Zlosnik. "Introduction." In *Gothic Kinship*, edited by Agnes Andeweg and Sue Zlosnik, 1–11. Manchester: Manchester University Press, 2013.

Anuario estadístico de cine mexicano 2019 / Statistical Yearbook of Cinema. Mexico City: Secretaría de Cultura / Instituto Mexicano de Cinematografía, 2020.

Bakhtin, Mikhail. "Folk Humor and Carnival Laughter." In *The Bakhtin Reader: Selected Writings of Bakhtin, Medvedev and Voloshinov*, edited by Pam Morris, 194–206. London: Arnold, 1994.

Baldick, Chris. *The Oxford Book of Gothic Tales*. Oxford: Oxford University Press, 1992.

Botting, Fred. *Gothic*. 2nd ed. London: Routledge, 2014.

Brandes, Stanley. "Is There a Mexican View of Death?" *Ethos* 31, no. 1 (2003): 127–44.

Brandes, Stanley. "The Day of the Dead, Halloween, and the Quest for Mexican National Identity." *Journal of American Folklore* 111, no. 442 (1998): 359–80.

Buse, Peter, and Andrew Stott. "Introduction: A Future for Haunting." In *Ghosts: Deconstruction, Psychoanalysis, History*, edited by Peter Buse and Andrew Stott, 1–20. Basingstoke, UK: Macmillan, 1999.

Byron, Glennis. "Introduction." In *Globalgothic*, edited by Glennis Byron, 1–10. Manchester: Manchester University Press, 2013.

Dalton, David S. "Liberation and the Gothic in Carlos Solórzano's *Las manos de Dios*." In *Latin American Gothic in Literature and Culture*, edited by Sandra Casanova-Vizcaíno and Inés Ordiz, 84–95. New York: Routledge, 2018.

Derrida, Jacques. *Specters of Marx: The State of the Debt, the Work of Mourning and the New International.* New York: Routledge, 1994.

Fernández, Laura. "Canta y No Llores: Life and Latinidad in Children's Animation." In *The Routledge Companion to Latina/o Popular Culture*, edited by Frederick Luis Aldama, 68–75. New York: Routledge, 2016.

Gutiérrez, Vicente. "Día de muertos no le tiene miedo a Coco." *El Economista*, October 16, 2018. https://www.eleconomista.com.mx/arteseideas/Dia-de-muertos-no-le-tiene-miedo-a-Coco-20181016-0150.html.

Lomnitz, Claudio. *Idea de la muerte en México*. Mexico: Fondo de Cultura Económica, 2006.

BBC Mundo. "México: James Bond inspira un desfile del Día de los Muertos," October 29, 2016. https://www.bbc.com/mundo/noticias-37813219.

Meyers, Helene. *Femicidal Fears: Narratives of the Female Gothic Experience*. Albany: State University of New York Press, 2001.

Ordiz, Inés, and Sandra Casanova-Vizcaíno. "Introduction: Latin America, the Caribbean, and the Persistence of the Gothic." In *Latin American Gothic in Literature and Culture*, edited by Sandra Casanova-Vizcaíno and Inés Ordiz, 1–12. New York: Routledge, 2018.

Paz, Octavio. *El laberinto de la soledad/Postdata/Vuelta a El laberinto de la soledad.* Mexico: Fondo de Cultura Económica, 2004.

Punter, David. *The Gothic Condition: Terror, History and the Psyche*. Cardiff: University of Wales Press, 2016.

Punter, David. *The Literature of Terror: A History of Gothic Fictions from 1765 to the Present Day. Volume 1: The Gothic Tradition.* 2nd ed. London: Longman, 1996.

Ribas-Casasayas, Alberto, and Amanda L. Petersen. "Introduction: Theories of the Ghost in a Transhispanic Context." In *Espectros: Ghostly Hauntings in Contemporary Transhispanic Narratives*, edited by Alberto Ribas-Casasayas y Amanda L. Petersen, 1–11. Lanham, MD: Bucknell University Press, 2016.

Spooner, Catherine. *Contemporary Gothic*. London: Reaktion Books, 2006.

Spooner, Catherine. *Post-Millenial Gothic: Comedy, Romance and the Rise of Happy Gothic*. London: Bloomsbury, 2017.

Walpole, Horace. *The Castle of Otranto: A Gothic Story*. Oxford: Oxford University Press, 1982.

Zavala, Paco. "Cumplió Cien años 'La Catrina' Imagen Creada por José Guadalupe Posada." *La Prensa San Diego*. February 17, 2012. https://laprensa.org/cumplio-cien-anos-la-catrina-imagen-creada-por-jose-guadalupe-posada.

Filmography

Arnaiz, Ricardo, dir. *La leyenda de la Nahuala*. 2007; Puebla, Mexico: Animex Producciones.

Gutiérrez, Jorge, R., dir. *The Book of Life*. 2014; Beverly Hills, CA: 20th Century Fox Home Entertainment, 2016. Blu-Ray.

Gutiérrez Medrano, Carlos, dir. *Día de muertos*. 2019; Mexico City: Zima Entertainment/Videocine Distribución, 2020. DVD.

Mendes, Sam, dir. *Spectre*. 2015; Beverly Hills, CA: 20th Century Fox Home Entertainment, 2016. Blu-Ray.

Unkrich, Lee, dir. *Coco*. 2017; Burbank, CA: Buenavista Home Entertainment, 2018. Blu-Ray.

Chapter 8

Border/lands of Belonging in Disney-Pixar's *Coco*

Molly F. Todd

One of the most captivating animated films released recently was Disney-Pixar's *Coco.* Although produced by a global (still US-based) corporation, it premiered in Mexico in Spanish, breaking box office records when it earned $57.9 million USD.[1] It later performed well among Latinx/diverse crowds in the United States and among moviegoers across the globe. For many viewers, the film was a representational success story—a thoughtful, culturally nuanced example of Mexican people and culture in the circulation of global mediascapes. It was seen as a homage or love letter to Mexico.[2] During the time of the movie's release, such a positive representation was particularly meaningful. *Coco* premiered when the US-Mexico border was a central focus of global and US media, and notably of ex-US president Donald Trump.[3] Portrayals of migrants fleeing from Customs and Border Protection's tear gas or running across the border in "caravans" became images that represented both the "invasion" and "crisis" at the border.[4] In her study of global border politics, Harsha Walia reminds us, "Such representations depict migrants and refugees as the *cause* of an *imagined* crisis at the border, when in fact, mass migration is the *outcome* of the *actual* crisis of capitalism, conquest, and climate change."[5] Nevertheless, the ex-president was notorious for spouting dehumanizing remarks and using inflammatory rhetoric in relation to the border and to Mexican people (among others), a fact that came through with the (incomplete) construction of a supposedly "impenetrable," "powerful" and "beautiful" border wall.[6]

In this context, *Coco* stood out as the antithesis to pejorative representations of Mexicans and Mexican people in global mediascapes. Rather than build walls, *Coco* has been celebrated as a bridge toward multicultural diversity.[7] Like many viewers, when I first saw the film and its colorful, intricate images and heard its vibrant soundscapes, I felt strong emotions like happiness and a yearning for belonging. At the time of viewing, I was living in my home state of Colorado and working on my master's thesis on the militarization of the US-Mexico border. Learning about for-profit detention centers, government-corporate military contracts, and border militarization as a for-profit industry, I knew that the ex-president's approach to the border, his rhetoric about the position of Mexicans—concurrently as less-than, as criminal, as "backwards"—and the images that followed them was not new, but rather a recent articulation of longer-standing patterns of US-Mexico border politics.[8] It is from that position that I came to the movie *Coco*, which shaped the lens from which I began to ponder the borders that appeared in the film.[9] I also came to the film as a second-language Spanish speaker who has been to Mexico and taken interest in the country's music, art, and cultural diversity that expands beyond its borders.

Indeed, *Coco* is not only a film about Mexico. In many ways, *Coco* is also a film about borders and border/lands.[10] It starts with a story of a family's struggle to draw a boundary at music and their child's pursuit of a musical career. That child was Mamma Coco, the great-grandmother of the film's protagonist, Miguel, and from whom the movie takes its title. For generations after Coco, the limits of what could be possible and what kind of life could be imagined were bounded by this restriction on music. Miguel, however, follows his heart across that border proclaiming "I am not like the rest of my family," and secretly practices his guitar to the tune of his idol Ernesto de la Cruz. Cruz's character—who dons a shiny white suit, a white sombrero, charming grin, and a smooth voice—was inspired by popular Mexican musicians Jorge Negrete and Pedro Infante, each of whom was a sonic fixture in Golden Age Mexican cinema.[11]

As Día de Muertos was approaching, Miguel's family, like many families across Mexico, had prepared an altar to remember and connect with their loved ones who had passed on to the other side. One night, Miguel's dog Dante jumps up on the altar to feast on the tasty meals placed there for the dead, and a struggle between them ensues. Miguel wrestles Dante away, but not before a photograph on the top of the altar comes tumbling down, cracking the glass of the frame and revealing the paper photograph underneath.

The photo, torn at the corner, introduces audiences to Mama Imelda, Miguel's great-great grandmother, standing next to a man who appears to be holding something. Although the tear in the photo edges right across the man's bust, missing the portion of the photograph with his face, Miguel notices a fold in the photograph. This edge reveals hidden information, as Miguel unfolds the photograph and sees a man holding a guitar. "Could this be Ernesto de la Cruz?" Miguel wonders. The white suit and guitar gleamed in Miguel's eyes: it must be! Confirming Miguel's underlying desire to play music, the unfolded photograph bridged Miguel to the musical world. From that moment on, he decided he would seek de la Cruz's blessing to play music since he was family, after all.

A few nights later, following his newfound confidence, Miguel decides to enter a singing contest, but he first needs to find a guitar. Running frantically through the graveyard, he spots one shining in a large pantheon[12] ahead and runs toward it, breaking the glass to enter and snatching the guitar. As fate would have it, Miguel realizes he has entered the pantheon of de la Cruz, and looking up at Cruz's portrait, he tells him he must borrow his guitar so that he can play in the plaza. At that moment, Miguel strums his guitar, and a wind blows through the structure, gently lifting and twirling the marigold petals at his feet. In that musical act, Miguel unknowingly crosses the border between the land of the living into the land of the dead and himself becomes imperceivable to those living on the other side.

The movie mobilizes an imaginary border between the land of the living (Mexico) and the southbound land of the dead as Miguel also navigates other borders like his familial boundaries with music or the "traditional" values his family and his own "modern" desires to leave that life behind and become a musician. Other symbolic, sensorial, and embodied borders emerge throughout the film, drawing on the mythology of the Mexican holiday Día de Muertos. *Coco*'s border/lands overflow with blurred boundaries between living beings and ghosts, magical creatures, and the liminal spaces between the land of the living and the land of the dead.

This chapter follows those borders, homing in on the border-crossing scene where characters encounter a border security checkpoint. Before beginning the discussion of that scene, the first section of this chapter discusses Mexican national cultural representation in a global marketplace, focusing on power by highlighting debates over cultural imperialism. In that discussion, I retain in view longer colonial projects of controlling national cultural narratives through authorship, including charges marking Disney as culturally imperialist, and connect Disney's more recent adaptation of authentic

Mexican representations to neoliberal inclusion. The second section of the chapter analyzes five still shots and the broader cinematic experience in one of the border-crossing scenes. In that section, I discuss the meaning of integrating neoliberal border security imagery with the Día de Muertos skeleton-ghost characters, when set in a context of Disney cultural production about the Mexican nations.[13] However, as I discuss below, despite being produced by Disney, *Coco* was made largely *by* Mexican or Mexican American cast members, writers, and artists—and arguably *for* those same crowds.[14]

Following Ignacio Sánchez-Prado, who has argued that cinema provides a unique window into "the social and cultural impact of neoliberalism in Mexico," this chapter explores the following questions:[15] What productive or performative effects do these nuanced, positive, and "authentic" representations of Mexicans and Mexican culture alongside a militarized border have in the neoliberal global economy? Do the border scene(s) and the border representations in Coco *normalize* and naturalize a militarized border (and one that is ultimately inhumane)? Or, working as a parody of border tensions and as an authentic representation of Greater-Mexican cultural practice and thought, does *Coco* ultimately challenge systems of separation and exclusion, moving audiences toward a more inclusive global cultural vision?

Overall, in this chapter, I argue that representation *matters*. It has productive effects, but these are not simply what is reported through the lens of a liberal multicultural identity politics. Representation can have subversive performative effects, like the power of seeing oneself represented and what futures can be imagined as a result, but representation can also normalize certain ideas about power, such as border checkpoints and a growing military apparatus, that ultimately further global inequality or what some have called global apartheid.[16] Marissa K. López alludes to this fact when she argues that "representational otherness," when divorced from "material inequalities," produces a type of "neoliberal aesthetics" that generally fails to resist neoliberal governance or power and instead validates the status quo in the global political economy.[17] Indeed, representation often facilitates certain openings or crossings, often of capital, while simultaneously facilitating other closings or forms of blockage and reinforcement, often (paradoxically) of people themselves.[18] Ultimately, I argue that *Coco* is neither a contemporary example of a veiled "cultural imperialism" committed by Disney, nor does it simply move Mexican, US, or global culture toward a happy, diverse, and globally inclusive multiculturalism with equity and dignity for all. Instead, I contend that *Coco* materializes neoliberal belonging and inclusion, thus incorporating Mexican people into a global cultural marketplace on certain terms as symbolized by the skeleton-ghosts.

Cultural Hegemony, Commodified Inclusion, and Multicultural Representation

Many reviews and academic publications about *Coco* thus far have focused on the topic of "authentic" Mexican national identity on a global stage, and the question of an authentic "Mexicanness," or *mexicanidad*, being represented in *Coco*.[19] Discourses of cultural authenticity, especially as expressed in a corporate media production, are part of longer debates about cultural representation and practices of "cultural imperialism" and cultural hegemony by media giants like Disney. They are also part of larger debates around cultural exchange and transmission across borders. Transculturation moves in many directions, not just from the "core" nations (and their hegemonic cultural producers like Disney), into the periphery.[20] Questions surrounding Disney's complicity, as well as break from, reproducing ethnocentric cultural stereotypes have been circulating since long before *Coco* came to be, and they have interrogated issues of power, domination, cultural hegemony, and the homogenization of global culture.

The argument that Disney's productions are a form of cultural imperialism or cultural appropriation is not new. In an important reflection during the Pinochet administration in Chile, Ariel Dorfman and Armand Mattelart drew connections between the ideology of Disney comics and American imperialism in their well-known book: *How to Read Donald Duck: Imperialist Ideology in the Disney Comic*. They viewed the imperialist and colonizing force of mainstream media as hegemonic and totalizing, fully normalizing the ideas of "Western" capitalism. Indeed, Disney has a long history of cultural blunders for which it has been criticized. From appropriation, to "brown-facing," to (mis)representation, to American Imperialism, Disney has been shown to produce "cultural" products that center Euro-centric norms and ideas while orientalizing or exoticizing the "Other."[21]

Antonio Gramsci argued that hegemony implied not simply power based on domination but also power based on "direction," which could be perpetuated through ideology and culture.[22] Culture is one channel by which the worldview of the capitalist class is legitimated and framed as being for the benefit of all people, rather than just for the benefit of capitalists. Gramsci states that "the realisation of a hegemonic apparatus, insofar as it creates a new ideological terrain, determines a *reform of consciousness and of methods of knowledge*."[23] His conception of hegemony focuses on relations of capital, whereby the knowledges and forms of consciousness or common sense mirror the values of the ruling class. Therefore, cultural hegemony goes to the level of what we can imagine, as cultural products interact with our consciousness and inform our beliefs. When viewed via a framework of hegemony, Disney's representations of cultural authenticity still ultimately orient audiences toward US norms and a homogenized (Anglocentric) vision of cultural inclusion. Does *Coco* facilitate the inclusion of "Mexicans" into the Disney world as a homogenous group that elides much of the cultural diversity that exists throughout the Mexican nations?[24] It is more complicated than that. (Post)colonial and decolonial scholarship demonstrates that alongside attempts at domination through culture is resistance, and that imposed cultural practices or norms are often reappropriated by subjugated populations toward their own means.[25]

In her discussion of embedded coloniality in *Mulan*, *Moana*, and *Coco* Michelle Anya Anjirbag has discussed hegemony in animated film through the homogenization of culture and the adaptation and assimilation into "Western," "developed" ways of life and cultural products.[26] Although she largely critiques the Disney corporation as an extension of coloniality, she does note that *Coco* "challenged the adhered-to production process of the studio and reconfigures in some ways the importance of opening space for the Other to represent itself and negotiate its own representation in mainstream production by hegemonic gatekeepers."[27] Overall, however, she questions how cultural production is shaped by and shapes a colonial matrix of power and considers how film can capture imaginary spaces, effectively extending the narrative reach of the corporations that produce film and the knowledges within them. She finds that Disney animation can present knowledges that confirm US-dominant ideologies and even transnational ideologies of the status quo. Furthermore, she positions Disney in the hegemonic culture of "American Caucasian, cis-gendered, straight, Anglo."[28]

Disney, to some extent, has addressed these issues by adding disclaimers on Disney+ to their older productions, which warn viewers the material could be racially offensive. The mega corporation, at surface level, seems to now be consistently aiming to better their cultural representations. Anjirbag also interrogated the ways in which cultural authenticity, or the inclusion of "culturally authentic" products, is a tool of corporate cultural producers like Disney to expand their reach into the marketplace.[29] Such critiques of "authentic" cultural inclusion allow for a more critical perspective of *Coco's* reception across audiences. For example, in preparation for marketing the film, Disney tried to trademark "Día de Los Muertos" when they included the holiday's name in a proposed title. The titling debacle raised concerns over mishandling and misrepresenting information of the cultural "Other" (that is, of Mexican people by the Anglo-American Disney corporation), reflecting past debates about Disney's role in cultural imperialism. While the intentions *may* have been to simply describe the film, the effect would have been a trademark giving Disney rights to the name of the Mexican holiday. Owning the name is part of owning the narrative, and owning the narrative is a form of owning and dominating knowledge production.

In some ways, Disney's actions surrounding the making of the film appeared to be another attempt at cultural subsumption by the corporation, like their Indigenous labor extraction in *Moana* that took place under the larger rhetoric of cultural authenticity.[30] There is history of extraction of creative labor and knowledges in colonial practices that is arguably mirrored in some of Disney's cultural products that garner profits for Disney, not the communities.[31] Another point of contention relates to the contributions of Afro-Mexicans to Mexican culture that are not explicitly referenced in the film, following larger patterns of subsuming Afro-Mexican histories into larger Mestizo nation-building projects.[32] However, *Coco* does include the music of Son Jarocho,[33] a musical form with Afro-Latino roots and histories of resistance to Spanish colonialism and transatlantic slavery.

The tunes, featured in songs such as "Un poco loco"[34] create aural sensations with stringed instruments and funky sounds reflective of the intermingling of cultures and musical knowledges. Son Jarocho first emerged in Veracruz, Mexico, when European colonial fleets carried enslaved Africans from the port in Havana to Veracruz, bringing along their musical knowledges. The music of son Jarocho is a sonic Afro-Latino tradition that enlivens Afro-Latino lifeworlds: "The histories of African-descended populations remained alive in embodied and cultural practices, specifically regional music and dance forms from several Mexican states. Among the most prominent of these living traditions is son Jarocho from Veracruz."[35]

The geographical and socioeconomic context of son Jarocho reveals an intermixing of Spanish, African, and Indigenous cultures that makes it at once all of those identities, as well as simply "Mexican." Just as Jacqueline Avila argues that Mexican "national" cinema is constructed transnationally in "cultural exchanges from across continents,"[36] the origins of what is considered "Mexican" national music is also transnational.[37] In *Coco* there are multiple layers of authorship across national boundaries that make up its narrative web, complicating the simplistic view that Disney has "colonized" the minds and hearts of the Mexican people.[38] Furthermore, what constitutes "Mexican" is not so clear, as national belonging does not equal homogenous racial, ethnic, or political identity.

One of the most outspoken critics of Disney's attempt to trademark Día de Muertos was Lalo Alcaraz, an American cartoonist who grew up along the US-Mexico border. In response, Alcaraz published a bookend cartoon of a dead mouse consisting only of bones, which reads, "Muerto Mouse—It's coming to trademark your cultura!"[39] His artwork reflects the concerns and critiques of cultural hegemony and cultural imperialism. However, Disney later hired Alcaraz as part of a team of cultural consultants to provide feedback for the production and marketing of the movie. Disney saw Alcaraz as someone whose "worldview is informed by tuning into Mexican perspectives,"[40] marking a cross-border weaving of culture that complicates such claims to hegemony.

In an interview about their work on *Coco*, Alcaraz and another consultant, Marcela Davison Avilés, describe their own embodied knowledge of Mexico and the border between Mexico and the US. The interview demonstrated that, with Alcaraz's participation, the movie *Coco* became very much about asserting its legitimacy as Mexican and as a representation of Mexicanness through strong and nuanced cultural ties. Both musical and symbolic references to Mexico's Golden Age cinema and to "Mexican" national music abound. Furthermore, connections to Mexico's Indigenous histories are especially prominent in the cempasúchil (marigold) flower and Miguel's dog, Dante, who is a *Xoloitzcuintli*, the Mexican hairless dog breed that gets its name from the Aztec language and is thought to be a spiritual protector or guide in the land of the dead.[41] In *Coco*'s land of the dead, there are also references to Aztec pyramids.

In the same interview, Alcaraz and Davison Avilés also pointed to the "dark-skinned characters, [and] indigenous-featured characters" in the film as evidence of a resistance to an identity politics in Mexico and Mexican media which is anti-Indigenous.[42] They are speaking to Mexican cinema, which often whitewashes its characters or relegates Indigenous characters to the periphery.[43] In other ways, discussions about representation need to interrogate power dynamics of narrative authority, particularly as they relate to Hollywood. If representation signified undoing systems of domination in Mexico and globally, then perhaps Alcaraz would have been brought back on as a consultant for *Frozen II*, which premiered in 2019.

In hiring cultural consultants who have lived on the US side of the US-Mexico border and who were outspoken about its motives about producing a film called *Día de los Muertos* at first, Disney created a legitimacy of Mexican representation while subsuming the intricacies of Mexicanness. Indeed, the titling error ultimately led the corporation to create a more "culturally authentic" product that was incredibly well-received (and profitable) due to its supposed *authenticity*. That said, it remains pertinent to contextualize these shifts in sensitivity to racism and cultural representation. This is especially prominent in *Coco*, which was hailed as a representational success story of cultural authenticity and care. It was praised for its attention to details of Mexican culture and customs, and for its engagement with Mexican, Mexican American and Chicano/a/x actors, contributors, and consultants including self-identified "fronterizos," or people who live(d) along the US-Mexico border themselves.[44] Disney's method of cultural representation in *Coco* shifted from one of explicit "Othering," and instead captured peoples' worlds through heartfelt representation and inclusion of culturally authentic representations that crossed borders.

Indeed, film can no longer be understood solely through the lens of the nation (if it ever could).[45] Rather, we must place it in conversation with transnational networks of power and the viewing audiences that these produce. *Coco* is a film arguably made *for* Mexican people and largely *by* people who identified as (Greater-) Mexican: a large majority of the actors, artists, and consultants self-identified as Mexican or Mexican American. Nevertheless, these contributors were already validated by their placement in Hollywood through the participation in a Disney production. It is a film that is at once global or transnational with local articulations, much like the process of globalization itself.[46] This understanding of local/global (what Néstor García Canclini calls "glocal") helps situate a nonessentialist perspective of "culture," including when "Mexican culture" is referenced in this chapter.[47]

Coco was released across global viewing audiences whose lives, in distinct ways and through local articulations, had been and are still being shaped by a political economic climate of a neoliberal capitalism with colonial continuities: "The rise of neoliberalism has conferred upon certain companies a level of power once held by political and religious institutions at the time of colonial expansion."[48] Scholars have taken interest in *how* this has taken place, or how neoliberalism has taken hold, both through culture and at the level of subjectivity. Ignacio Sánchez Prado defines it as "a cultural signifier that constitutes social and cultural fields beyond the mere economy."[49] It has affected the audience's individual and communal sense of self. Indeed, the field of cultural representation is one space in which viewing audiences build their frameworks of meaning. In Mexico, changes to both the ways in which films were produced and consumed led to the erosion of national cinema, including a shift from a nationalized film industry to one open to private corporate producers.[50] Sánchez Prado notes that "the late 1980s revealed the remnants of a fading cultural geography of cinema."[51]

The audiences that came to see *Coco*, whether from Mexico or elsewhere in the world, have largely come to sense themselves as those who find meaning through consumption and commodification, or what Wendy Brown calls *Homo oeconomicus*.[52] According to Brown, neoliberalism has commodified all areas of life, not just the economic. People increasingly see themselves as individuals competing for global resources (including the value attached to belonging) and find belonging beyond national identity. Following Brown, Luca Mavelli's analysis of the commodification of citizenship argues that the logic of the market has produced a neoliberal economy of belonging, where "belonging, inclusion and exclusion are increasingly becoming a function of an individual's, or a group's, capacity to contribute to the country's financial viability, economic competitiveness, international reputation, moral standing, and self-understanding, and emotional well-being."[53] In this political economy of neoliberal belonging and exclusion—which evidences colonial continuities—inclusion is increasingly commodified through documentation practices, including the citizenship regimes and the commodification of citizenship that Mavelli discusses. Regimes of documentation shape subjectivity and daily life practices. Sarah Horton argues that "documents and bureaucratic requirements may be viewed as political technologies that help transform migrants into particular kinds of subjects."[54] In the section that follows, I consider the border crossing scene in the film, and consider photographs as a form of documentation that shape the behavior of the characters.

Borderlands (of imagination) in *Coco* // Securitizing *Coco's* border/lands

In the introduction of this chapter, I briefly detailed one of the prominent border scenes in *Coco*, when Miguel unknowingly crosses into the liminal land of the dead. In the land of the dead, glowing skeleton bodies represent memories of passed-on loved ones, familial bonds that those in the land of the living will have the chance to remember during Día de Muertos. In *Coco*, when living relatives place a photograph of the dead on their altars, the border between the two lands is opened. Without the photographs documenting the familial bonds on the altar and facilitating the process of remembering, the border stays closed.

For Miguel, his own journey to return to the land of the living led him on a musical path to find Ernesto de la Cruz. Along the way, he encounters a whimsical skeleton named Héctor, who promises to help him in exchange for Miguel placing his photo on the ofrenda. This would be the only way that Héctor himself could cross the border to visit his loved ones. Eventually, Héctor's photo is placed on the ofrenda, but not before he attempts to cross over into the land of the living "illegally."

In this scene, Miguel walks across the marigold bridge with Hector toward the border checkpoint that serves as the dividing line between the land of the living and the land of the dead. His eyes fill with wonder as he looks around at all the "spirit creatures," or "*alibrijes*," flying around the magical world, a liminal space where the living and the dead meet. The vibrancy of Día de Muertos and "Mexican" mythology travel the path of the alibrijes, floating and scurrying around viewers, pressing upon them with their bright colors: all the while Hector and Miguel make their way across the bridge and border checkpoint with celebratory sounds of families reuniting in the background.

In this moment, an affect of enchantment and sensations of joy meet a more disciplined soundscape of the border checkpoint. A Border Patrol agent announces that the crossers should have their documents ready for reentry. Perhaps more sobering is the announcement "if you are experiencing travel issues, agents at the department of family reunions are here to assist you." The skeleton agents are smiling, and although they are doing serious work, the affect is still bright and upbeat. The objects in the screen are almost glowing. Nevertheless, the agents at work are wearing uniforms familiar to some eyes as US Customs and Border Protection (CBP), touting long blue sleeves and a military aesthetic. The border crossing point in the film has similarities with the customs offices found at official ports of entry, like El Paso/Juarez or PedWest in San Isidro. That said, it is worth noting that the officials here are dead, and the border is meant to keep people in, not out.

Next, viewers are introduced to border security technology when a family walks into the scene. The Border Patrol agent tells them to step right up. A machine scans their bones to somehow see beneath the surface of the skeleton-spirit figures, as shown in figure 8.1 "Scanning Bones." A light 'ting' that sounds like a hotel desk bell indicates the family was approved to cross. They breathe a sigh of relief, smile, and move through. Following the family is Héctor's encounter, where we continue to get a better sense of the border. In figure 8.2, "Frida," Héctor plays with the Border Patrol agent, posing as Frida Kahlo in an attempt to sneak across the border. Figure 8.3 "Unauthorized," shows his surprise when his fake identity is discovered. A large red X appears on the screen with a blaring buzz behind it, reminding viewers that even in the spiritual world there are some who are not allowed, some who are "Other," and some who do not belong. Despite the abrupt sense of regulation of Héctor's phantasmic, skeletal body, the character does not express much fear. Perhaps rightly so, because in figure 8.4 "You're caught!" the Border Patrol agent smiles mischievously as she sarcastically remarks "Sorry, Frida." She seems amused by Héctor. They are playing a game. Her comments and tone suggest she knows he is trying to pose as someone else, but she does not call for his arrest. Instead, she lets the game continue. In figure 8.5, "Admission of Guilt," Héctor removes his disguise to show the Border Patrol agent his real identity and tries to charm her into allowing him to cross. The agent simply responds, "no foto on the ofrenda, no crossing the bridge."

Figure 8.1. A machine scans their bones to see beneath the surface of the skeleton-spirit figures. *Source:* Unkrich, Lee, dir. *Coco*, 2017; Burbank, CA: Buenavista Home Entertainment, 2018. Blu-Ray.

Figure 8.2. Héctor plays with the Border Patrol agent, posing as Frida Kahlo in an attempt to sneak across the border. *Source:* Unkrich, Lee, dir. *Coco*, 2017; Burbank, CA: Buenavista Home Entertainment, 2018. Blu-Ray.

Figure 8.3. Héctor expresses surprise when his identity is discovered. *Source:* Unkrich, Lee, dir. *Coco*, 2017; Burbank, CA: Buenavista Home Entertainment, 2018. Blu-Ray.

Figure 8.4. Border Patrol agent smiles mischievously and says, "Sorry, Frida." *Source:* Unkrich, Lee, dir. *Coco*, 2017; Burbank, CA: Buenavista Home Entertainment, 2018. Blu-Ray.

Figure 8.5. Héctor removes his disguise to show the Border Patrol his real identity. *Source:* Unkrich, Lee, dir. *Coco*, 2017; Burbank, CA: Buenavista Home Entertainment, 2018. Blu-Ray.

It is interesting that this scene debuted during a time when networks of political power, both globally as well as between Mexico and the US, were intently focused on border militarization, securitization, and the construction of border walls. Reading the borderlands in this scene helps us to follow Sanchez Prado's method for reading film, which asks where "the film links itself with the imaginary networks of political power that sustain the political system."[55] The representation of the border in the film is a site where we can trace these networks, and the border scene highlights the film's global position and the global position of Mexicans. I argue that although this scene acts as a parody of border security, the images nevertheless fit within, or reproduce larger discourses of neoliberal border politics with colonial and imperial continuities. Such discourses include those already mentioned—invasion and crisis—both of which correspond to the idea that borders need to be secured through militarization.

Militarization of the border/lands, including the various iterations of wall construction along the US-Mexico border, is representative of larger global trends toward militarizing borders and carceral geographies.[56] Constructing border walls is *part of*, not counter to, the process of neoliberal globalization.[57] Indeed, since 1989, over seventy border walls have been constructed or are in the process of being constructed in countries throughout the world.[58] Rather than understand this militarization as a response to various "border crises," it can better be understood as a response to a crisis of displacement,[59] whereby neoliberal reforms (among other things) produce social, political, and economic insecurity that cause populations and individuals to leave their homes. In Mexico, the country opened its economic borders to both the United States and Canada when it signed the North American Free Trade Agreement (NAFTA) in 1993. With NAFTA came the privatization of national industry, from farmland to film. It opened "domestic industries in Mexico to a global regime of production."[60] Going into effect on January 1, 1994, the agreement established the liberalization of capital and trade across national borders among those countries. Although the trilateral agreement opened trade between countries, it devalued the peso and flooded the Mexican market with US-subsidized corn, devastating the livelihood of farmers there, especially in the southern states of Veracruz and Chiapas.[61] Accordingly, the displacement caused by NAFTA's implementation has disproportionately affected poor rural farmers and Indigenous groups in Mexico, including Maya, Mixtec, and Zapotec.[62]

The liberalization of capital flows across borders that accompanied NAFTA did not equal the freedom of movement or equality of mobility across those same borders. NAFTA has been accompanied by increased militarization of the US-Mexico border that has been building since the 1980s. This increased securitization connects to longer histories of US-Mexico border formation, including anti-immigrant policies and oppressive, racialized practices. The US government uses "smart technologies," and tends to take on an "enforcement first" approach that largely ignores the structural causes of border crossing in the first place.[63] A recent immigration bill that lists border security technologies exemplifies this startling approach: "86 integrated fixed towers, 286 fixed camera systems, 232 mobile surveillance systems, 4,595 unattended ground sensors, 820 handheld equipment devices, 416 personal radiation detectors, 104 radiation isotope identification devices, 62 mobile automated targeting systems, (and) 53 fiber-optic tank inspection scopes."[64] The long list of security technologies mentioned above—not even a comprehensive list—is indicative of the Department of Homeland Security's (DHS) seemingly limitless budget, which was $40.6 billion at the time of *Coco*'s release, and which increased to $52 billion by 2022.[65]

DHS expenditures at and beyond the border aim to enforce a strategy of deterrence. The intention is to make border crossing so perilous that it would deter populations from making the journey. The idea is that because the "safe" areas to cross the border (urban areas) are militarized, migrants who desire to cross over without documentation will not do so. In this strategy, the deterrent is not just apprehension at border checkpoints, but more boldly it is the high risk of death if one should pass through the desert or attempt to swim around the ocean barrier of the Californias. However, it has not prevented undocumented immigration.[66] Instead, it is a strategy that intends deadly consequences, while at the same time, producing capitalist value.[67] This has been called a necropolitics and necrocitizenship.[68] Necropolitics produce dead bodies alongside discourses about who is expendable, or the exception. A necropolitical border strategy, or a biopolitical strategy that lets particular bodies die, performs through cultural productions on a global scale. Literature on border films and on the media representation of border crossers as dead bodies points to the political significance of the overrepresentation of the border crosser as victimized or as a body that experiences pain, violence, and death.[69] Furthermore, these filmed bodies become a place in which society can deposit its negative affect. Miguel Diaz-Barriga and Margaret Dorsey have argued that there is a "normalization of militarism and military engagement within Mexican American culture."[70] They specifically look at the connections between performances of citizenship and necropolitics, or what they call *necrocitizenship*—death and death making in citizenship practices. In their formulations, even practices of "resistance" to militarized border regimes can end up reaffirming (neoliberal) militarized subjectivities.

In *Coco*, if a character's photo is not on the ofrenda they cannot cross the border, just like those crossing into the United States from Mexico cannot do so without the proper documents. Similarly, the US-Mexico border keeps migrants who work in the US from returning home. The photo on the ofrenda serves as a connection between the land of the living and the land of the dead. It is through the memory of family members that their spirits survive. If they cannot cross the border, they will not be able to visit their loved ones; eventually they will be forgotten, and their spirit will not live on. Not being able to cross over then also implies being forgotten. This border and these border agents can determine who we forget. We see this as Héctor's character begins to deteriorate as he slowly fades away and becomes transparent. The more time that passes in which he can't cross, the closer the death of Héctor's spirit becomes.

There is something perhaps eerie about this in the larger geopolitical context of border politics and immigration, a context that produces literal skeletons. Taking a closer look at figures 8.2 and 8.3, "Frida" and "Unauthorized," viewers are confronted with an image of the Mexican national icon Frida Kahlo. Images of Kahlo and her work are some of the most well-known and commodified images of Mexican national culture. In this scene, Kahlo is brought into contemporary border security practices. In figure 8.2, we see Frida through the screen of a biometric scanning device, one used to ensure she can legally cross. In figure 8.3, we see her being marked as unauthorized. Although viewers also know that it is Héctor behind the floral headdress, Kahlo's familiar image nevertheless becomes enmeshed in larger border discourses where images of border militarization and "crisis" circulate regularly. On a larger scale, these securitized skeletons become incorporated into Mexican understandings of the holiday.

These images correspond with the idea of a need to securitize borders. They fit within discourses of "invasion" and crisis—larger hegemonic discourses of neoliberal border politics with colonial and imperial continuities. The border checkpoint in the film mirrors border security, border guards, border walls, and border technologies in the nonanimated world and represents borders as a point to be crossed but also as a point of detention and blockage. The Border Patrol agents use similar security technologies to those used on the US-Mexico border, and on many other borders across the world. They hold the power to determine if potential crossers have the right documents or not. While this is a depiction of crossing over from the land of the living to the land of the dead, it nevertheless comes at a time when border crossing is on the minds of many people across the US-Mexico borderlands and globally.

Conclusion

In *Coco*, the photographs serve as a form of documentation that shapes the behavior of the characters in the film. The practice of displaying photos on the altar is at once one of remembering during Día de Muertos and a practice of self-management through documentation in a regime of border security. By looking to the border scene as a hegemonic imaginary of borders in a neoliberal era—one that is militarized, controlled, and that separates families—the ways in which the film operated through neoliberal belonging and exclusion becomes clearer. This is how inclusion works in the neoliberal political economy: it happens on terms often defined by those in power. Although *Coco* tells a heartwarming story that integrates nuanced images and sensory experiences of Mexican culture into Disney's global cultural marketplace, it also integrates them across that story as both dead and securitized.

At the same time, this chapter has aimed to balance its critique of neoliberal belonging and its colonial continuities by highlighting that cultural production, including the movie *Coco*, cannot be understood through the locus of the nation. The movie was Mexican, American, and transnational all at once. It had localized connections to national representation in Mexico while at the same time being seen as a global production. The images and soundscapes in this film, and the affects they produce, take on distinct meaning across contexts, even for national groups: the images of border checkpoints may be completely commonplace for residents of Tijuana, for example, many of whom cross back and forth between the US and Mexico daily. The same referents may have different meaning for migrants from all over the world who have come to the US-Mexico border seeking asylum: an entirely different meaning to those who have crossed with the privilege and mobility of a US passport (or another meaning to those who never crossed at all). Despite the diversity of meaning-making, a consideration of the border scene set within a discussion of the larger global political economy provides a more critical view of *Coco*'s reception, highlighting the limits of a neoliberal, multicultural identity politics.

Notes

1. Box Office Mojo, *Coco* (Box Office Mojo, 2017). https://www.boxofficemojo.com/release/rl3983050241/.

2. Jacqueline Avila, "Memorias de Oro: Music, Memory, and Mexicanidad in Pixar's Coco (2017)." *Americas: A Hemispheric Music Journal* 29, no. 1 (2020): 1–23; Arturo Morales Campos, "Prototipos mexicanos y el conflicto migratorio en el filme Coco, de Walt Disney." *Sincronía* 25, no. 79 (2021).

3. For a study that focuses specifically on the movie's resonance during the presidency of Donald Trump, see Sandra L. López Varela, "Approaching Pixar's *Coco* during the Trump Era," *iMex Revista: México Interdisciplinario* 9, no. 18 (2020).

4. See for example, Tara Law, "The Story Behind the Photo of a Family Running from Tear Gas at the U.S.-Mexico Border," *Time*, November 27, 2018, https://time.com/5464560/caravan-mexico-border-iconic-photo/; Dakin Andone, Patrick Oppmann, and Natalie Gallón, "Migrant Caravan Resumes March North from Mexico-Guatemalan Border," CNN, October 22, 2018, https://www.cnn.com/2018/10/21/americas/migrant-caravan-mexico/index.html.

5. Harsha Walia, *Border and Rule: Global Migration, Capitalism, and the Rise of Racist Nationalism* (Chicago: Haymarket), 3.

6. Walker, Victoria. "Trump Says He Will Build 'Impenetrable, Physical, Tall, Powerful, Beautiful Border" *Washington Post*, August 31, 2016, https://www.washingtonpost.com/video/politics/trump-says-he-will-build-impenetrable-physical-tall-powerful-beautiful-border/2016/08/31/34eceacc-6fb6-11e6-993f-73c693a89820_video.html.

7. Avila, "Memorias de Oro."

8. See Molly F. Todd, *Borders, Art, and Imagination: Journeys with 'The Frontera Project' and 'Mare from the Inside'* (PhD diss., Virginia Tech, 2023); Joseph Nevins, *Operation Gatekeeper and Beyond: The War on" Illegals" and the Remaking of the US–Mexico Boundary* (London: Routledge, 2010).

9. The seed of this essay came from a course during my PhD program at Virginia Tech. I would like to thank Drs. María del Carmen Caña Jiménez, Audrey Reeves, and Vinodh Venkatesh for their feedback on early versions of this paper.

10. My use of the term border/lands builds from Gloría Anzaldúa as well as others who have used her work to think about cultural exchange. Border/lands are territorial, cultural, linguistic, spiritual, and embodied; they are the unfolding and folding of different borders and cultural meanings together across time and space. See Gloria Anzaldúa, *Borderlands/La Frontera: The New Mestiza* (San Francisco: Aunt Lute Books, 1987); Todd, *Borders, Art, and Imagination* (Blacksburg: VT Publishing 2023); José David Saldívar, *Border Matters: Remapping American Cultural studies* (Berkeley: University of California Press, 1997).

11. Richard Corliss, "Learning Pedro Infante" *Time*, April 15, 2007; *Yucatan Times*, "She Was the Inspiration Behind Disney's Coco," *Yucatan Times*, October 19, 2022, https://www.theyucatantimes.com/2022/10/she-was-the-inspiration-behind-disneys-coco/.

12. In this case, pantheon, or *panteón*, refers to a built structure in a cemetery and/or the cemetery itself.

13. Many scholars have at least alluded to a multiplicity of Mexican nations—particularly a hegemonic, *mestizo* Mexico and an array of Indigenous Mexicos that exist beyond the purview of the *mestizo* state. Certainly, most of these studies have centered on *mestizo* Mexico's attempts to impose itself on the other nations. See Guillermo Bonfil Batalla, *Mexico Profundo: Reclaiming a Civilization* (Austin: University of Texas Press, 1996); Claudio Lomnitz, *Deep Mexico, Silent Mexico: An Anthropology of Nationalism* (Minneapolis: University of Minnesota Press, 2001); David S. Dalton, *Mestizo Modernity: Race, Technology, and the Body in Postrevolutionary Mexico* (Gainesville: University of Florida Press), 4–7. More recently, thinkers like Theodore W. Cohen have asserted an Afro-Mexican nation as well. See Theodore W. Cohen, *Finding Afro-Mexico: Race and Nation after the Revolution* (Cambridge, UK: Cambridge University Press).

14. An especially important Mexican nation to the current study is the Chicanx community, which is both deeply related to, yet distinct from, the Mexican nations south of the Río Grande.

15. Ignacio M. Sánchez Prado, *Screening Neoliberalism: Transforming Mexican Cinema 1988–2012* (Nashville, TN: Vanderbilt University Press, 2014), 6.

16. Angela Davis, *Freedom Is a Constant Struggle: Ferguson, Palestine, and the Foundations of a Movement* (Chicago, IL: Haymarket Books, 2016); Sarah B. Horton, "Migrants, Bureaucratic Inscription, and Legal Recognition," in *Paper Trails: Migrants, Documents, and Legal Insecurity*, ed. Sarah B Horton and Josiah Heyman (Durham, NC: Duke University Press, 2020), 34.

17. Marissa K. López, *Racial Immanence: Chicanx Bodies Beyond Representation* (New York: New York University Press. 2019), 4. For an in-depth discussion of neoliberal aesthetics, see Walter Benn Michaels, *The Beauty of the Social Problem: Photography, Autonomy, Economy* (Chicago: University of Chicago Press, 2015), 63.

18. Sandro Mezzadra and Brett Neilson, *Border as Method, or, the Multiplication of Labor* (Durham, NC: Duke University Press, 2013).

19. Avila, "Memorias de Oro"; Yunuen Ysela Mandujano Salazar, "Coco, el discurso de autenticidad y la reproducción de estereotipos a través del mito de la Mexicanidad," in *Más allá del mundo de ensueño: desenmascarando los mensajes de los películas y su significación social*, ed. Yunuén Ysela Mandujano Salazar (Ciudad Juárez: Universidad Autónomo de Ciudad de Juárez, 2021).

20. Arjun Appadurai, *Modernity at Large: Cultural Dimensions of Globalization* (Minneapolis: University of Minnesota Press, 1996); Diana Taylor, *The Archive and*

the Repetoire: Performing Cultural Memory in the Americas (Durham, NC: Duke University Press, 2003).

21. Anjirbag, "Reforming Borders of the Imagination," 152. Ariel Dorfman and Armand Mattelart, *How to Read Donald Duck: Imperialist Ideology in the Disney Comic*, trans. David Kunzle (New York: International General, 1971), 12.

22. Antonio Gramsci. *Selections from the prison notebooks*. (New York: International Publishers, 1971), xiv.

23. Gramsci, *Selections from the Prison Notebooks*, 365.

24. Michelle Anya Anjirbag, "Reforming Borders of the Imagination: Diversity, Adaptation, Transmediation, and Incorporation in the Global Disney Film Landscape," *Jeunesse: Young People, Texts, Cultures* 11, no. 2 (2019).

25. Roberto D. Hernández, *Coloniality of the U-S / Mexico Border: Power, Violence, and the Decolonial Imperative* (Tucson: University of Arizona Press, 2020); Daniel Nemser, *Infrastructures of Race: Concentration and Biopolitics in Colonial Mexico* (Austin: University of Texas Press, 2017); Mary Louise Pratt, "Arts of the Contact Zone." *Profession* (1991): 33–40; Diana Taylor, *The Archive and the Repertoire: Performing Cultural Memory in the Americas* (Durham, NC: Duke University Press, 2003).

26. Anjirbag, "Reforming Borders of the Imagination."

27. Anjirbag, "Reforming Borders of the Imagination," 166.

28. Anjirbag, "Mulan and Moana: Embedded Coloniality and the Search for Authenticity in Disney Animated Film," *Social Sciences* 7, no. 11 (2018).

29. Anjirbag "Reforming Borders of the Imagination"; Anjirbag, "Mulan and Moana: Embedded Coloniality and the Search for Authenticity in Disney Animated Film."

30. Ida Yoshinaga, "Disney's Moana, the Colonial Screenplay, and Indigenous Labor Extraction in Hollywood Fantasy Films," *Narrative Culture* 6, no. 2 (2019): 188.

31. There are multiple layers of colonization in Mexico's history. Mexico was colonized by Spain, including histories of slavery and the dispossession and erasure of Indigenous peoples. However, the US-Mexico relationship is also one of imperialism, settler colonialism, and is also informed by global historical processes of coloniality. Therefore, we can understand the coloniality/modernity matrix to be scaffolded and complex.

32. Christine B. Arce, *Mexico's Nobodies: The Cultural Legacy of the Soldadera and Afro-Mexican Women* (Albany: State University of New York Press, 2016).

33. Mandalit del Barco, "Mexico, Music and Family Take Center Stage in 'Coco.'" *NPR*, November 20, 2017, https://www.npr.org/2017/11/20/564385036/mexico-music-and-family-take-center-stage-in-coco.

34. Brian Truitt, "Everything You Need to Know about the Mexican Cultural References in Pixar's 'Coco'" *USA Today*, November 21, 2017, https://www.usatoday.com/story/life/movies/2017/11/20/everything-you-need-know-mexican-cultural-references-pixars-coco/879113001/.

35. Micaela Díaz-Sánchez and Alexandro D. Hernández. "The Son Jarocho as Afro-Mexican Resistance Music," *Journal of Pan African Studies* 6, no. 1 (2013): 192.

36. Jaqueline Avila. *Cinesonidos: Film, Music and National Identity during Mexico's Epoca de Oro* (Stanford, CA: Stanford University Press, 2019).

37. Alejandro L. Madrid, ed., *Transnational Encounters: Music and Performance at the U.S.-Mexico Border* (New York: Oxford University Press, 2011).

38. It is important to also note that Mexicans are not a homogenous group, and they occupy many different identity positions.

39. Lalo Alcaraz, *Muerto Mouse: It's Coming to Take Your Cultura*, Lalo Alcaraz Art Shop, 2013. https://lalo-alcaraz-art-shop.myshopify.com/products/muerto-mouse-print.

40. Elizabeth Castro, "When *Coco* feels Like Home: Film as Homenaje," *Harvard Kennedy School Journal of Hispanic Policy* 30 (2018): 33.

41. Kristin Romey, "This Hairless Mexican Dog Has a Storied, Ancient Past," *National Geographic Online*, November 2022.

42. Castro, "When *Coco* Feels Like Home: Film as Homenaje," 34.

43. For a discussion of the aesthetic preference for European genetics and culture in Mexican cinema, see Mónica García Blizzard, *The White Indians of Mexican Cinema: Racial Masquerade throughout the Golden Age* (Albany: State University of New York Press, 2022).

44. Castro, "When *Coco* Feels Like Home: Film as Homenaje," 37.

45. Avila, *Cinesonidos,* 2019; Michael Shapiro. *Methods and Nations: Cultural Governance and the Indigenous Subject* (New York: Routledge, 2004).

46. Arjun Appadurai, *Modernity at Large: Cultural Dimensions of Globalization* (Minneapolis: University of Minnesota Press, 1996).

47. For a discussion of glocal discourses in Latin America, see Néstor García Canclini, *Latinoamericanos buscando lugar en este siglo* (Buenos Aires: Paidós, 2002), 80–81.

48. Anjirbag, "Reforming Borders of the Imagination," 160.

49. Sánchez Prado, *Screening Neoliberalism*, 7.

50. Jacobo Asse Dayan, "Güeros: Social Fragmentation, Political Agency and the Mexican Film Industry under Neoliberalism," *Norteamérica* 12, no. 1 (2017).

51. Sánchez Prado, *Screening Neoliberalism*, 2.

52. Wendy Brown, *Undoing the demos: neoliberalism's stealth revolution* (New York: Zone Books, 2015).

53. Luca Mavelli, "Citizenship for Sale and the Neoliberal Political Economy of Belonging," *International Studies Quarterly*, 62, no. 3 (2018): 482–93.

54. Horton, "Migrants, Bureaucratic Inscription, and Legal Recognition," 13.

55. Sánchez Prado, *Screening Neoliberalism*, 12.

56. See Davis, *Freedom Is a Constant Struggle*; Miguel Díaz-Barriga and Margaret E. Dorsey, *Fencing in Democracy: Necrocitizenship and the US-Mexico Border Wall* (Durham: Duke University Press, 2020).

57. See Dalton, *Robo Sacer: Necroliberalism and Cyborg Resistance in Mexican and Chicanx Dystopias* (Nashville, TN: Vanderbilt University Press, 2023), introduction.

58. Díaz-Barriga and Dorsey, *Fencing in Democracy*, 9.

59. Walia, *Border and Rule.*

60. Walia, *Border and Rule*, 50.

61. Ila Nicole Sheren, *Portable Borders: Performance Art and Politics on the U.S. Frontera since 1984* (Austin: University of Texas Press, 2015), 12; Cristina Tzintzún, Arnulfo Manríquez, and Carlos Pérez de Alejo, *Presente! Latin@ Immigrant Voices in the Struggle for Racial Justice / Voces Inmigranted Latin@s en la lucha por la justicia racial* (New York: AK Press).

62. Walia, *Border and Rule*, 51.

63. Alfonso Gonzalez, *Reform without Justice: Latino Migrant Politics and the Homeland Security State* (New York: Oxford University Press, 2014), 137.

64. Todd Miller, *Border Patrol Nation: Dispatches on the Frontlines of Homeland Security* (San Francisco: City Lights, 2014), 29.

65. US Department of Homeland Security, *Budget-in-brief Fiscal Year 2017* (2017), https://www.dhs.gov/sites/default/files/publications/FY2017BIB.pdf; US Department of Homeland Security, *Fiscal Year 2022 Budget in Brief* (2022), https://www.dhs.gov/sites/default/files/publications/dhs_bib_-_web_version_-_final_508.pdf.

66. Wayne A. Cornelius, "Death at the Border: Efficacy and Unintended Consequences of US Immigration Control Policy," *Population and Development Review* 27, no. 4 (2001).

67. Abraham Acosta, *Thresholds of Illiteracy: Theory, Latin America, and the Crisis of Resistance* (New York: Fordham University Press, 2014), chapter 5.

68. Achilles Mbembe, *Necropolitics*, trans. Steven Corcoran (Durham, NC: Duke University Press, 2019).

69. Adrián Pérez-Melgosa, "Low-Intensity Necropolitics: Slow Violence and Migrant Bodies in Latin American Films." *Arizona Journal of Hispanic Cultural Studies* 20, no. 1 (2016): 219–20.

70. Barriga and Dorsey, *Fencing in Democracy*, 12.

Bibliography

Acosta, Abraham. *Thresholds of Illiteracy: Theory, Latin America, and the Crisis of Resistance.* New York: Fordham University Press, 2014.

Alcaraz, Lalo. *Muerto Mouse: It's Coming to Take Your Cultura.* Lalo Alcaraz Art Shop, 2013. https://lalo-alcaraz-art-shop.myshopify.com/products/muerto-mouse-print.

Andone Dakin, Patrick Oppmann, and Natalie Gallón. "Migrant Caravan Resumes March North from Mexico-Guatemalan Border." CNN, 2018, October 22. https://www.cnn.com/2018/10/21/americas/migrant-caravan-mexico/index.html.

Anjirbag, Michelle. "Mulan and Moana: Embedded Coloniality and the Search for Authenticity in Disney Animated Film." *Social Sciences* 7, no. 11 (2018). https://doi.org/10.3390/socsci7110230.

Anjirbag, Michelle Anya. "Reforming Borders of the Imagination: Diversity, Adaptation, Transmediation, and Incorporation in the Global Disney Film Landscape." *Jeunesse: Young People, Texts, Cultures* 11, no. 2 (2019): 151–76. https://doi.org/10.1353/jeu.2019.0021.

Appadurai, Arjun. *Modernity at Large: Cultural Dimensions of Globalization.* Minneapolis: University of Minnesota Press, 1996.

Arce, B. Christine. *Mexico's Nobodies: The Cultural Legacy of the Soldadera and Afro-Mexican Women.* Albany: SUNY Presa, 2016.

Asse Dayan, Jacobo. "Güeros: Social Fragmentation, Political Agency and the Mexican Film Industry under Neoliberalism." *Norteamérica* 12, no. 1 (2017): 137–68 https://doi.org/10.20999/nam.2017.a005.

Avila, Jacqueline. *Cinesonidos: Film, music and national identity during Mexico's Epoca de Oro.* Stanford, CA: Stanford University Press, 2019.

———. "Memorias de Oro: Music, Memory, and Mexicanidad in Pixar's Coco (2017)." *Americas: A Hemispheric Music Journal* 29, no. 1 (2020): 1–23. https://doi.org/10.1353/ame.2020.0009.

del Barco, Mandalit "Mexico, Music and Family take center stage in 'Coco.'" *NPR* (Nov. 20, 2017), https://www.npr.org/2017/11/20/564385036/mexico-music-and-family-take-center-stage-in-coco.

Bonfil Batalla, Guillermo. *Mexico Profundo: Reclaiming a Civilization.* Austin: University of Texas Press, 1996.

Box Office Mojo. *Coco.* Box Office Mojo, 2017. https://www.boxofficemojo.com/release/rl3983050241/.

Brown, Wendy. *Undoing the Demos: Neoliberalism's Stealth Revolution.* New York: Zone Books, 2015.

Castro, Elizabeth. "When *Coco* Feels Like Home: Film as Homenaje." *Harvard Kennedy School Journal of Hispanic Policy* 30 (2018): 33–38.

Cohen, Theodore W. *Finding Afro-Mexico: Race and Nation after the Revolution.* Cambridge, UK: Cambridge University Press, 2020.

Cornelius, Wayne A. "Death at the Border: Efficacy and Unintended Consequences of US Immigration Control Policy." *Population and Development Review* 27, no. 4 (2001): 661–85. https://doi.org/10.1111/j.1728–4457.2001.00661.x.

Dalton, David S. *Mestizo Modernity: Race, Technology, and the Body in Postrevolutionary Mexico.* Gainesville: University of Florida Press, 2018.

———. *Robo Sacer: Necroliberalism and Cyborg Resistance in Mexican and Chicanx Dystopias.* Nashville, TN: Vanderbilt University Press, 2023.

Davis, Angela. *Freedom Is a Constant Struggle: Ferguson, Palestine, and the Foundations of a Movement.* Chicago: Haymarket, 2016.

Díaz-Barriga, Miguel, and Margaret E. Dorsey. *Fencing in Democracy: Necrocitizenship and the US-Mexico Border Wall.* Durham, NC: Duke University Press, 2020.

Dorfman, Ariel, and Armand Mattelart. *How to Read Donald Duck.* New York: International General, 1975.

García Blizzard, Mónica. *The White Indians of Mexican Cinema: Racial Masquerade throughout the Golden Age.* Albany: State University of New York Press, 2022.

García Canclini, Nésetor. *Latinoamericanos buscando lugar en este siglo.* Buenos Aires: Paidós, 2022.

Gonzalez, Alfonso. *Reform without Justice: Latino Migrant Politics and the Homeland Security State.* New York: Oxford University Press, 2014.

Gramsci, Antonio. *Selections from the prison notebooks.* New York: International Publishers, 1971.

Hernández, Roberto D. *Coloniality of the U-S / Mexico Border: Power, Violence, and the Decolonial Imperative.* Tucson: University of Arizona Press, 2020.

Horton, Sarah B. "Migrants, Bureaucratic Inscription, and Legal Recognition," in *Paper Trails: Migrants, Documents, and Legal Insecurity*, edited by Sarah B. Horton and Josiah Heyman, 1–26. Durham, NC: Duke University Press, 2020.

Law, Tara. "The Story Behind the Photo of a Family Running from Tear Gas at the U.S.-Mexico Border." *Time*, 2018, November 27. https://time.com/5464560/caravan-mexico-border-iconic-photo/.

Lomnitz, Claudio. *Deep Mexico, Silent Mexico: An Antrhopology of Nationalism.* Minneapolis: University of Minnesota Press, 2001.

López, Marissa K. *Racial Immanence: Chicanx Bodies Beyond Representation.* New York: New York University Press, 2019.

López Varela, Sandra L. "Approaching Pixar's Coco during the Trump Era." *iMex Revista: México Interdisciplinario* 9, no. 18 (2022): 130–44.

Madrid, Alejandro L., ed. *Transnational Encounters: Music and Performance at the U.S.-Mexico Border.* New York: Oxford University Press, 2011.

Mandujano Salazar, Yunuen Ysela. "Coco, el discurso de autenticidad y la reproducción de estereotipos a través del mito de la Mexicanidad." In *Más allá del mundo de ensueño: desenmascarando los mensajes de los películas y su significación social*, edited by Yunuén Ysela Mandujano Salazar, 13–30. Ciudad Juárez, CHIH: Universidad Autónomo de Ciudad de Juárez, 2021.

Mavelli, Luca. "Citizenship for Sale and the Neoliberal Political Economy of Belonging," *International Studies Quarterly*, 62, no. 3 (2018): 482–93.

Mbembe, Achille. *Necropolitics*, translated by Steven Corcoran. Durham, NC: Duke University Press, 2019.

Mezzadra, Sandro, and Brett Neilson. *Border as Method, or, the Multiplication of Labor.* Durham, NC: Duke University Press, 2013.

Michaels, Walter Benn. *The Beauty of a Social Problem: Photography, Autonomy, Economy.* Chicago: University of Chicago Press, 2015.

Miller, Todd. *Border Patrol Nation: Dispatches on the Frontlines of Homeland Security.* San Francisco: City Lights, 2014.

Morales Campos, Arturo. "Prototipos mexicanos y el conflicto migratorio en el filme Coco, de Walt Disney." *Sincronía* 25, no. 79 (2021): 475–98. https://doi.org/10.32870/sincronia.axxv.n79.25a21.

Nemser, Daniel. *Infrastructures of Race: Concentration and Biopolitics in Colonial Mexico.* Austin: University of Texas Press, 2017.

Nevins, Joseph. *Operation Gatekeeper and Beyond: The War on "Illegals" and the Remaking of the US–Mexico Boundary.* London: Routledge, 2010.

Pérez-Melgosa, Adrián. "Low-Intensity Necropolitics: Slow Violence and Migrant Bodies in Latin American Films." *Arizona Journal of Hispanic Cultural Studies* 20, no. 1 (2016): 217–36. https://doi.org/10.1353/hcs.2016.0048.

Pratt, Mary Louise. "Arts of the Contact Zone." *Profession* (1991): 33–40.

Romey, Kristen. "This Hairless Mexican Dog has a storied, Ancient past," *National Geographic Online* (November 2022).

Saldívar, José David. *Border matters: Remapping American cultural studies.* Berkeley: University of California Press, 1997.

Sánchez Prado, Ignacio M. *Screening Neoliberalism: Transforming Mexican Cinema 1988–2012.* Nashville, TN: Vanderbilt University Press, 2014.

Shapiro, Michael. *Methods and Nations: Cultural Governance and the Indigenous Subject.* New York: Routledge, 2004.

Sheren, Ila Nicole. *Portable Borders: Performance Art and Politics on the U.S. Frontera since 1984.* Austin: University of Texas Press, 2015.

Taylor, Diana. *The Archive and the Repertoire: Performing Cultural Memory in the Americas.* Durham, NC: Duke University Press, 2003.

Todd, Molly F. *Borders, Art, and Imagination: Journeys with 'The Frontera Project' and 'Mare from the Inside.'* PhD diss., Virginia Tech, 2023.

Truitt, Brian. "Everything You Need to Know about the Mexican Cultural References in Pixar's 'Coco' " *USA Today*, November 21, 2017, https://www.usatoday.com/story/life/movies/2017/11/20/everything-you-need-know-mexican-cultural-references-pixars-coco/879113001/.

Tzintzún, Cristina, Arnulfo Manríquez, and Carlos Pérez de Alejo. *Presente! Latin@ Immigrant Voices in the Struggle for Racial Justice / Voces Inmigranted Latin@s En La Lucha Por La Justicia Racial.* New York: AK Press, 2014.

US Department of Homeland Security, *Budget-in-brief fiscal year 2017*, (2017), https://www.dhs.gov/sites/default/files/publications/FY2017BIB.pdf.

US Department of Homeland Security, *Fiscal Year 2022 Budget in brief*, (2022), https://www.dhs.gov/sites/default/files/publications/dhs_bib_-_web_version_-_final_508.pdf.

Walia, Harsha. 2021. *Border and Rule: Global Migration, Capitalism, and the Rise of Racist Nationalism.* Chicago: Haymarket Books.

Walker, Victoria. "Trump says he will build 'impenetrable, physical, tall, powerful, beautiful border," *Washington Post*, August 31, 2016, https://www.washingtonpost.com/video/politics/trump-says-he-will-build-impenetrable-physical-tall-powerful-beautiful-border/2016/08/31/34eceacc-6fb6-11e6-993f-73c693a89820_video.html.

Yoshinaga, Ida. "Disney's Moana, the Colonial Screenplay, and Indigenous Labor Extraction in Hollywood Fantasy Films." *Narrative Culture* 6, no. 2 (2019): 188–215.

Yucatan Times. "She Was the Inspiration Behind Disney's *Coco*." *Yucatan Times*, October 19, 2022. https://www.theyucatantimes.com/2022/10/she-was-the-inspiration-behind-disneys-coco/.

Contributors

Enrique Ajuria Ibarra is associate professor at Universidad de las Américas Puebla, Mexico. He has previously published several articles and book chapters on Mexican Gothic and horror cinema. He is editor-in-chief of the peer-reviewed journal *Studies in Gothic Fiction* and currently exploring the Gothic in the Archie Comics Universe and continues studying Gothic and horror in Mexican film and literature.

Katherine Bundy is a Cuban American scholar, creative, and practicing web professional in Montreal, Canada. She writes, creates, and speaks about the intersections between emerging technologies, posthumanism, and cultural production—especially film and animation. As a founder of a film festival and a feminist wrestling collective in the South, Kate is committed to generating significance between theory and (creative) praxis. www.katherinebundy.com

David S. Dalton is Ruth G. Shaw Humanities Fellow, associate professor of Spanish and Latin American studies, and director of Latin American studies at the University of North Carolina, Charlotte. He is the author of *Robo Sacer: Necroliberalism and Cyborg Resistance in Mexican and Chicanx Dystopias* (2023) and *Mestizo Modernity: Race, Technology, and the Body in Postrevolutionary Mexico* (2018). He has also edited several books and special editions in journals. These include: *Anti-Catholicism in the Mexican Revolution, 1913–1940* (2024); *Imagining Latinidad: Digital Diasporas and Public Engagement Among Latin American Migrants* (2023); *Healthcare in Latin America: History, Society, Culture* (2022); *El cine de luchadores* (*Revista de Literatura Contemporánea Mexicana*, 2021); and *The Transatlantic Undead: Zombies in Hispanic and Luso-Brazilian Literatures* (*Alambique*, 2018). He has published over thirty-five articles and book chapters on different aspects of Mexican and Latin American studies.

Yunuen Ysela Mandujano-Salazar is a professor and researcher in the Department of Social Sciences at the Autonomous University of Ciudad Juarez (Mexico). She holds a PhD in social sciences focusing on cultural studies and a master's degree in studies of Asia and Africa, specialty Japan. She is a Mexican National System of Researchers (SNI) member. Some of her recent publications include *Beyond the Male Idol Factory. The Construction of Gender and National Ideologies in Japan through Johnny's Jimusho* (2024), *Más allá del mundo de ensueño: desdenmascarando los mensajes de las películas y su significación social* (2021, editor) and 'YouTube channels of Mexicans living in Japan: virtual communities and bi-cultural imagery construction' in *Imagining Latinidad: Digital Diasporas and Public Engagement Among Latin American Migrants* (2023).

Rodrigo Figueroa Obregón is an assistant professor of Spanish at New Mexico State University. He specializes in nineteenth-, twentieth-, and twenty-first-century Mexican literature. He has published several articles on Mexican *modernismo* and avant-garde. His research interests also extend to popular culture, sports, and music. His theoretical approaches include urban studies, technology studies, posthumanism, and body studies. He has also published three poetry volumes in Mexico and the United States, as well as a drama and several short stories.

Sofia Paiva de Araujo is an independent scholar with an interest in Mexican and Brazilian memorial cinemas.

Elissa J. Rashkin is a research professor in cultural and communication studies at the Universidad Veracruzana, Mexico. Her current work encompasses representation, memory, and agrarian struggle; imagemaking and the Anthropocene; and cultural production by women in Mexico and Latin America. Earlier projects include *Women Filmmakers in Mexico: The Country of Which We Dream* (2001) and *The Stridentist Movement in Mexico: The Avant-Garde and Cultural Change in the 1920s* (2009), both also published in Mexico, as well as other texts on Mexican and international film, photography, literature, and cultural history.

Molly F. Todd is a teaching assistant professor in sociology and international affairs at the University of Colorado Boulder. Her research employs collaborative methods across sites in Brazil, Mexico, and the United States to observe and participate in the ways that artistic production navigates and shapes border politics and their imaginaries. She has published several articles reflecting these efforts, as well as a chapter in the edited volume *Maré from the Inside: Art, Culture, and Politics in Rio de Janeiro, Brazil* (2021).

Vinodh Venkatesh is a professor of Spanish at Virginia Tech University. He is the author of three books: *Capitán Latinoamérica: Superheroes in Cinema, Television, and Web Series* (2020), *New Maricón Cinema: Outing Latin American Film* (2016), and *The Body as Capital: Masculinities in Contemporary Latin American Fiction* (2015). He has also coedited with María del Carmen Caña Jiménez *Horacio Castellanos Moya: El diablo en el espejo* (2016), and *Crisis TV: Hispanic Television Narratives after 2008* (2024). He is the author of over forty articles on contemporary Latin American and Spanish cinema and literature. Venkatesh serves on several editorial boards, including *Chasqui*, *Romance Notes*, *Hispanófila*, *Hispania*, and *Journal of Men's Studies*.

Index

Note: page numbers followed by *f* refer to figures.

aesthetics, 109, 188; anime, 156–57, 159; of animation, 111; of cinema, 108; of *Kalimán Regresa*, 119; negative, 185; neoliberal, 198, 214n17; online, 127; of the superhero, 113; Tezuka's, 151; Web 2.0 and, 132

Aguirre Beltrán, Gonzalo, 61

Ajuria Ibarra, Enrique, 17, 21n24, 121n21

Alexander, Sofía, 157, 159–60, 163. *See also* Crunchyroll; *Onyx Equinox*

Ambriz, Arturo "Vonno," 84, 99n9

Ánima Estudios, 2, 12, 16, 78n49, 189n8

animated cinema, 2–6, 11–12, 14–15, 18, 21n21, 49, 84, 114, 127, 132; Hollywood, 39; international, 34; Mexican, 22n35, 31; NAFTA and, 48

anime, 15, 17, 149–65, 166–67n18. *See also* Crunchyroll; manga; *otaku*

Animex Producciones, 55, 89–90, 189n8

Arnaiz, Ricardo, 19n8, 55–56, 59–60, 78n49, 112; *La leyenda del Chupacabras*, 71, 78n49; *Nikté*, 90. *See also* Animex Producciones; *La leyenda de la Nahuala*

Aurrecoechea, Juan Manuel, 6–7, 13, 22n33

auteurs, 141; Mexican, 24n73

authenticity, 59, 157, 203; cultural, 199–201, 203

Bartra, Roger, 33–34

blackness, 67, 70, 77n35

Blank, Grant, 128, 144n3

The Book of Life (Gutiérrez), 4, 17, 21n24, 71, 74n4, 176–78, 180–84, 188

border/lands, 196–97, 209, 212, 213n10

borders, 108, 130, 157, 196–97, 199, 203, 209–12, 213n10; militarization of, 196, 209–11; securitization of, 209–10. *See also* US-Mexico border

Brandes, Stanley, 175, 181

Buchan, Suzanne, 109, 120n7

Bukatman, Scott, 111, 120n18

Calderón, Felipe, 71, 101n39

CANACINE (National Chamber of the Cinematographic Industry), 31, 176

capitalism, 129, 195, 199, 203
Carrera, Carlos, 7; *Ana y Bruno*, 5, 21n25; *El héroe*, 10
Cartucho: Relatos de la lucha en el norte de México (Campobello), 91, 95, 97, 101n40
casonas, 69–71
censorship, 31, 78n52, 129, 140
El Chapulín Animado, 17, 109, 117
El Chapulín Colorado, 108, 111, 117–18
chingón/chingado, 16, 92, 101n50
Cholodenko, Alan, 109–10, 112
cinema, 4–6, 18, 108–10, 198; animation and, 112; children's, 13; commercial, 4–5, 12, 18, 107; cultural geography of, 204; family, 3; global, 141; Golden Age, 16, 46, 84, 87, 92, 100n22 (*see also* Mexican cinema: Golden Age); low, 21n28; mainstream channels of, 127; nationalism and, 151; neoliberal, 34; Paz and, 76n24; post-NAFTA, 44; postrevolutionary, 97; realistic, 152; of the Revolution, 84, 98n5; El Santo's, 117; superheroes and, 108; traditional, 158; US, 153, 184; world, 1, 11. *See also* animated cinema; Mexican cinema
citizenship, 83–84, 86, 90–91, 95–97, 98n4, 204; necrocitizenship, 210; practices, 211
Claymation, 6, 22n34
Coco (Unkrich and Molina), 15, 71, 74n4, 107, 157–58, 164–65, 176–78, 195–212; Day of the Dead in, 182, 184, 188, 196–98, 205, 212; ethics of representation in, 18, 190n26
coloniality, 200, 215n31
Colorados, 85, 89, 93, 95, 97
commercialism, 4, 21n21
corruption, 84, 118, 128–30, 139; political, 130–31, 137, 140, 143
Cosentino, Olivia, 5, 43
COVID-19 pandemic, 11, 78n49, 145n15
Crofton, Donald 110–11
Cruz Rodríguez, Ana, 7, 22n35
Crunchyroll, 155, 159–60
Cuarón, Alfonso, 42, 122n36
cyberculture, 138; studies, 128
cyberspace, 128–33, 136, 139–40, 144n3

Dalton, David S., 16, 39, 41–42, 76n24, 98nn4–5, 169n45, 190n34; *robo sacer*, 128, 134, 145n17
Day of the Dead (Día de Muertos), 17–18, 55, 176–84, 187–88, 189n5, 189n8; in *The Book of Life*, 4; *catrina* and, 190n19; in *Coco*, 182, 184, 188, 196–98, 205, 212; Disney and, 202; in *La leyenda de la Nahuala*, 57–59, 72; *¡Viva la muerte!* and, 9
DC, 107, 115, 161
death, 18, 40–41, 62, 86, 175, 178–85, 187–88; borders and, 210
década perdida, 108, 112
defeat, 37, 39, 44, 47, 63, 68, 92, 101n48
De la Mora, Sergio, 38, 40, 46–47, 100n22
De la Reguera, Ana, 4, 177
Del Castillo, Kate, 4, 177
Del Toro, Guillermo, 1, 4–5, 15, 19n5, 115; *Ana y Bruno* and, 21n25; *The Book of Life* and, 177; *Pinocchio*, 1, 3*f*, 4, 6, 10, 19n1; *Simpsons* and, 21n22
Derrida, Jacques, 63, 178, 183
Día de Muertos (Gutiérrez Medrano), 18, 74n4, 177–78

difference, 65, 91, 109; social, 71
Disney, 1, 8, 12–15, 107, 112, 116, 197–203, 212. See also *Coco*; Pixar
Domínguez-Ruvalcaba, Héctor, 33, 46, 94
double entendre/*albures*, 21n28, 31–32, 36, 48, 68, 121n31
Dragon Ball, 154, 156, 159
DreamWorks, 2, 10, 14, 112
Drug War, 72, 90, 101n39, 134, 136

Engels, Friedrich, 47–48
Esch, Sophie, 86, 91, 94–95
Estrada, Jorge, 101n40; *Un mundo maravilloso*, 5; *La revolución de Juan Escopeta*, 16, 83–94, 98
experimental animation, 127–29, 132, 141–43

Fernández, Emilio, 12, 24n73, 87, 88*f*
Figueroa, Gabriel, 12–13, 87, 88*f*
film studies, 109; animated, 6–7; Mexican, 3, 6
Flash (Adobe), 6, 121n24, 143
Foucault, Michel, 70, 75n17, 77n38, 78n47
Fuego Nuevo, 55, 57–58, 62

García Canclini, Néstor, 112, 203, 216n47
gender, 34, 40, 56, 62, 84–85, 91; hierarchy, 86; ideology, 48; norms, 16, 114; oppression, 73n3; roles, 114, 121n27
Germany, 132, 134, 136
ghosting, 16, 56, 64
ghosts, 57, 63–64, 68, 70, 178, 184, 197; of the Drug war, 72; skeleton-ghosts, 199
Golden Age, 3, 12, 17, 43, 83–84, 87, 100n20, 196; *Coco* and, 202; masculinity and, 46, 92, 100n22; *mexicanidad* and, 16
Gómez Bolaños, Roberto, 111, 117. See also *El Chapulín Animado*; *El Chapulín Colorado*
Good Neighbor Policy, 13, 24n81
Gothic, the, 18, 178–80, 182–83, 187–88, 190n26, 190n34
Gothic fiction, 179, 183, 185, 191n35; European, 187
Gothic motifs, 185–86
Gothic texts, 181–82, 185, 191n35
Guadalajara, 1, 10, 177
Gunning, Tom, 110

Haraway, Donna, 134, 145n18
haunting, 178, 183–84
hegemony, 65, 199–200; capitalist, 138; cultural, 199–200, 202; Disney's, 8; of masculinity, 33, 116
heterotopia, 69–71, 73, 77n38, 78n47
Hidalgo, Miguel, 56, 77n33
Hind, Emily, 46, 135, 145n20
Hollywood, 6, 11–15, 18, 24n73, 108, 112, 121n27, 127, 177, 203; animated cinema, 39; authenticity and, 157; Japan and, 153; representation and, 202; representations of Mexicans in, 160, 165; stereotypes, 164
horror, 178, 181–83, 185, 187–88, 189n8; aesthetic of, 136; internet, 145n15
Huevocartoon, 6, 16, 23n65, 31–34, 36, 37*f*, 44–48, 116
Huevos congelados, 23n65, 31
Huerta, Victoriano, 85

identity politics, 198, 202, 212
IMCINE (Instituto Mexicano de Cinematografía), 2, 10–11, 22n34
immigration, 43, 210–11

imperialism, 215n31; American, 199; cultural, 197–99, 201–2
inclusion, 203–4, 212; cultural, 200; neoliberal, 198
Infante, Pedro, 47, 88–89, 100n24, 196
internet, 18, 32, 128–30, 136, 138, 140, 155; access to, 127, 145n11, 149–50, 155–56; celebrities, 134; commercial, 31; horror, 133, 145n15; meme culture, 131; tradition and, 74n11; use, 17, 145n11
Inquisition, 61–62, 64, 77n36, 77n40
Irwin, Robert McKee, 24n81, 33, 46, 85, 91, 93, 102
Iwabuchi, Koichi, 152–53, 167n21

Japan, 149–57, 167n18; reconstruction of, 151; traditional cultural elements of, 153

Kahlo, Frida, 206, 207*f*, 211
Kalimán, 108, 119
kinship, 180, 183, 185, 187–88

La leyenda de la Llorona, 2, 78n49
La leyenda de la Nahuala (Arnaiz), 12, 16, 19n8, 55–60, 62–73, 76n21, 90, 112, 189n8
Long, Mary, 139, 146n26
lucha libre, 121n24; cinema, 76n24
Luna, Diego, 4, 177

machismo, 38, 46, 83, 162
MacLaird, Misha, 5–6
manga, 119, 149–52, 155–57, 159, 166–67n18
manhood, 33, 38, 40, 48, 85–87, 95, 97; Mexican, 100n22
mariachi, 36, 41, 73n4, 161–62, 176, 180
Marshall, John, 129, 144n3
Martínez González, Roberto, 61, 75n17
martyrdom, 37, 74n4
Marvel, 107, 115
Marx, Karl, 47–48
masculinity, 16, 32–36, 38, 43–48, 49n1, 85–86, 88–94, 96–97; displacement of, 116; hypermasculinity, 33, 99n6; Mexican, 16, 32–34, 36, 42, 45, 88, 92, 94; nonviolent, 83, 97; violent, 35, 84, 89, 93 (see also *pelado*)
mestizaje, 88, 175
Mexican cinema, 1, 3–6, 11–12, 15, 21n24, 67, 89, 109, 201–2; animation and, 2, 10, 112; erosion of, 204; European genetics and culture in, 216n43; Good Neighbor Policy and, 24n81; masculinity in, 88; middle class and, 99n10; NAFTA and, 40, 43; violence in, 84. *See also* Golden Age
Mexican film industry, 2–3, 5, 7, 10, 18, 22n39, 204
mexicanidad/Mexicanness, 15–16, 24n73, 25n89, 34, 38, 112, 187, 199, 202–3
Mexican Independence, 55–56, 59, 67, 71–72; bicentenary of, 83–84, 89; War of, 71, 76n32
Mexican Revolution, 8, 16, 24n73, 56, 74n4, 83, 86, 90–91, 94–95, 101n40; animation and, 97; centenary of, 84, 89; cinema of, 84, 98, 98n5, 99n9
mobility, 209, 212
modernity, 34, 73n3, 86, 179, 215n31
Mora, Carl, 3, 21n21, 24n73
mummies, 113–14, 189n8

NAFTA (North American Free Trade Agreement), 43–44, 48, 209–10; Mexican cinema after, 40, 42, 44

Napier, 160, 164, 165, 166, 180
narcos, 133–36
nahualismo, 60–62, 74n5, 76n21
nationalism, 151; cultural, 84
Negrete, Jorge, 88, 196
neoliberalism, 198, 203–4
Netflix, 1–2, 11, 15, 113, 117, 122n36, 122n38, 158–59
network effects, 129–30
nihonseikusai, 153, 167n21
Núñez, Güicho, 129, 137–40, 142–43. See also *Retrato politico*

Onyx Equinox (Alexander), 17, 150, 157, 159–60, 162–65
otherness, 15; representational, 198
Ordóñez, Samanta, 34, 42, 94
Orozco, Victor, 129–36, 142–43; *Reality 2.0*, 127–34, 136, 143
otaku, 149–50, 152, 156–57, 164, 167n18; communities, 155–56
Otero, Solimar, 72, 74n5
Otra película de huevos y un pollo, 31–32, 38–42

Participatory Web, 128–31, 134, 136, 140–41. *See also* Web 2.0
Paz, Octavio, 32–35, 76n24, 101n50; "la Chingada," 46; on Day of the Dead, 189n5; on death in Mexico, 175; "Los hijos de la Malinche," 16; *The Labyrinth of Solitude*, 37, 51n47, 63; on Mexican masculinity, 92; *pachuco*, 44. *See also* chingón/chingado
pelado, 32, 44, 88–89
Peña Nieto, Enrique, 130, 137, 139, 144n7, 144n10
Pitman, Thea, 128–29, 139, 144n11
Pixar, 2, 14–15, 34, 112, 146n30, 177; *Finding Nemo*, 34, 49n17. See also *Coco*
platforms, 11, 17, 117, 128–30, 134; application, 138; gaming, 135; participatory, 143; social media, 130–31; streaming, 11, 16, 141, 164–65; video-hosting, 129, 131
Powerhouse Animation Studios, 158
Price, Brian, 5, 36–37, 101n48
PRI (Partido Revolucionario Institucional), 115–16, 139, 144n7, 144n10
Puebla, 55–57, 60, 62, 65, 67, 70, 77n35, 189n8; Callejón del Muerto, 74n6; Diocese of, 76n32; government of, 74n9; legendary, 77n40. *See also* Fuego Nuevo

Quetzalcoatl, 62, 163

racism, 65, 78n52, 203
Ramírez-Berg, Charles, 24n73, 99n6, 100n20
Ramos, Samuel, 32–34, 44, 46, 92. See also *pelado*
Rashkin, Elissa, 16, 121n21
Reisdorf, Bianca, 128, 144n3
representation, 62, 118, 198, 202, 212; of the border, 209–10; of children, 97; cultural, 61, 163, 177, 197–99, 203–4; of Day of the Dead, 176, 184; Disney and, 199–200, 203; ethics of, 18; of gender, 121n27; Indigenous, 165; Mexican, 150, 157, 160, 164, 190n26, 195, 197–98, 203; Mexicanist, 76n21; of Mexicanness, 202
Retrato politico (Núñez), 17, 127, 129, 131, 137–40, 143
Revoltoso (Ambriz), 84, 99n9
Ribot, Daniel, 115, 121n29
Riva Palacio Alatriste, Gabriel, 2, 14, 31, 34; *Un gallo con muchos huevos*, 14, 31–32, 44–46, 48. *See also*

Riva Palacio Alatriste, Gabriel *(continued)* Huevocartoon; *Huevos congelados*; *Otra película de huevos y un pollo*; *Una película de huevos*
Riva Palacio Alatriste, Rodolfo, 2, 31, 34. *See also* Huevocartoon; *Huevos congelados*; *Otra película de huevos y un pollo*; *Una película de huevos*
Rodríguez, Álvaro, 158, 168n37. See also *Seis Manos/Six Hands*
Rodríguez Bermúdez, Manuel, 6–11, 31
rotoscoping, 129, 131, 137, 143

Sahagún, Bernardo de, 61–63, 75n15
Sánchez Prado, Ignacio M., 2, 4–6, 25n89, 99n10, 101n46, 107–8, 120n6, 198, 203–4, 209; *Screening Neoliberalism*, 5
El Santo, 108, 111, 113–15, 117, 121n28
Santo contra los clones, 113, 115, 117, 121n24, 122n37
El Santos vs. La Tetona Mendoza, 17, 109, 115, 118
Seis Manos/Six Hands (Graeber and Rodríguez), 150, 157–60, 162, 165, 167, 169, 170, 171
Serdán family, 56, 74n4
Sifuentes-Jáuregui, Ben, 35, 93
Sierra Silva, Pablo Miguel, 67, 70
The Simpsons, 4, 21–22, 137–38
Soler, Gabilondo, 13–14; Cri-Cri, 13–14, 67
son jarocho, 67, 201
Sony, 107, 153–55, 159
Spectre (Mendes), 180–81, 184
Spooner, Catherine, 179, 181, 190n26
streaming, 11–12, 15–17, 21n18, 23n65, 107, 109, 164; anime and, 141, 156, 158; market, 117; short films and, 141; superheroes and, 122n36. *See also* Crunchyroll; Netflix; Viz
Studio Ghibli, 112, 151
superheroes, 107–9, 111–16, 118–19, 120n6, 122n36
superhero genre, 17, 110, 112–13, 115, 117, 121n24, 122n38

Taylor, Claire, 128–29, 139, 144n11
Tezcatlipoca, 62, 163
Tezuka, Osamu, 151
Todd, Molly Frances, 18, 168n32, 190n26
trauma, 90–91, 94, 97; foundational, 64
Trino, 115–17. *See also* El Santo
Trump, Donald, 195, 213n3

Ugalde, Victor, 10, 23n64
Una película de huevos, 2, 5, 11–12, 20n9, 23n64, 31–32, 34–38, 40, 112–13
United States, 13, 42–43, 153, 209, 211; animation and, 8; anime and, 149–50, 152, 154, 156–58, 165; Cinco de Mayo in, 73n4; *Coco* in, 195; cultural diversity in, 188; Day of the Dead in, 176–77; FIFA World Cup in, 154; film festivals in, 9; Halloween in, 181; internet in, 145n11; Occupy movement in, 130; police murder in, 78n52; streaming services and, 15
US-Mexico border, 195–96, 202–3, 209–12; militarization of, 196, 209–11

Vázquez Hernández, Luis Gabriel, 7, 10
Venkatesh, Vinodh, 16, 119n6
Veracruz, 67, 74n6, 75n21, 76n32, 77nn35–36, 201, 209

Villa, Pancho, 84–86, 89, 95
violence, 18, 32–36, 64, 72, 83–86, 90–98, 99n15, 130, 136, 139, 152, 155, 159, 210; epistemic, 86, 92; exotic, 24n73; gun, 84, 91, 95; masculine, 85; masculinity and, 33–34, 94; narco-violence, 128–29, 132–36, 143; Revolutionary, 88, 91; sexual, 166n18
Viz, 156, 158, 165, 169, 177, 181, 194, 197, 207, 209

Warner Brothers, 13, 107
Web 1.0, 128–29, 144n2
Web 2.0, 17, 128–32, 134–36, 138–43, 145n15
witchcraft, 39, 62, 65, 75–76n21, 77n36, 165, 185
Woodside, Julián, 55, 65, 68

Yo Soy 132 movement (#YoSoy132), 130–31, 139, 144n10, 146n26
YouTube, 107, 117, 131–33, 135–36; channels, 164; communities, 135

Zacatecas, 85–87, 89, 95

www.ingramcontent.com/pod-product-compliance
Ingram Content Group UK Ltd.
Pitfield, Milton Keynes, MK11 3LW, UK
UKHW040134050425
457011UK00005B/29